SOMETHING UNDER THE BED
IS DROOLING

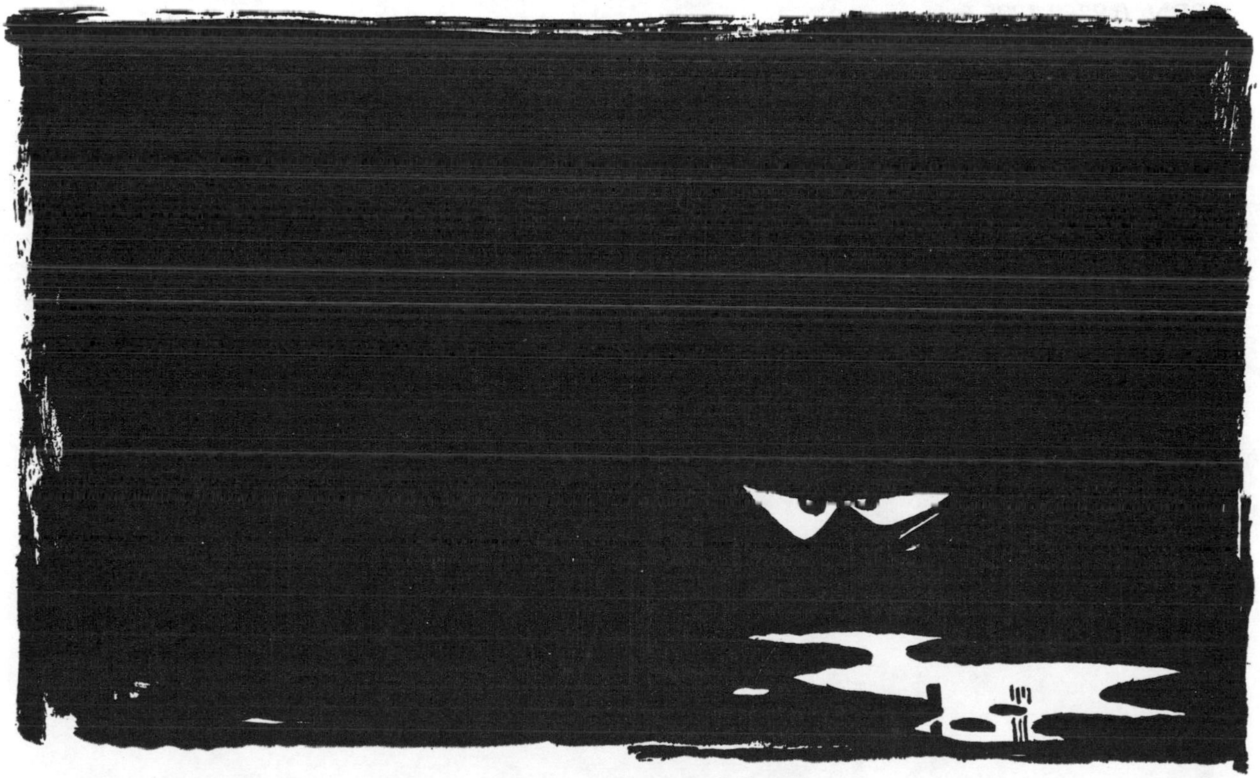

A Calvin and Hobbes Collection by Bill Watterson
Foreword by Pat Oliphant

Andrews and McMeel
A Universal Press Syndicate Company
Kansas City • New York

Calvin and Hobbes is syndicated internationally by Universal Press Syndicate.

Something Under the Bed Is Drooling copyright © 1988 by Universal Press Syndicate. All rights reserved. Printed in the United States of America. No part of this book may be used or reproduced in any manner whatsoever without written permission except in the case of reprints in the context of reviews. For information write Andrews and McMeel, a Universal Press Syndicate Company, 4900 Main Street, Kansas City, Missouri 64112.

ISBN: 0-8362-1825-6

Library of Congress Catalog Card Number: 87-73254

First Printing, February 1988
Sixth Printing, April 1990

ATTENTION: SCHOOLS AND BUSINESSES

Andrews and McMeel books are available at quantity discounts with bulk purchase for educational, business, or sales promotional use. For information write to: Special Sales Department, Andrews and McMeel, 4900 Main Street, Kansas City, Missouri 64112.

Foreword

There is a mystical quality to Bill Watterson's work. What we have here is no mere comic strip. It possesses a dimension which was found once upon a time in George Herriman's Krazy Kat and, later, in Walt Kelly's Pogo. That, however, was long ago, and since their passing, there has been nothing in the world of cartoon art to replace them. Now, we have Calvin and Hobbes.

There are no mealy-mouths or namby-pamby characters in this strip. The kid is delightfully and dedicatedly rotten. The mother and the father (no names are given or necessary) live alongside their offspring in a state of agitated wonderment at what they must have done to deserve this child. The kid, for his part, lives a good 70 percent of his time in a world I remember well from my own childhood, peopled with unspeakable creatures of the imagination, and the rest of the time in a real world peopled with other unspeakables (the teacher, the girl, the school thug). Refuge from the latter world is found in the former. And then there's the goofy stuffed tiger. A gentle soul, he is much smarter than the kid, whose brashness he leavens with a wry, endearing wisdom.

There are many comic strips out there, a few good, some average, a great many merely background clutter. All have their own cast of characters, engaging or not, all glued and patched together with dialogue, some good, some not. Very few bright stars appear who possess that peculiar magic which can provoke comparison with the best of the past. Looking at the work of our two comparisons, Herriman and Kelly, we can see a wedding of idea and art rarely seen these days, a feeling that words can enhance art and art can do the same for the written — that a carefully wrought blend of these ingredients can create a degree of enchantment which bespeaks genius.

You want magic?

Watterson the alchemist has conjured forth a work of subtlety, character, and depth far out of proportion to his tender years. I wish him long life, and may the powers of his sorcery never diminish.

You want magic?

This is a collection of the sorcerer's recipes for changing simple ink and paper into the purest gold. Humbly allow me to present Calvin (the kid) and Hobbes (the tiger). This book is magic.

— PAT OLIPHANT

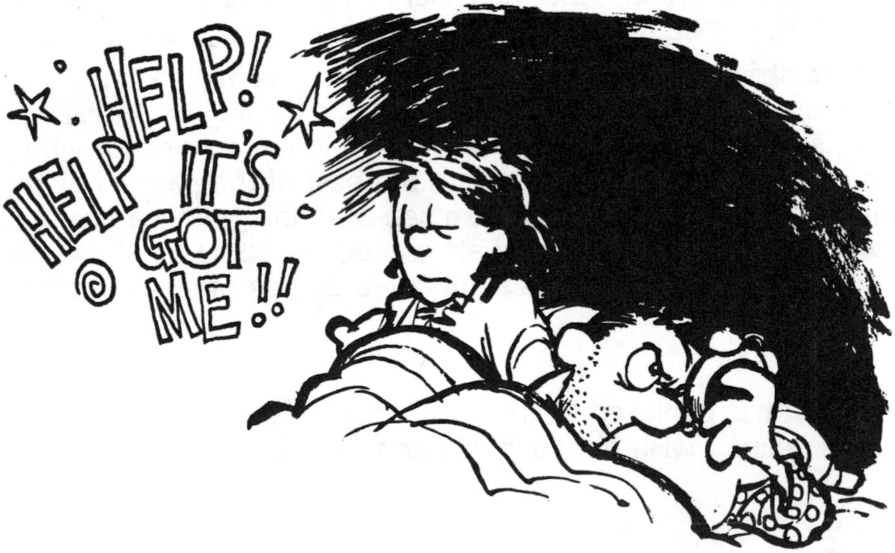
HELP! HELP IT'S GOT ME!!

To Mom and Dad

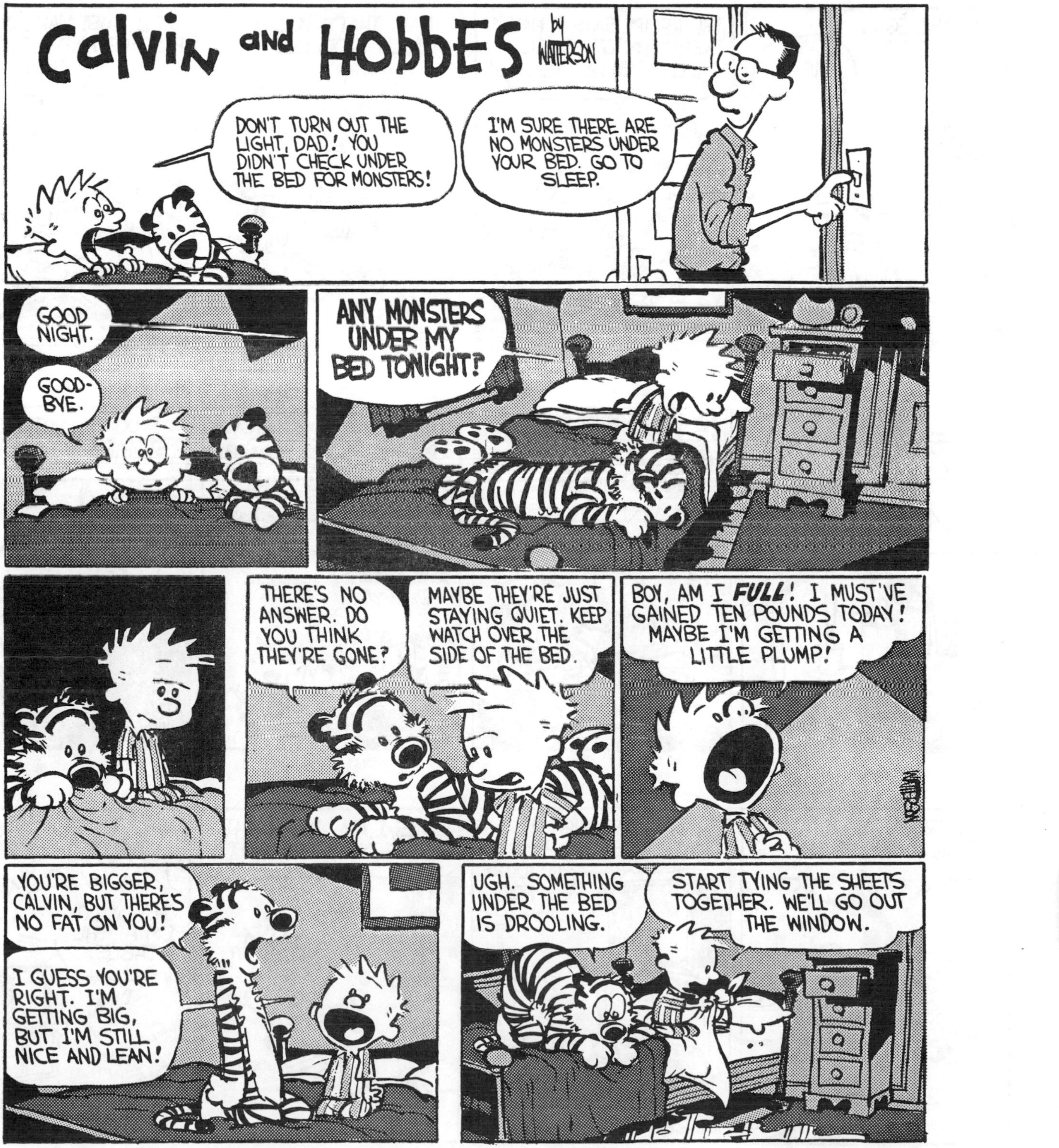
Calvin and HobbES
by WATTERSON
DON'T TURN OUT THE LIGHT, DAD! YOU DIDN'T CHECK UNDER THE BED FOR MONSTERS!
I'M SURE THERE ARE NO MONSTERS UNDER YOUR BED. GO TO SLEEP.
GOOD NIGHT.
GOOD-BYE.
ANY MONSTERS UNDER MY BED TONIGHT?
THERE'S NO ANSWER. DO YOU THINK THEY'RE GONE?
MAYBE THEY'RE JUST STAYING QUIET. KEEP WATCH OVER THE SIDE OF THE BED.
BOY, AM I **FULL**! I MUST'VE GAINED TEN POUNDS TODAY! MAYBE I'M GETTING A LITTLE PLUMP!
YOU'RE BIGGER, CALVIN, BUT THERE'S NO FAT ON YOU!
I GUESS YOU'RE RIGHT. I'M GETTING BIG, BUT I'M STILL NICE AND LEAN!
UGH. SOMETHING UNDER THE BED IS DROOLING.
START TYING THE SHEETS TOGETHER. WE'LL GO OUT THE WINDOW.

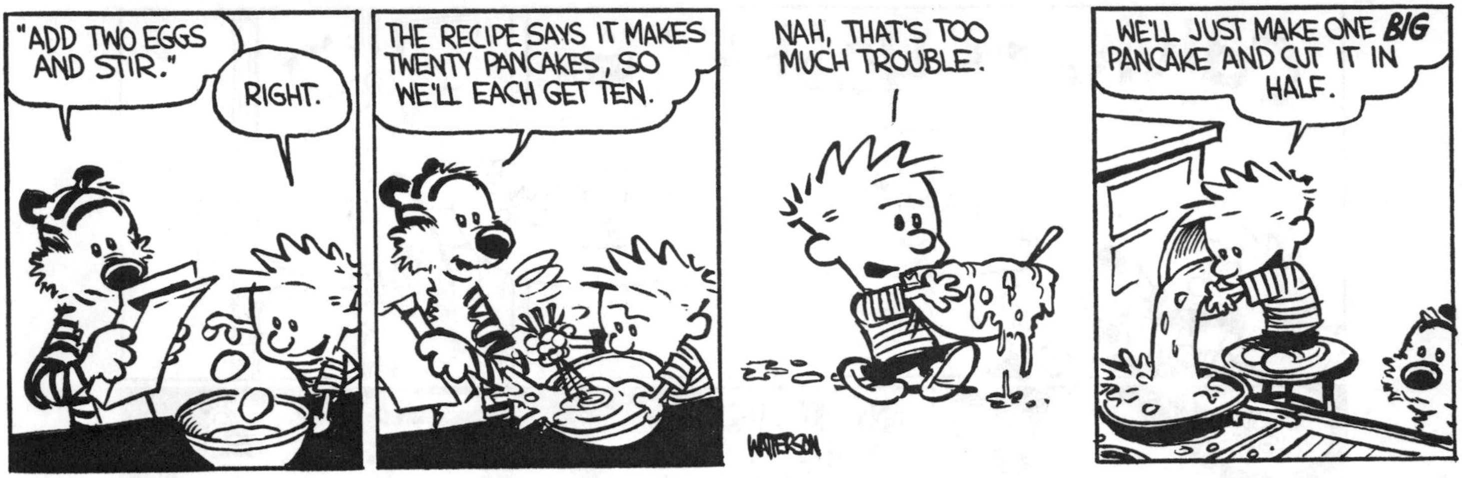
"ADD TWO EGGS AND STIR."
RIGHT.
THE RECIPE SAYS IT MAKES TWENTY PANCAKES, SO WE'LL EACH GET TEN.
NAH, THAT'S TOO MUCH TROUBLE.
WATTERSON
WE'LL JUST MAKE ONE BIG PANCAKE AND CUT IT IN HALF.

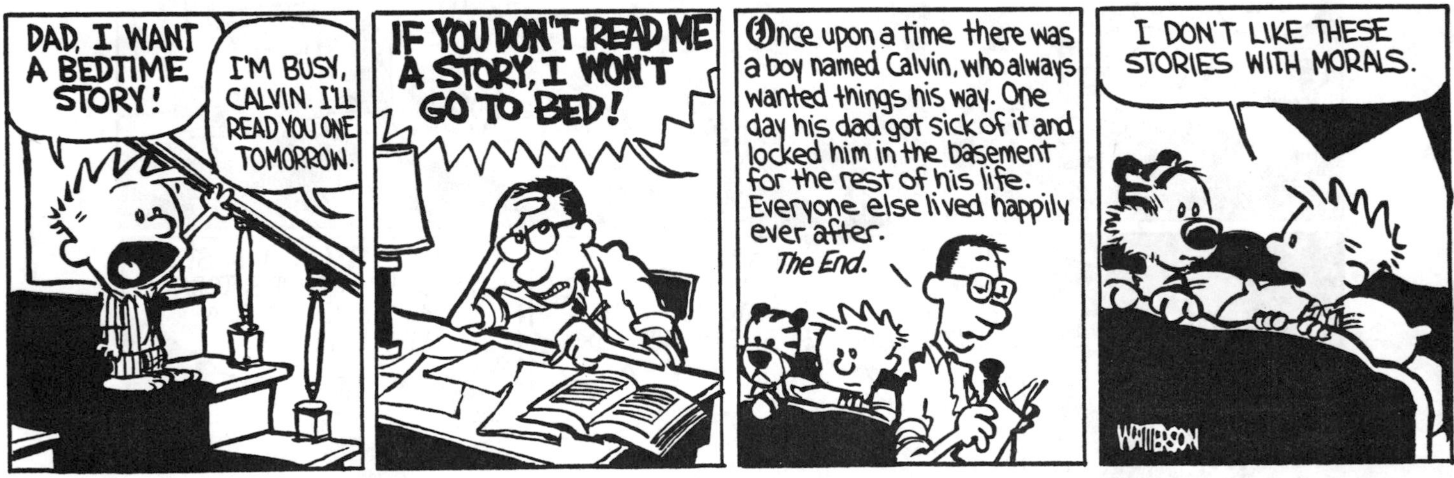
DAD, I WANT A BEDTIME STORY!
I'M BUSY, CALVIN. I'LL READ YOU ONE TOMORROW.
IF YOU DON'T READ ME A STORY, I WON'T GO TO BED!
Once upon a time there was a boy named Calvin, who always wanted things his way. One day his dad got sick of it and locked him in the basement for the rest of his life. Everyone else lived happily ever after.
The End.
I DON'T LIKE THESE STORIES WITH MORALS.
WATTERSON

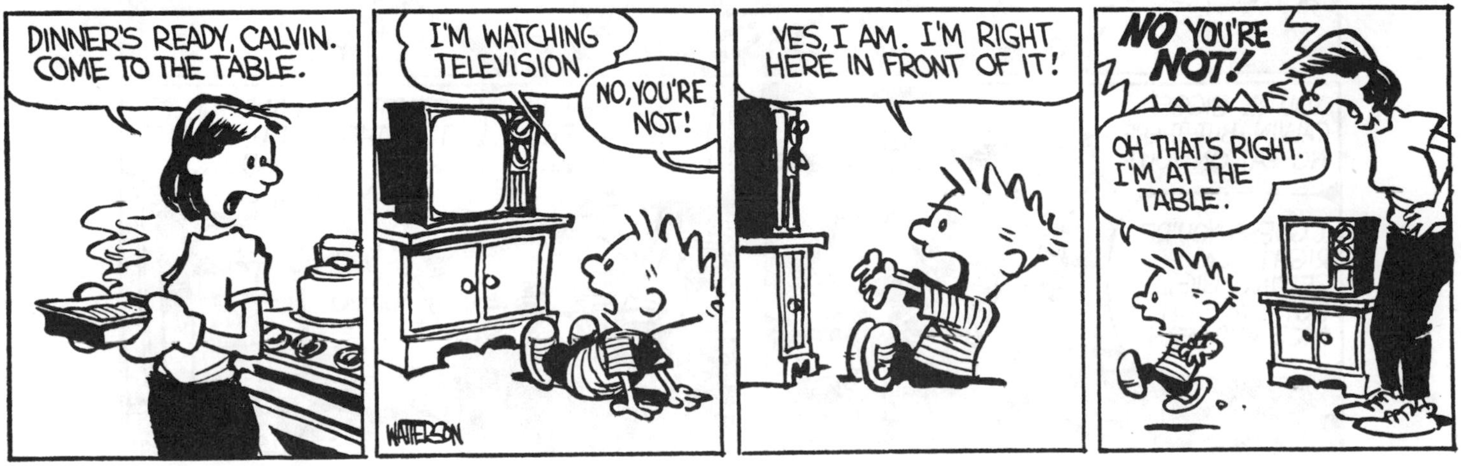
DINNER'S READY, CALVIN. COME TO THE TABLE.
I'M WATCHING TELEVISION.
NO, YOU'RE NOT!
WATTERSON
YES, I AM. I'M RIGHT HERE IN FRONT OF IT!
NO YOU'RE NOT!
OH THAT'S RIGHT. I'M AT THE TABLE.

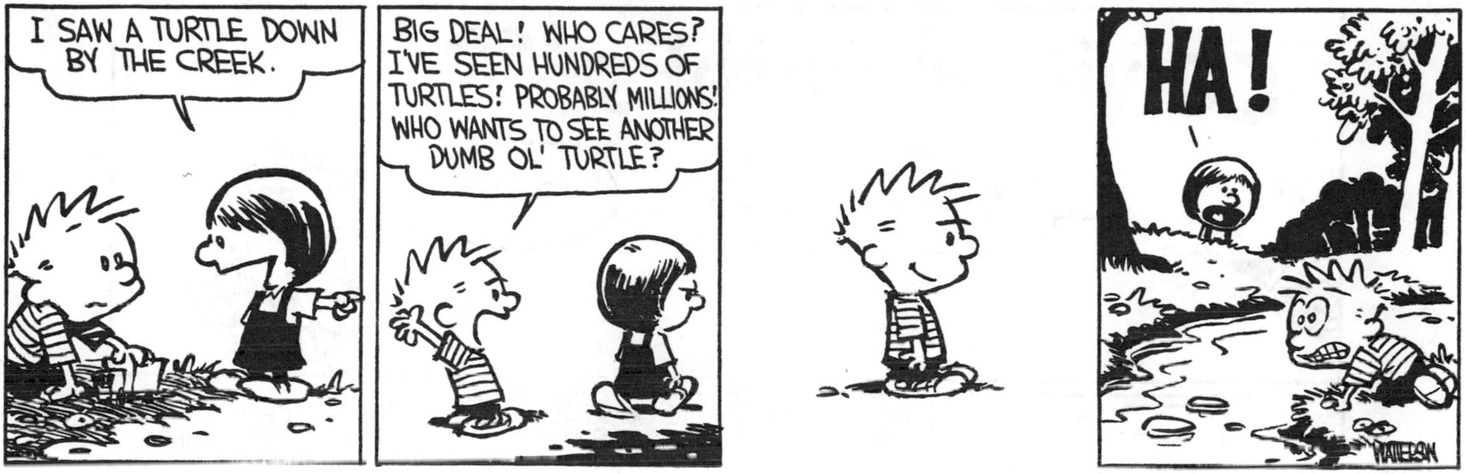
I SAW A TURTLE DOWN BY THE CREEK.
BIG DEAL! WHO CARES? I'VE SEEN HUNDREDS OF TURTLES! PROBABLY MILLIONS! WHO WANTS TO SEE ANOTHER DUMB OL' TURTLE?
HA!
WATTERSON

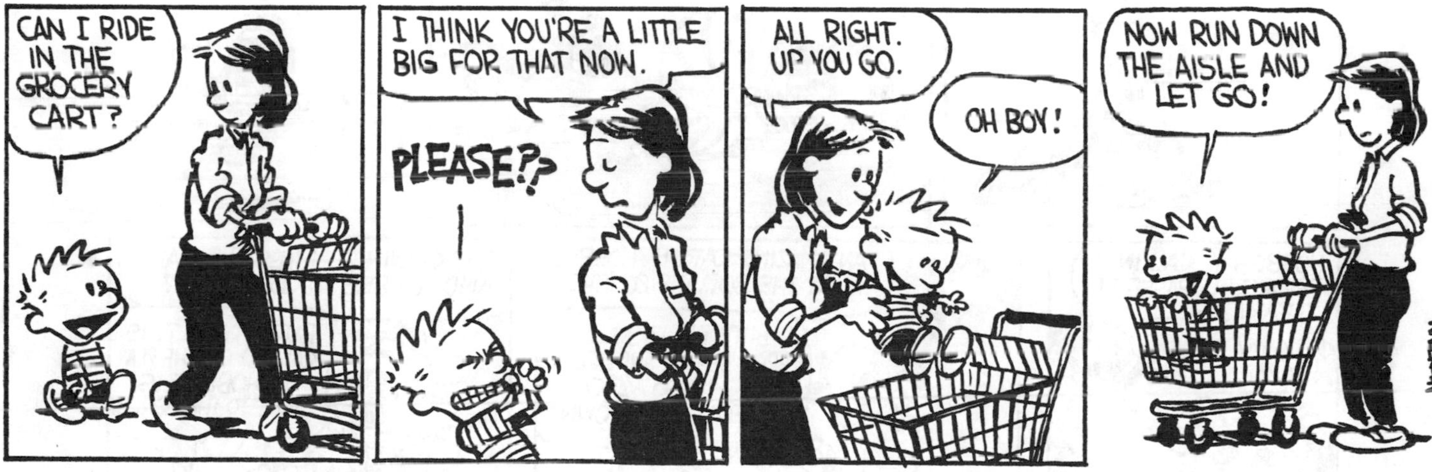
CAN I RIDE IN THE GROCERY CART?
I THINK YOU'RE A LITTLE BIG FOR THAT NOW.
PLEASE?!
ALL RIGHT. UP YOU GO.
OH BOY!
NOW RUN DOWN THE AISLE AND LET GO!
WATTERSON

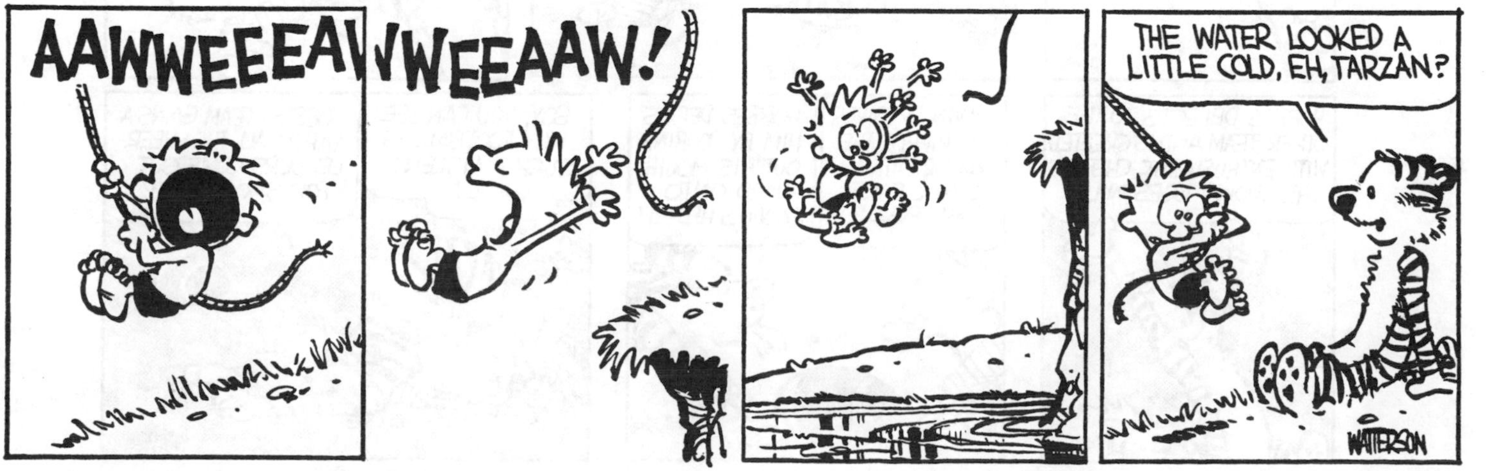
AAWWEEEAWWEEAAW!
THE WATER LOOKED A LITTLE COLD, EH, TARZAN?
WATTERSON

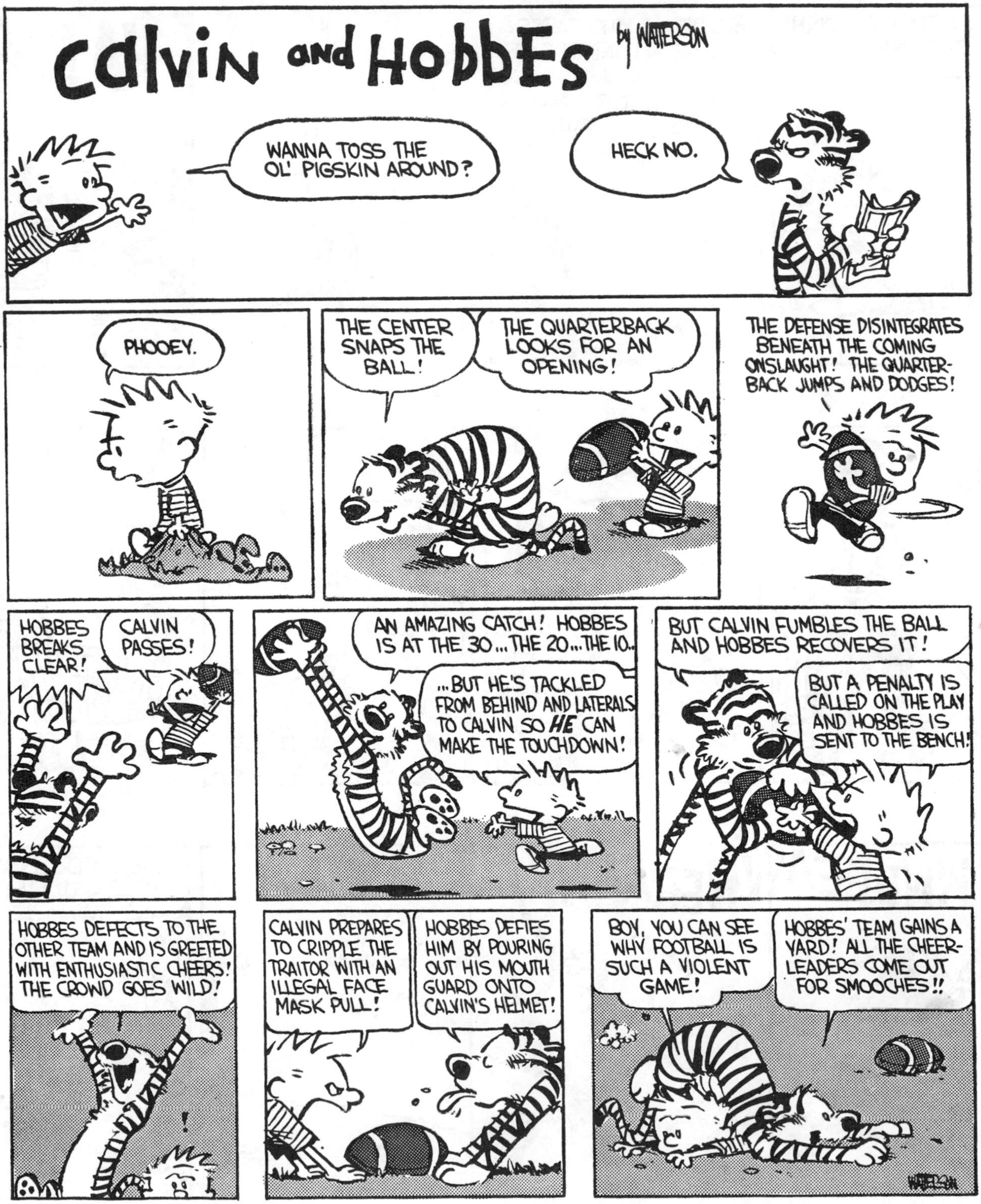
Calvin and HOBBES
by WATTERSON
WANNA TOSS THE OL' PIGSKIN AROUND?
HECK NO.
PHOOEY.
THE CENTER SNAPS THE BALL!
THE QUARTERBACK LOOKS FOR AN OPENING!
THE DEFENSE DISINTEGRATES BENEATH THE COMING ONSLAUGHT! THE QUARTER-BACK JUMPS AND DODGES!
HOBBES BREAKS CLEAR!
CALVIN PASSES!
AN AMAZING CATCH! HOBBES IS AT THE 30... THE 20... THE 10...
...BUT HE'S TACKLED FROM BEHIND AND LATERALS TO CALVIN SO HE CAN MAKE THE TOUCHDOWN!
BUT CALVIN FUMBLES THE BALL AND HOBBES RECOVERS IT!
BUT A PENALTY IS CALLED ON THE PLAY AND HOBBES IS SENT TO THE BENCH!
HOBBES DEFECTS TO THE OTHER TEAM AND IS GREETED WITH ENTHUSIASTIC CHEERS! THE CROWD GOES WILD!
CALVIN PREPARES TO CRIPPLE THE TRAITOR WITH AN ILLEGAL FACE MASK PULL!
HOBBES DEFIES HIM BY POURING OUT HIS MOUTH GUARD ONTO CALVIN'S HELMET!
BOY, YOU CAN SEE WHY FOOTBALL IS SUCH A VIOLENT GAME!
HOBBES' TEAM GAINS A YARD! ALL THE CHEER-LEADERS COME OUT FOR SMOOCHES!!
WATTERSON

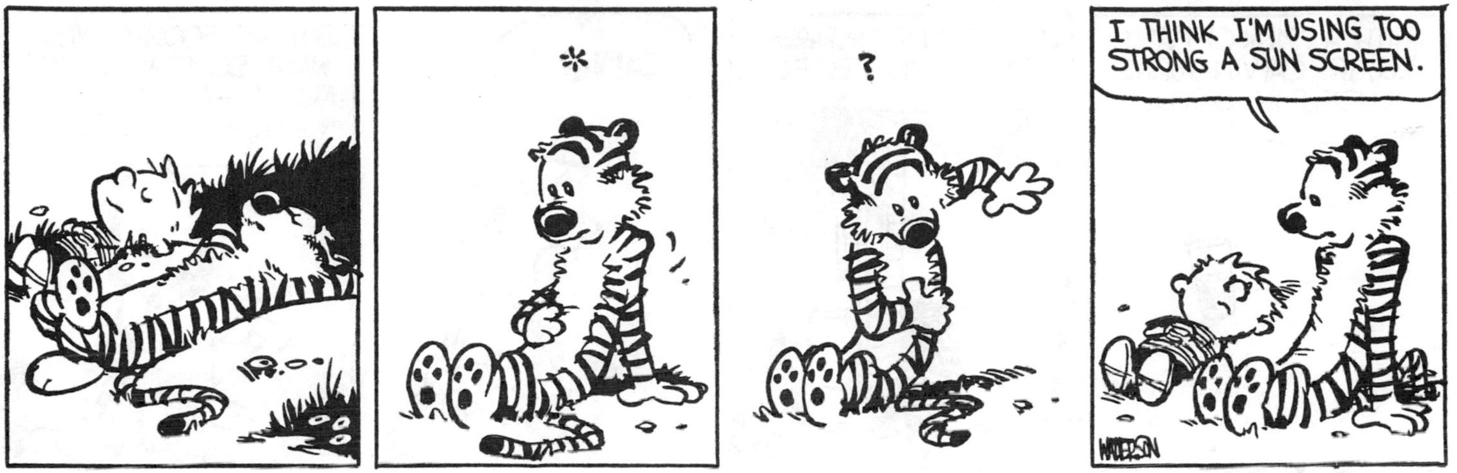
*
?
I THINK I'M USING TOO STRONG A SUN SCREEN.
WATTERSON

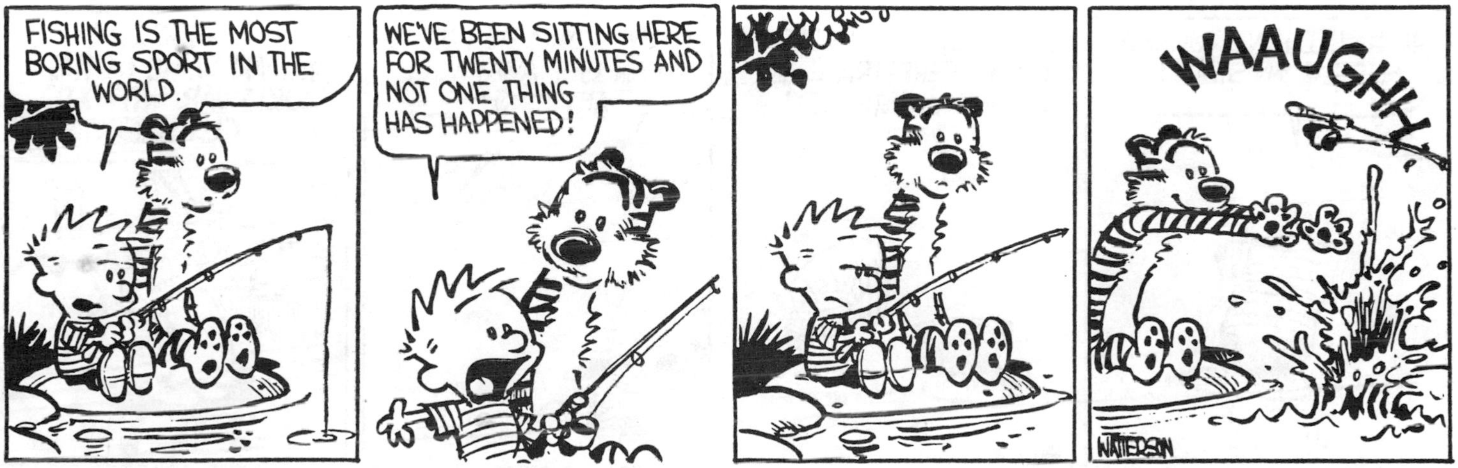
FISHING IS THE MOST BORING SPORT IN THE WORLD.
WE'VE BEEN SITTING HERE FOR TWENTY MINUTES AND NOT ONE THING HAS HAPPENED!
WAAUGHH
WATTERSON

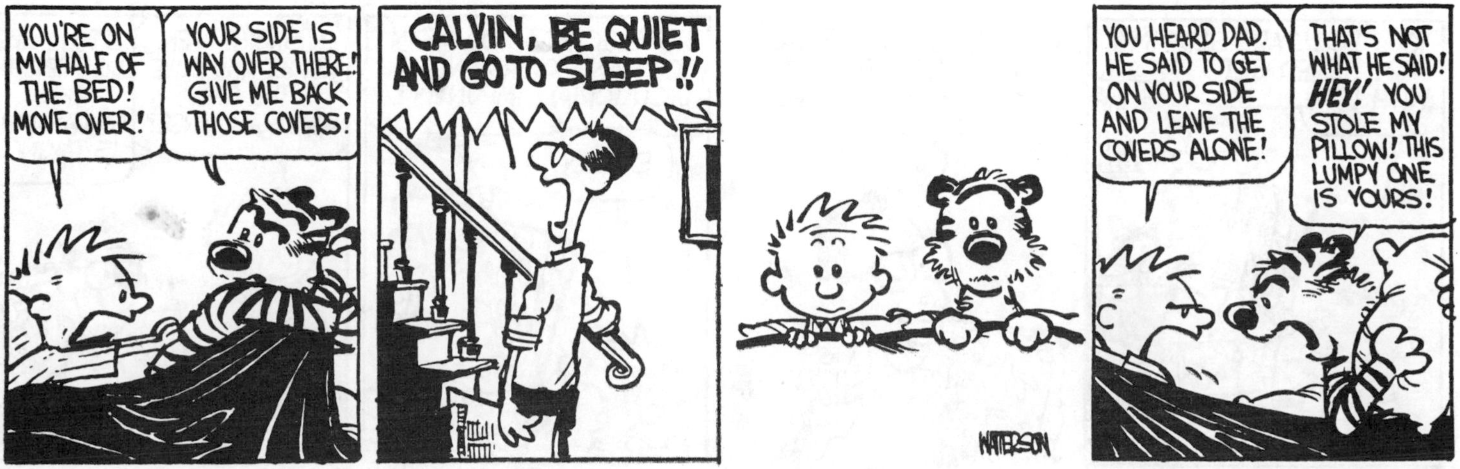
YOU'RE ON MY HALF OF THE BED! MOVE OVER!
YOUR SIDE IS WAY OVER THERE! GIVE ME BACK THOSE COVERS!
CALVIN, BE QUIET AND GO TO SLEEP!!
YOU HEARD DAD. HE SAID TO GET ON YOUR SIDE AND LEAVE THE COVERS ALONE!
THAT'S NOT WHAT HE SAID! HEY! YOU STOLE MY PILLOW! THIS LUMPY ONE IS YOURS!
WATTERSON

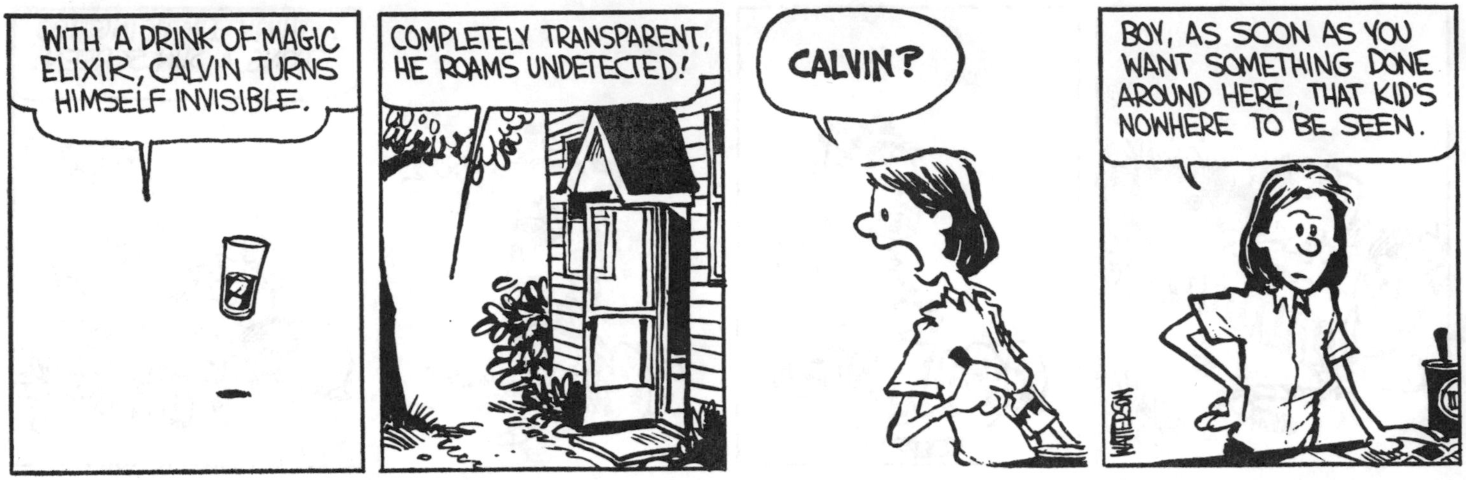
WITH A DRINK OF MAGIC ELIXIR, CALVIN TURNS HIMSELF INVISIBLE.
COMPLETELY TRANSPARENT, HE ROAMS UNDETECTED!
CALVIN?
BOY, AS SOON AS YOU WANT SOMETHING DONE AROUND HERE, THAT KID'S NOWHERE TO BE SEEN.
WATTERSON

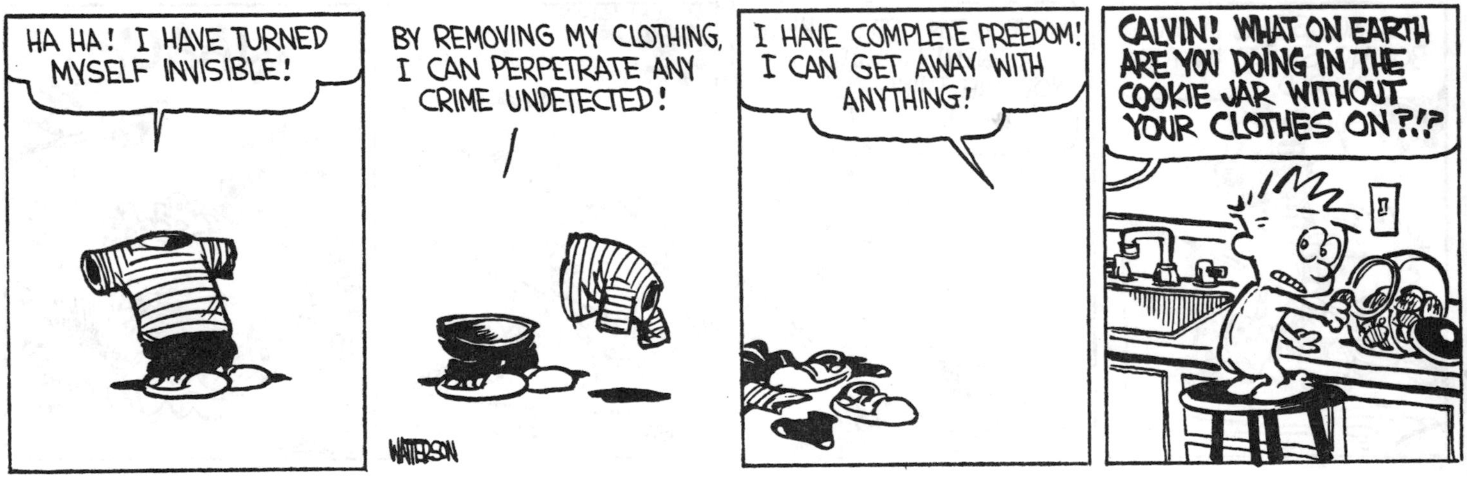
HA HA! I HAVE TURNED MYSELF INVISIBLE!
BY REMOVING MY CLOTHING, I CAN PERPETRATE ANY CRIME UNDETECTED!
WATTERSON
I HAVE COMPLETE FREEDOM! I CAN GET AWAY WITH ANYTHING!
CALVIN! WHAT ON EARTH ARE YOU DOING IN THE COOKIE JAR WITHOUT YOUR CLOTHES ON?!?

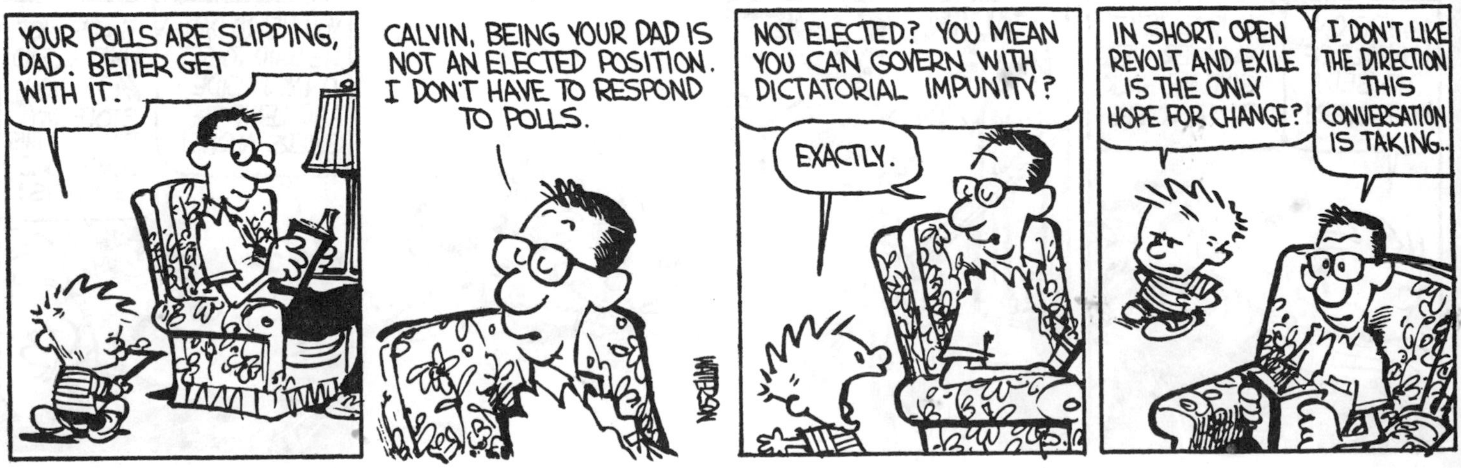
YOUR POLLS ARE SLIPPING, DAD. BETTER GET WITH IT.
CALVIN, BEING YOUR DAD IS NOT AN ELECTED POSITION. I DON'T HAVE TO RESPOND TO POLLS.
WATTERSON
NOT ELECTED? YOU MEAN YOU CAN GOVERN WITH DICTATORIAL IMPUNITY?
EXACTLY.
IN SHORT, OPEN REVOLT AND EXILE IS THE ONLY HOPE FOR CHANGE?
I DON'T LIKE THE DIRECTION THIS CONVERSATION IS TAKING..

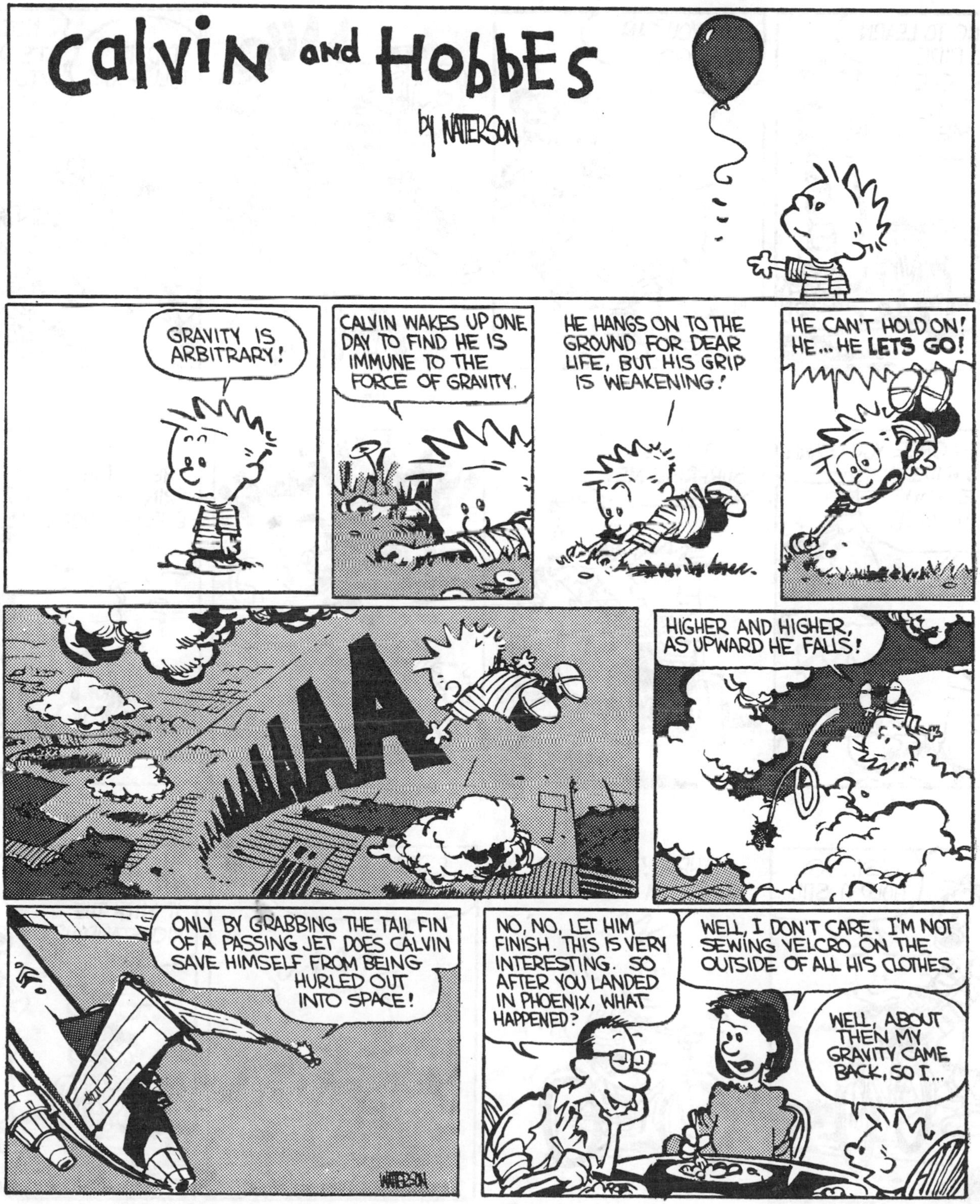
Calvin and Hobbes
by WATTERSON
GRAVITY IS ARBITRARY!
CALVIN WAKES UP ONE DAY TO FIND HE IS IMMUNE TO THE FORCE OF GRAVITY.
HE HANGS ON TO THE GROUND FOR DEAR LIFE, BUT HIS GRIP IS WEAKENING!
HE CAN'T HOLD ON! HE... HE LETS GO!
AAAAAAAA
HIGHER AND HIGHER, AS UPWARD HE FALLS!
ONLY BY GRABBING THE TAIL FIN OF A PASSING JET DOES CALVIN SAVE HIMSELF FROM BEING HURLED OUT INTO SPACE!
WATTERSON
NO, NO, LET HIM FINISH. THIS IS VERY INTERESTING. SO AFTER YOU LANDED IN PHOENIX, WHAT HAPPENED?
WELL, I DON'T CARE. I'M NOT SEWING VELCRO ON THE OUTSIDE OF ALL HIS CLOTHES.
WELL, ABOUT THEN MY GRAVITY CAME BACK, SO I...

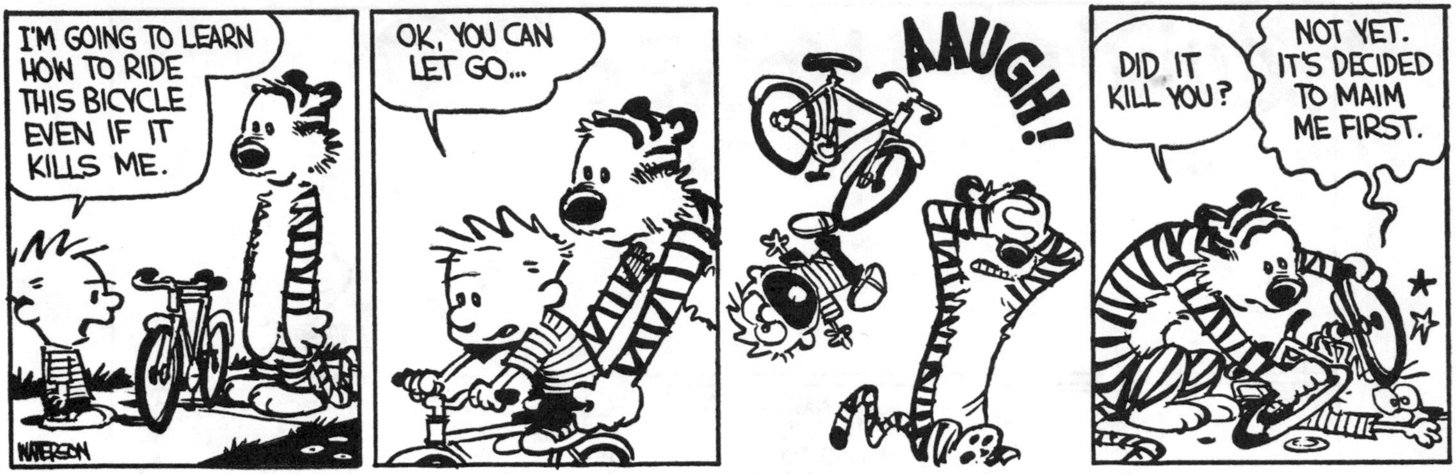
I'M GOING TO LEARN HOW TO RIDE THIS BICYCLE EVEN IF IT KILLS ME.
OK, YOU CAN LET GO...
AAUGH!
DID IT KILL YOU?
NOT YET. IT'S DECIDED TO MAIM ME FIRST.

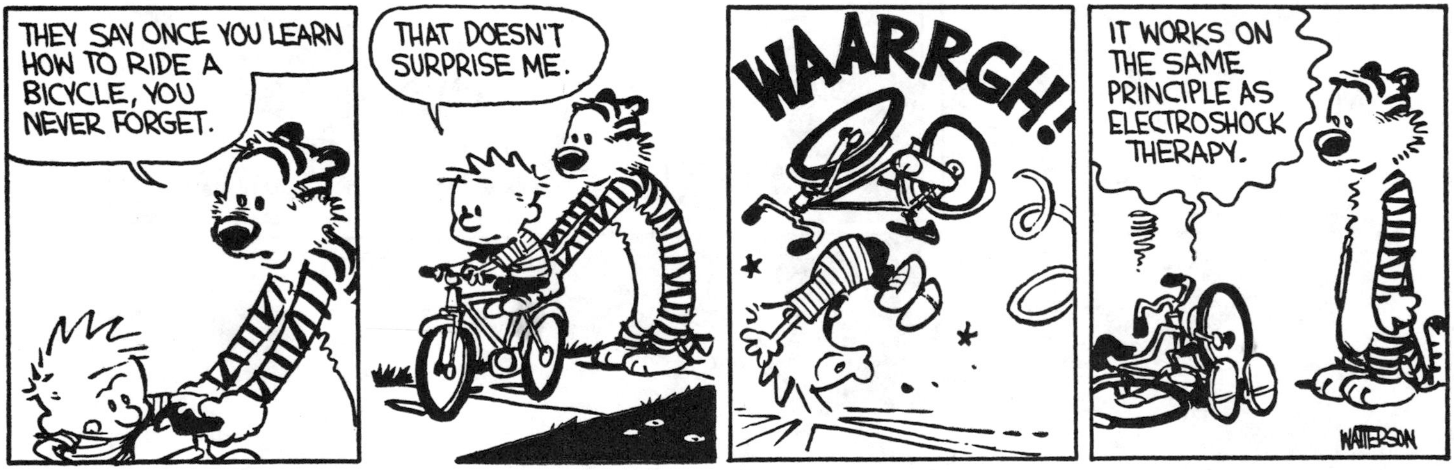
THEY SAY ONCE YOU LEARN HOW TO RIDE A BICYCLE, YOU NEVER FORGET.
THAT DOESN'T SURPRISE ME.
WAARRGH!
IT WORKS ON THE SAME PRINCIPLE AS ELECTROSHOCK THERAPY.

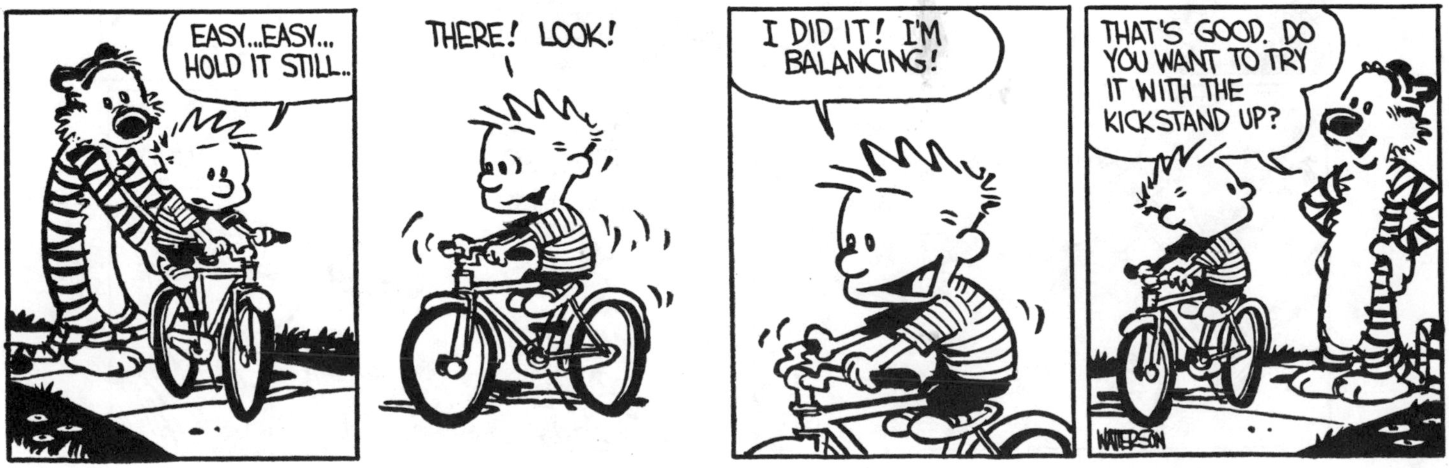
EASY...EASY... HOLD IT STILL..
THERE! LOOK!
I DID IT! I'M BALANCING!
THAT'S GOOD. DO YOU WANT TO TRY IT WITH THE KICKSTAND UP?

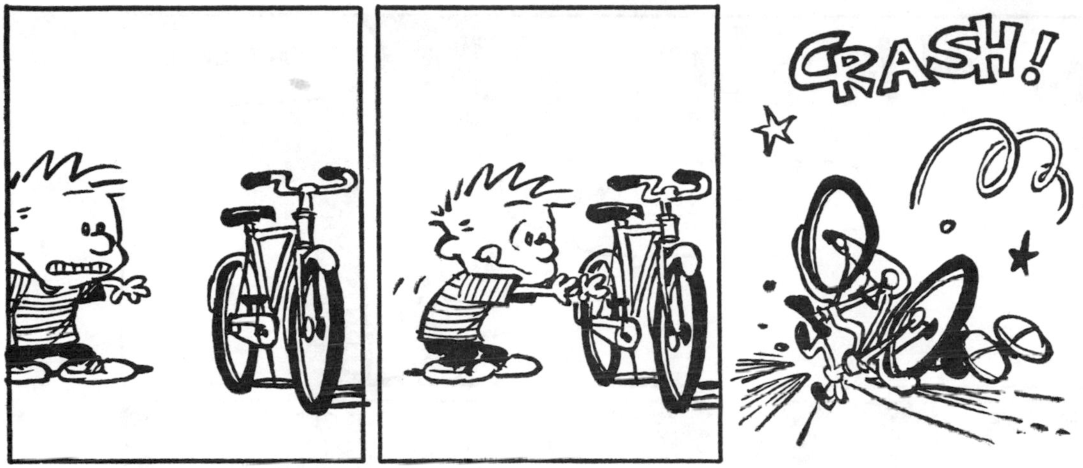
CRASH!
IT JUMPED ME!!

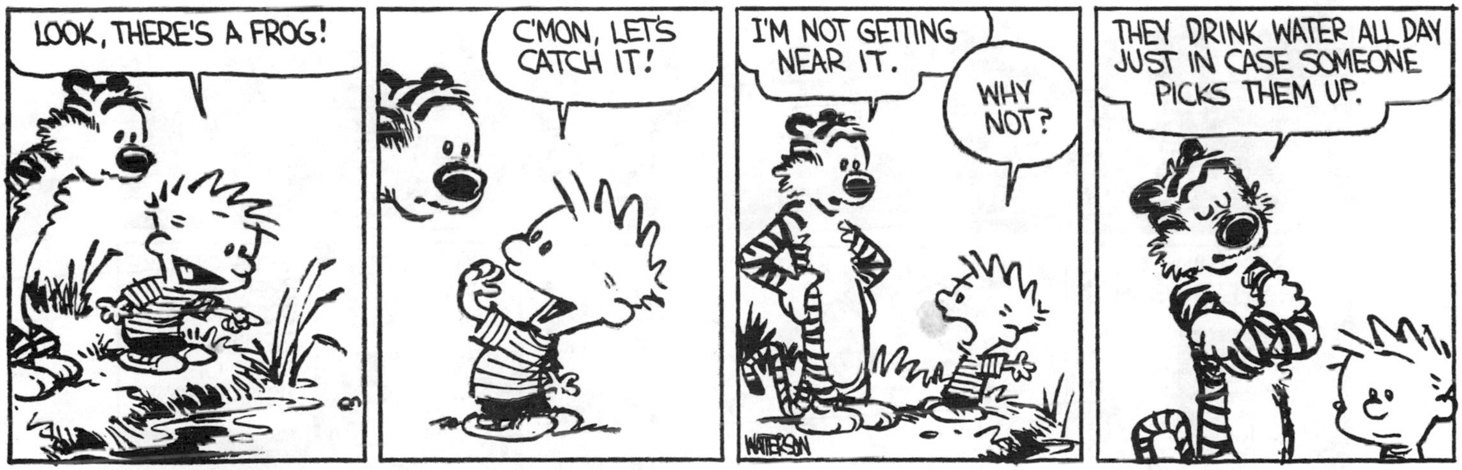
LOOK, THERE'S A FROG!
C'MON, LET'S CATCH IT!
I'M NOT GETTING NEAR IT.
WHY NOT?
THEY DRINK WATER ALL DAY JUST IN CASE SOMEONE PICKS THEM UP.

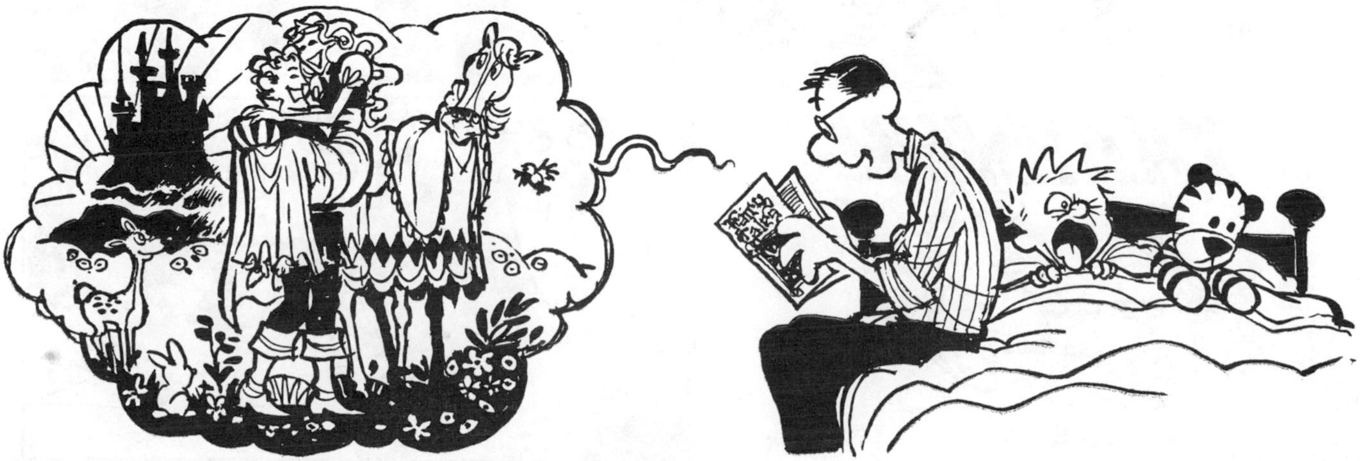

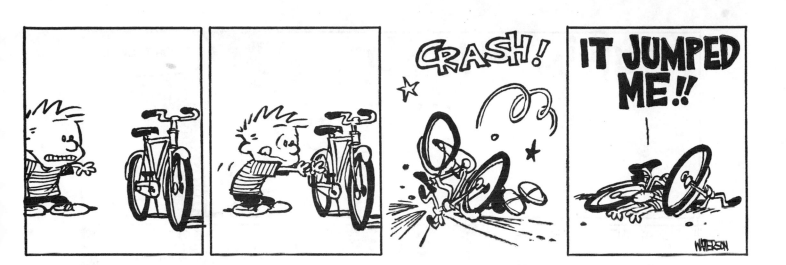

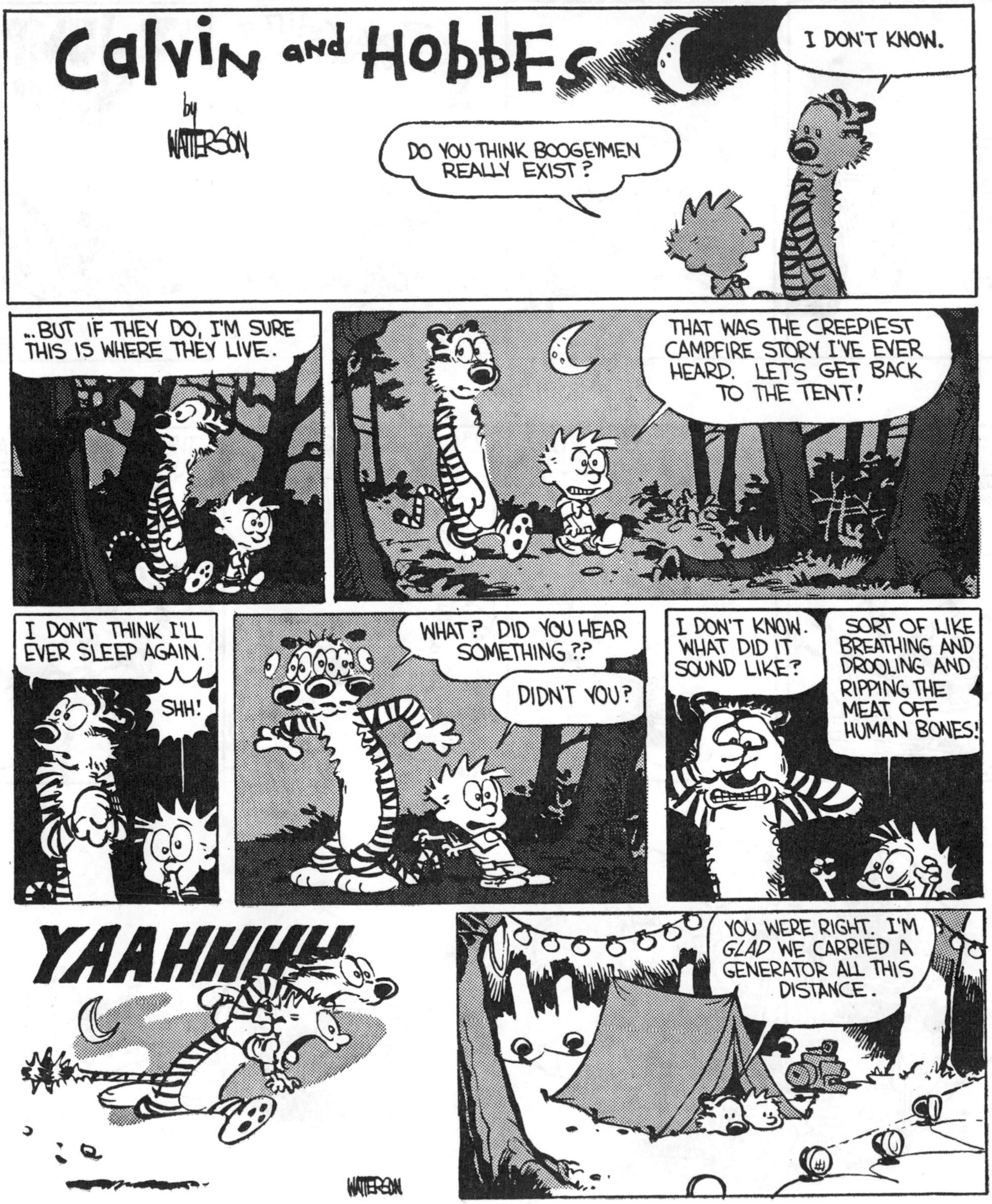
Calvin and Hobbes
by WATTERSON
DO YOU THINK BOOGEYMEN REALLY EXIST?
I DON'T KNOW.
..BUT IF THEY DO, I'M SURE THIS IS WHERE THEY LIVE.
THAT WAS THE CREEPIEST CAMPFIRE STORY I'VE EVER HEARD. LET'S GET BACK TO THE TENT!
I DON'T THINK I'LL EVER SLEEP AGAIN.
SHH!
WHAT? DID YOU HEAR SOMETHING??
DIDN'T YOU?
I DON'T KNOW. WHAT DID IT SOUND LIKE?
SORT OF LIKE BREATHING AND DROOLING AND RIPPING THE MEAT OFF HUMAN BONES!
YAAHHHH
YOU WERE RIGHT. I'M GLAD WE CARRIED A GENERATOR ALL THIS DISTANCE.
WATTERSON

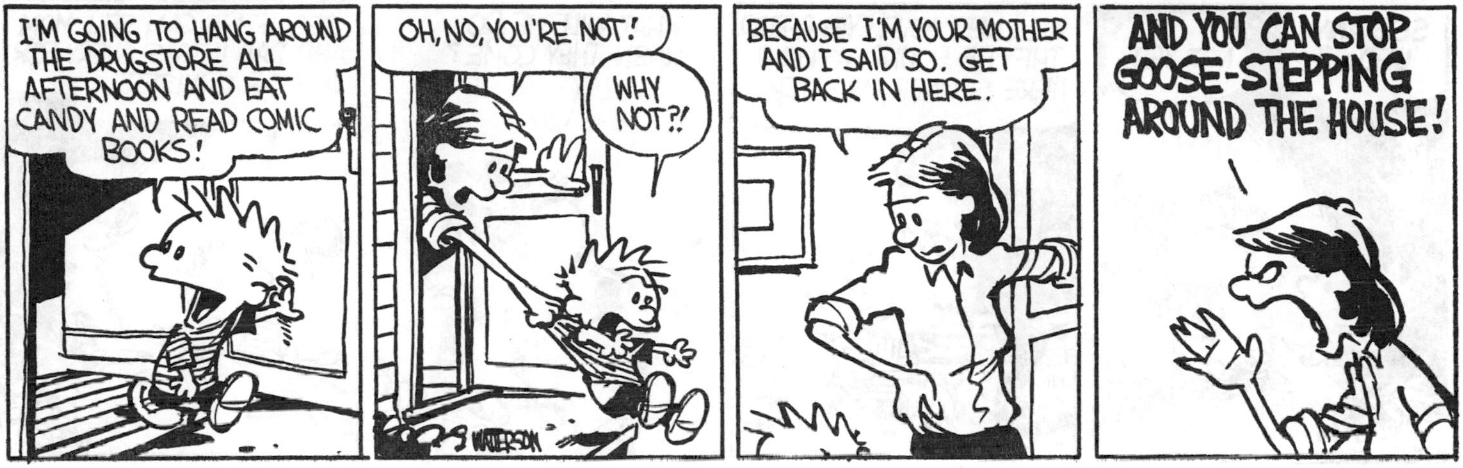
I'M GOING TO HANG AROUND THE DRUGSTORE ALL AFTERNOON AND EAT CANDY AND READ COMIC BOOKS!
OH, NO, YOU'RE NOT!
WHY NOT?!
BECAUSE I'M YOUR MOTHER AND I SAID SO. GET BACK IN HERE.
AND YOU CAN STOP GOOSE-STEPPING AROUND THE HOUSE!
WATTERSON

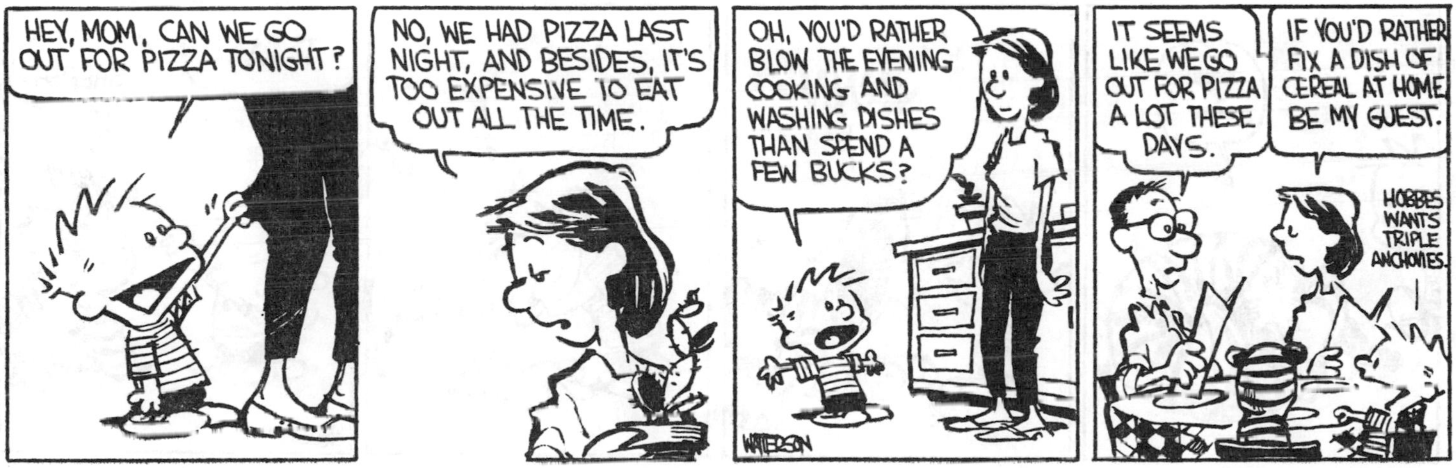
HEY, MOM, CAN WE GO OUT FOR PIZZA TONIGHT?
NO, WE HAD PIZZA LAST NIGHT, AND BESIDES, IT'S TOO EXPENSIVE TO EAT OUT ALL THE TIME.
OH, YOU'D RATHER BLOW THE EVENING COOKING AND WASHING DISHES THAN SPEND A FEW BUCKS?
WATTERSON
IT SEEMS LIKE WE GO OUT FOR PIZZA A LOT THESE DAYS.
IF YOU'D RATHER FIX A DISH OF CEREAL AT HOME, BE MY GUEST.
HOBBES WANTS TRIPLE ANCHOVIES.

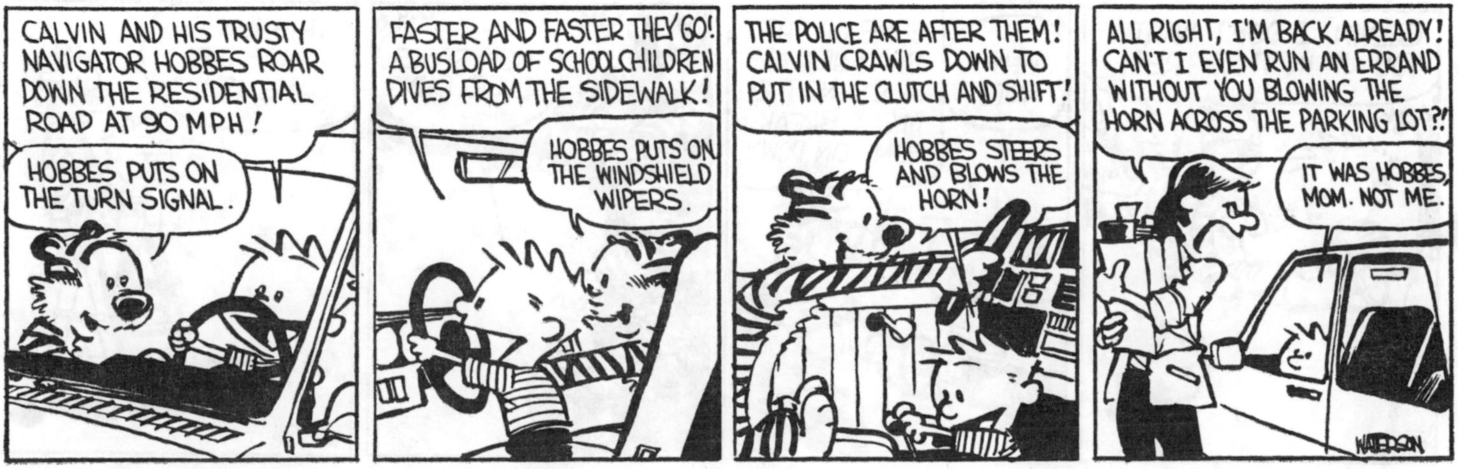
CALVIN AND HIS TRUSTY NAVIGATOR HOBBES ROAR DOWN THE RESIDENTIAL ROAD AT 90 MPH!
HOBBES PUTS ON THE TURN SIGNAL.
FASTER AND FASTER THEY GO! A BUSLOAD OF SCHOOLCHILDREN DIVES FROM THE SIDEWALK!
HOBBES PUTS ON THE WINDSHIELD WIPERS.
THE POLICE ARE AFTER THEM! CALVIN CRAWLS DOWN TO PUT IN THE CLUTCH AND SHIFT!
HOBBES STEERS AND BLOWS THE HORN!
ALL RIGHT, I'M BACK ALREADY! CAN'T I EVEN RUN AN ERRAND WITHOUT YOU BLOWING THE HORN ACROSS THE PARKING LOT?!
IT WAS HOBBES, MOM. NOT ME.
WATTERSON

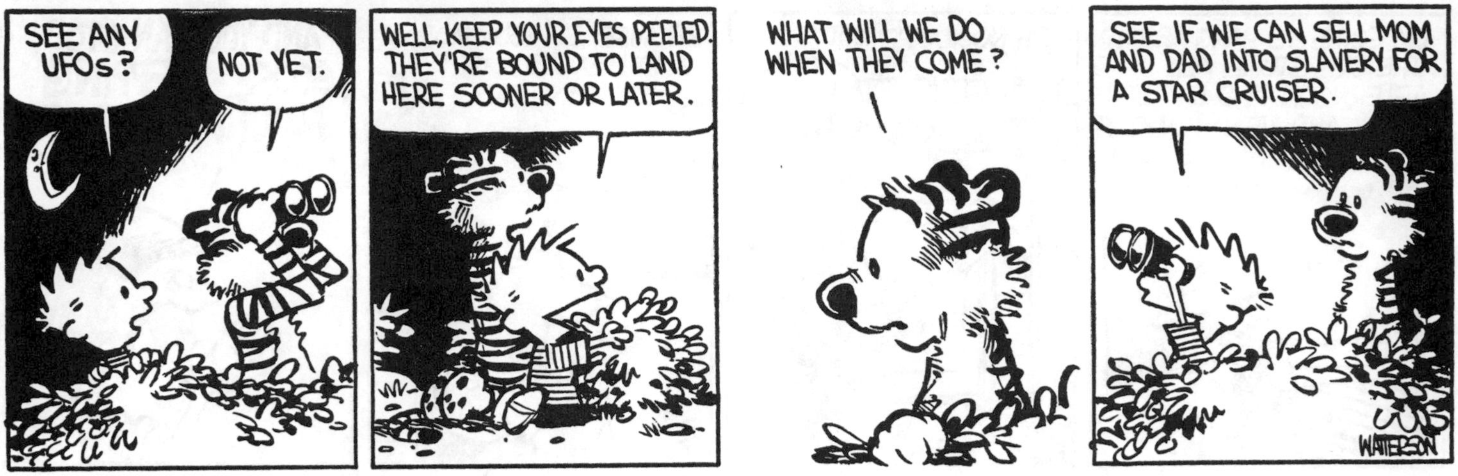
SEE ANY UFOs?
NOT YET.
WELL, KEEP YOUR EYES PEELED. THEY'RE BOUND TO LAND HERE SOONER OR LATER.
WHAT WILL WE DO WHEN THEY COME?
SEE IF WE CAN SELL MOM AND DAD INTO SLAVERY FOR A STAR CRUISER.
WATTERSON

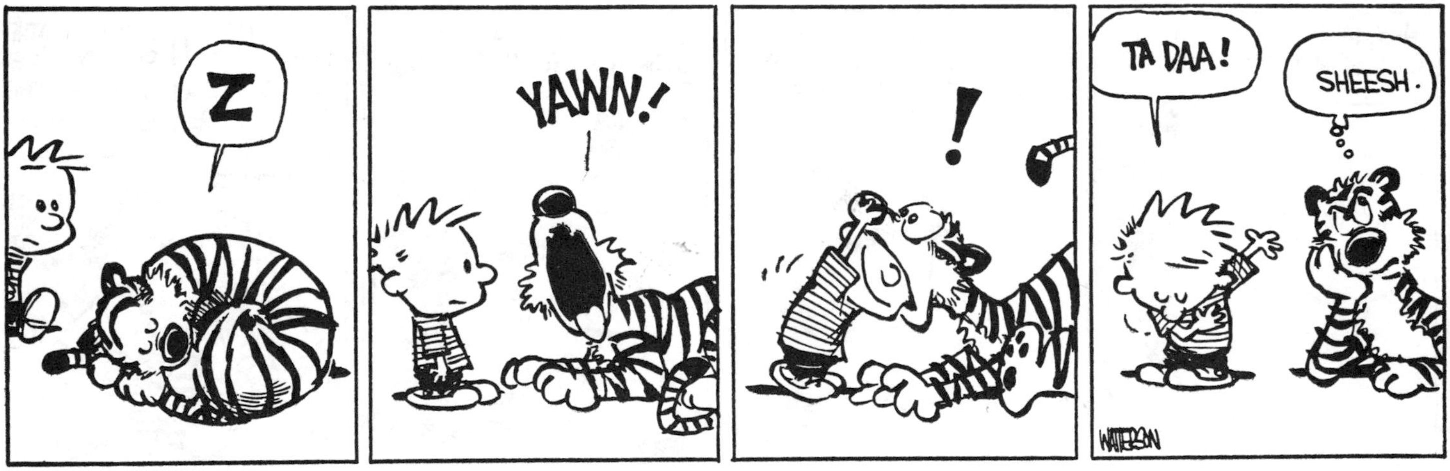
Z
YAWN!
!
TA DAA!
SHEESH.
WATTERSON

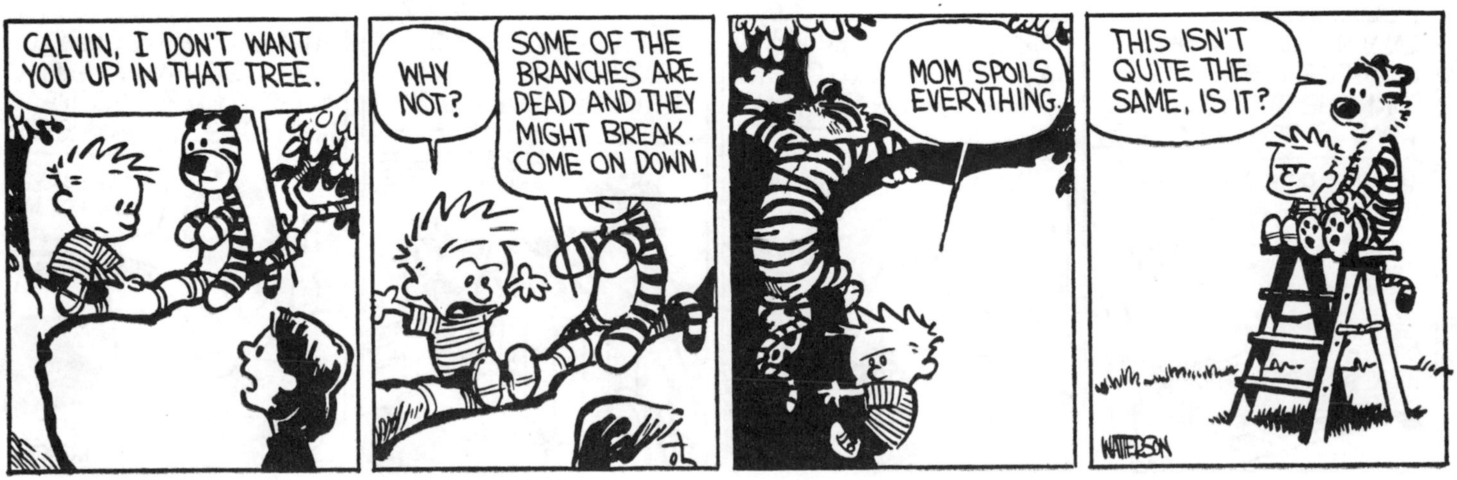
CALVIN, I DON'T WANT YOU UP IN THAT TREE.
WHY NOT?
SOME OF THE BRANCHES ARE DEAD AND THEY MIGHT BREAK. COME ON DOWN.
MOM SPOILS EVERYTHING.
THIS ISN'T QUITE THE SAME, IS IT?
WATTERSON

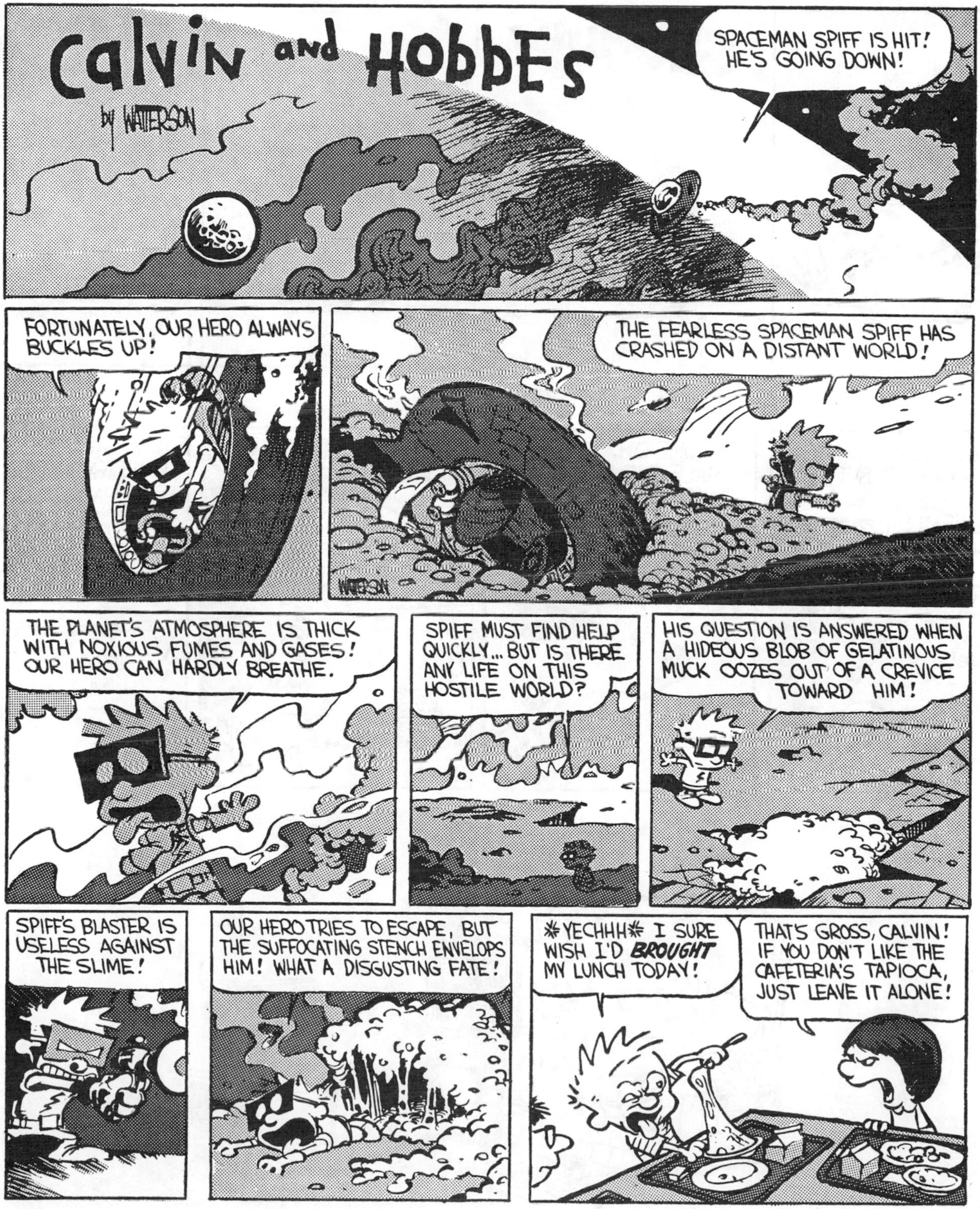
Calvin and HOBBES
by WATTERSON
SPACEMAN SPIFF IS HIT! HE'S GOING DOWN!
FORTUNATELY, OUR HERO ALWAYS BUCKLES UP!
THE FEARLESS SPACEMAN SPIFF HAS CRASHED ON A DISTANT WORLD!
WATTERSON
THE PLANET'S ATMOSPHERE IS THICK WITH NOXIOUS FUMES AND GASES! OUR HERO CAN HARDLY BREATHE.
SPIFF MUST FIND HELP QUICKLY... BUT IS THERE ANY LIFE ON THIS HOSTILE WORLD?
HIS QUESTION IS ANSWERED WHEN A HIDEOUS BLOB OF GELATINOUS MUCK OOZES OUT OF A CREVICE TOWARD HIM!
SPIFF'S BLASTER IS USELESS AGAINST THE SLIME!
OUR HERO TRIES TO ESCAPE, BUT THE SUFFOCATING STENCH ENVELOPS HIM! WHAT A DISGUSTING FATE!
YECHHH I SURE WISH I'D BROUGHT MY LUNCH TODAY!
THAT'S GROSS, CALVIN! IF YOU DON'T LIKE THE CAFETERIA'S TAPIOCA, JUST LEAVE IT ALONE!

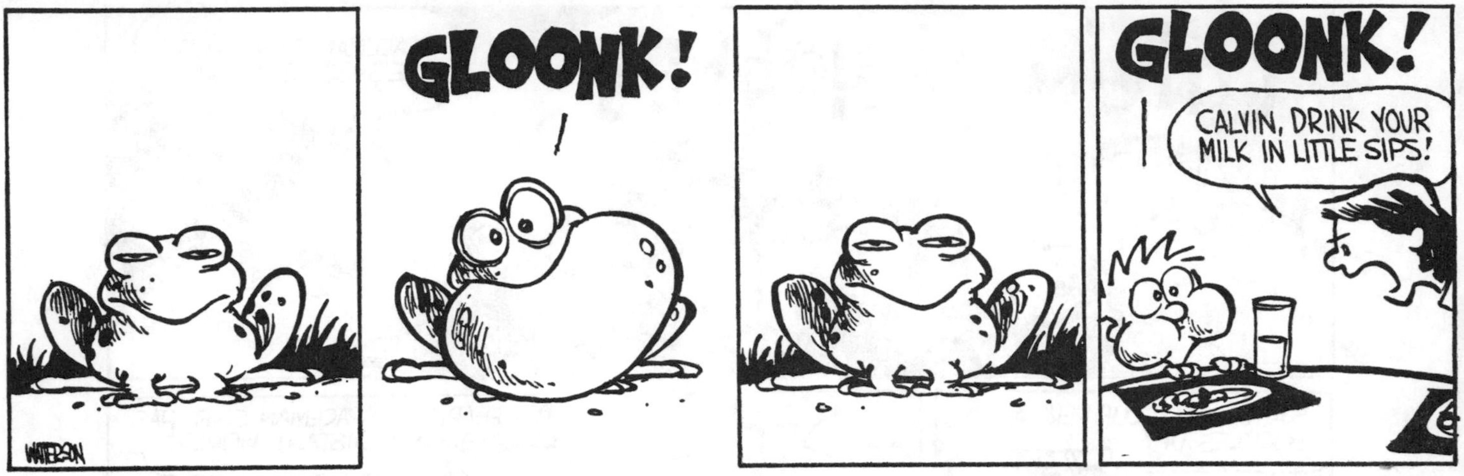
WATERSON
GLOONK!
GLOONK!
CALVIN, DRINK YOUR MILK IN LITTLE SIPS!

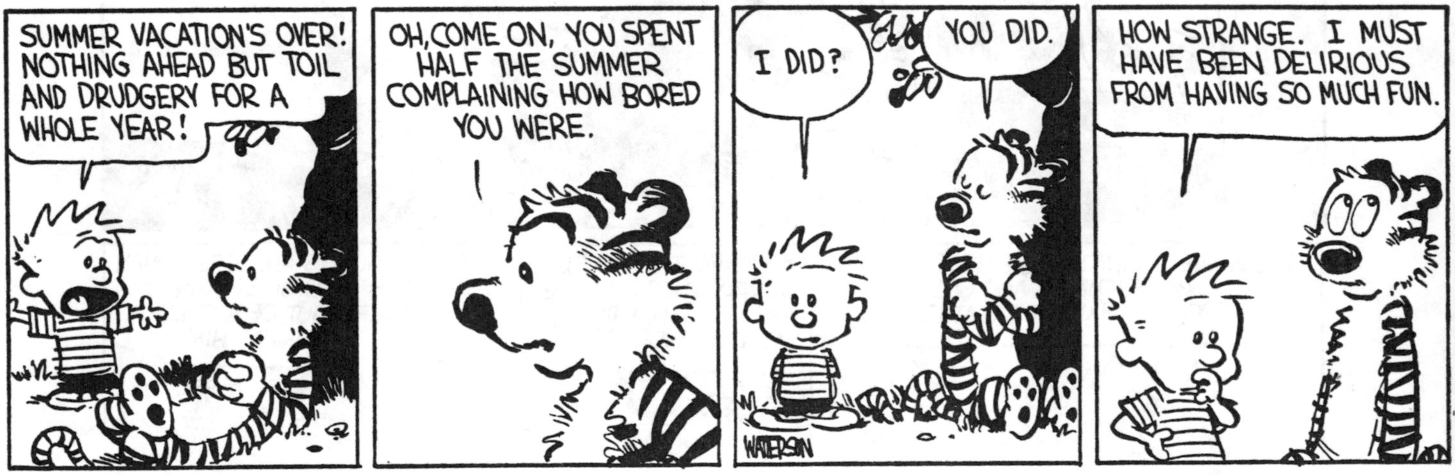
SUMMER VACATION'S OVER! NOTHING AHEAD BUT TOIL AND DRUDGERY FOR A WHOLE YEAR!
OH, COME ON, YOU SPENT HALF THE SUMMER COMPLAINING HOW BORED YOU WERE.
I DID?
YOU DID.
WATERSON
HOW STRANGE. I MUST HAVE BEEN DELIRIOUS FROM HAVING SO MUCH FUN.

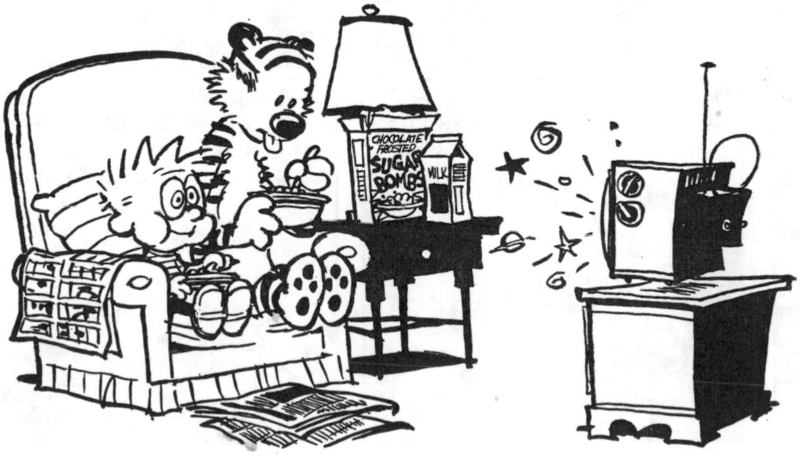
CHOCOLATE FROSTED
MILK

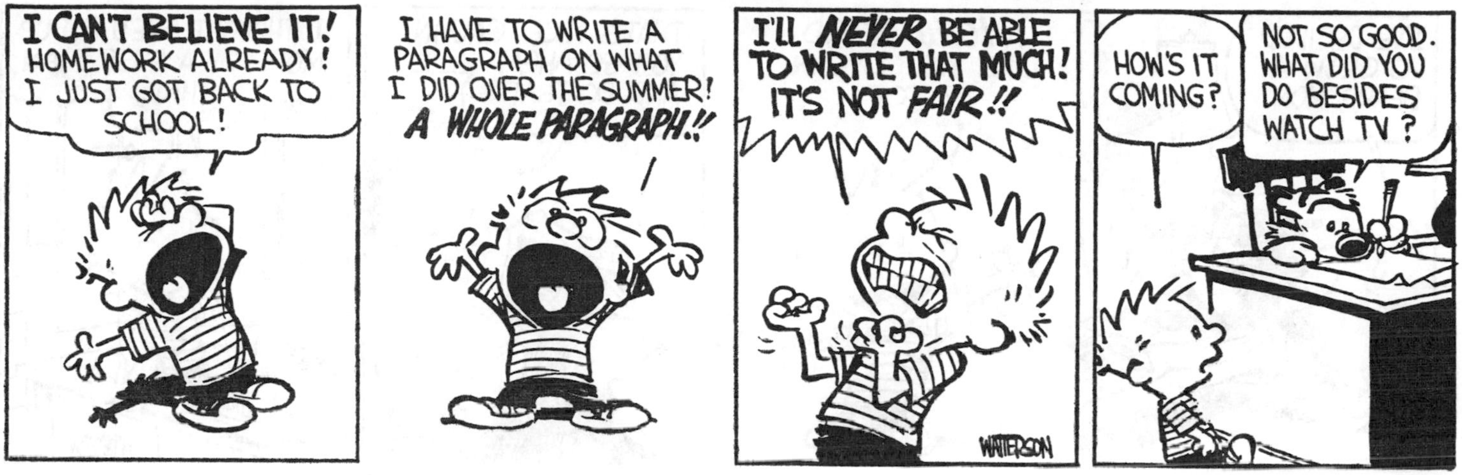
I CAN'T BELIEVE IT! HOMEWORK ALREADY! I JUST GOT BACK TO SCHOOL!
I HAVE TO WRITE A PARAGRAPH ON WHAT I DID OVER THE SUMMER! A WHOLE PARAGRAPH!!
I'LL NEVER BE ABLE TO WRITE THAT MUCH! IT'S NOT FAIR!!
WATERSON
HOW'S IT COMING?
NOT SO GOOD. WHAT DID YOU DO BESIDES WATCH TV?

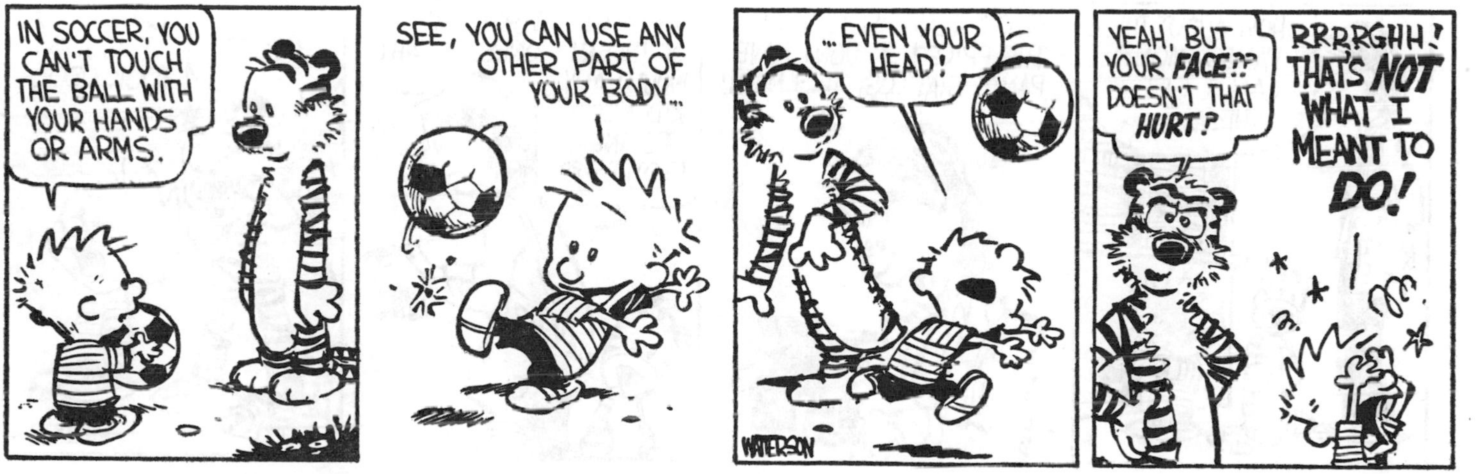
IN SOCCER, YOU CAN'T TOUCH THE BALL WITH YOUR HANDS OR ARMS.
SEE, YOU CAN USE ANY OTHER PART OF YOUR BODY...
...EVEN YOUR HEAD!
WATERSON
YEAH, BUT YOUR FACE?!? DOESN'T THAT HURT?
RRRRGHH! THAT'S NOT WHAT I MEANT TO DO!

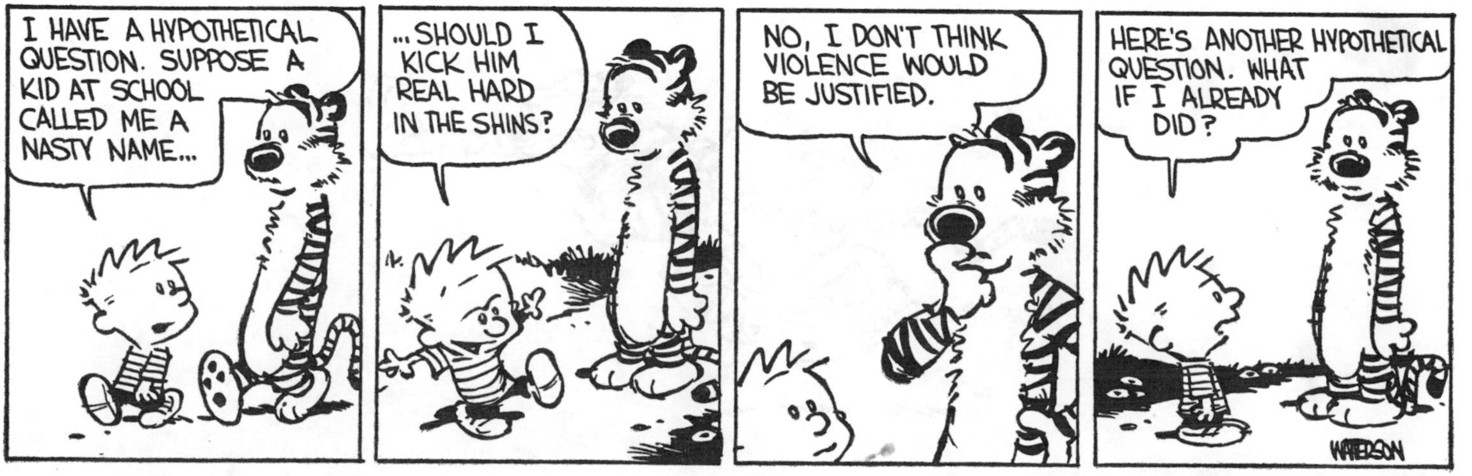
I HAVE A HYPOTHETICAL QUESTION. SUPPOSE A KID AT SCHOOL CALLED ME A NASTY NAME...
...SHOULD I KICK HIM REAL HARD IN THE SHINS?
NO, I DON'T THINK VIOLENCE WOULD BE JUSTIFIED.
HERE'S ANOTHER HYPOTHETICAL QUESTION. WHAT IF I ALREADY DID?
WATERSON

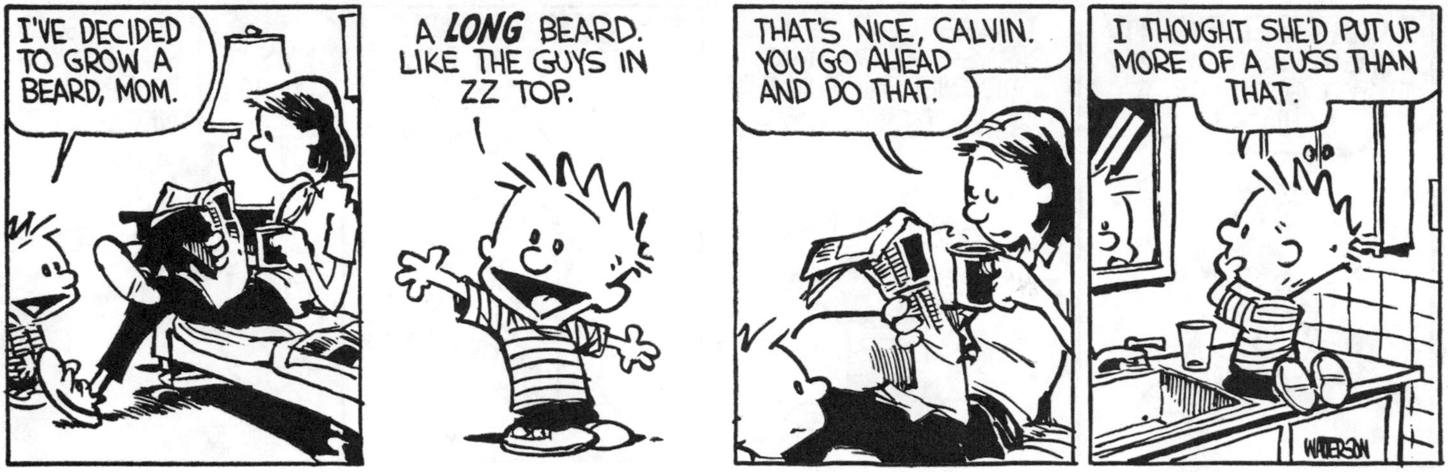
I'VE DECIDED TO GROW A BEARD, MOM.
A **LONG** BEARD. LIKE THE GUYS IN ZZ TOP.
THAT'S NICE, CALVIN. YOU GO AHEAD AND DO THAT.
I THOUGHT SHE'D PUT UP MORE OF A FUSS THAN THAT.
WATERSON

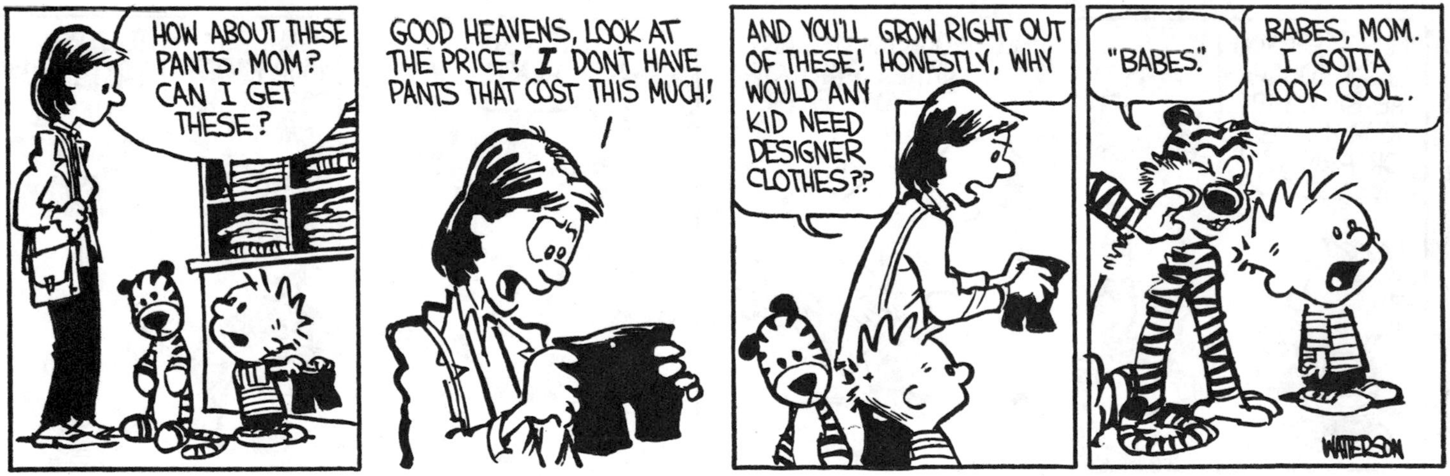
HOW ABOUT THESE PANTS, MOM? CAN I GET THESE?
GOOD HEAVENS, LOOK AT THE PRICE! *I* DON'T HAVE PANTS THAT COST THIS MUCH!
AND YOU'LL GROW RIGHT OUT OF THESE! HONESTLY, WHY WOULD ANY KID NEED DESIGNER CLOTHES??
BABES, MOM. I GOTTA LOOK COOL.
"BABES."
WATERSON

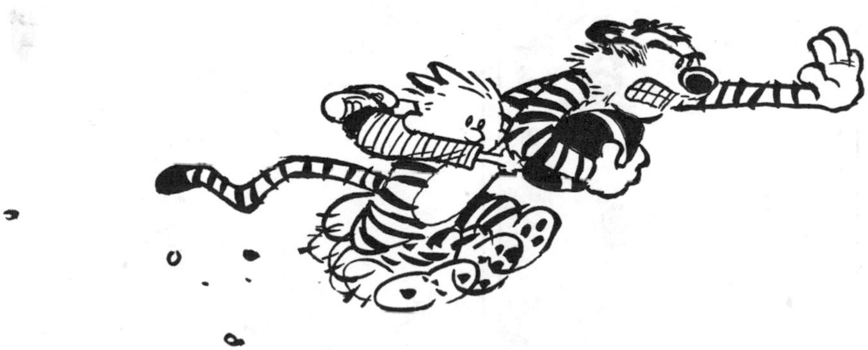

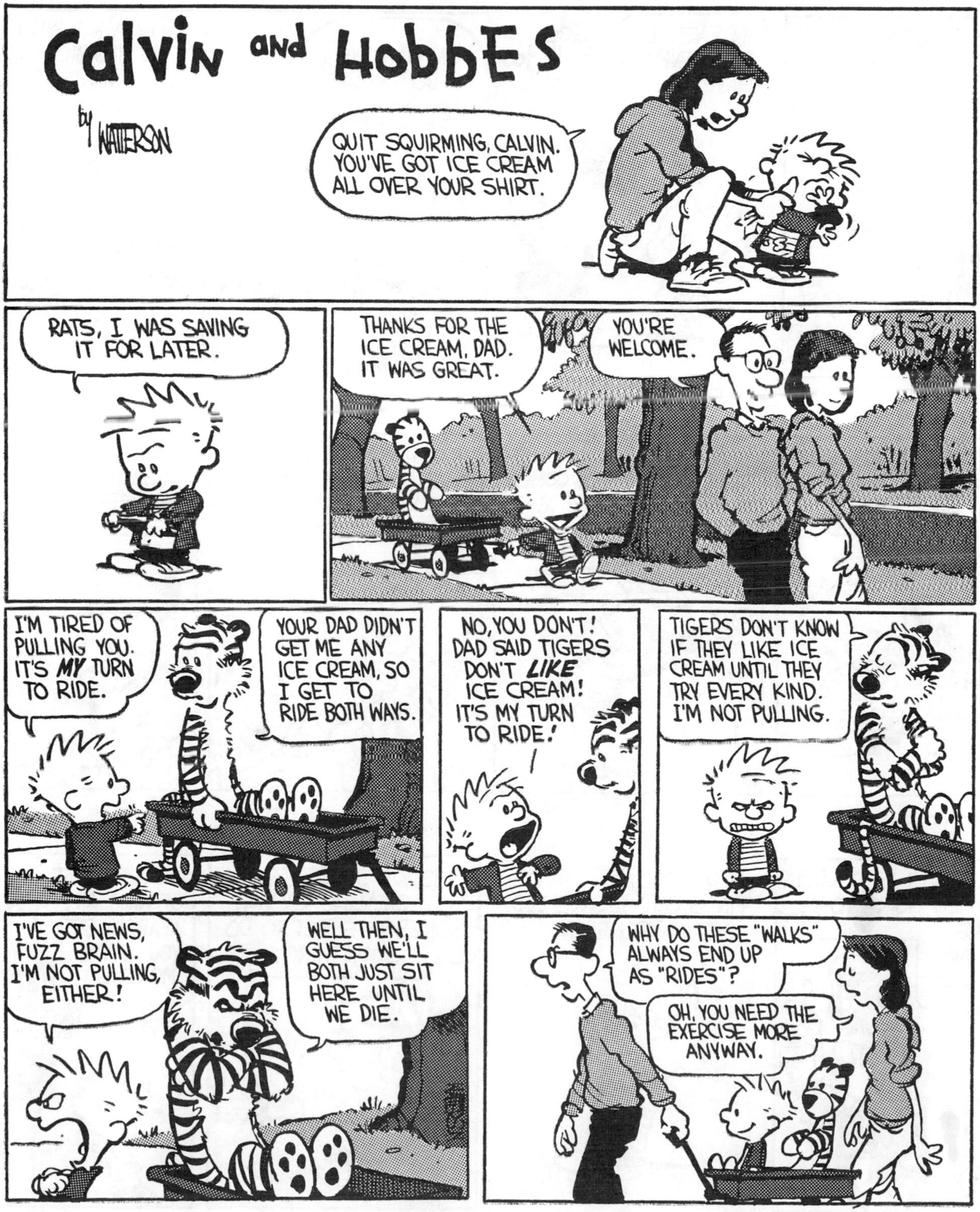
Calvin and HobbES
by WATTERSON
QUIT SQUIRMING, CALVIN. YOU'VE GOT ICE CREAM ALL OVER YOUR SHIRT.
RATS, I WAS SAVING IT FOR LATER.
THANKS FOR THE ICE CREAM, DAD. IT WAS GREAT.
YOU'RE WELCOME.
I'M TIRED OF PULLING YOU. IT'S *MY* TURN TO RIDE.
YOUR DAD DIDN'T GET ME ANY ICE CREAM, SO I GET TO RIDE BOTH WAYS.
NO, YOU DON'T! DAD SAID TIGERS DON'T ***LIKE*** ICE CREAM! IT'S MY TURN TO RIDE!
TIGERS DON'T KNOW IF THEY LIKE ICE CREAM UNTIL THEY TRY EVERY KIND. I'M NOT PULLING.
I'VE GOT NEWS, FUZZ BRAIN. I'M NOT PULLING, EITHER!
WELL THEN, I GUESS WE'LL BOTH JUST SIT HERE UNTIL WE DIE.
WHY DO THESE "WALKS" ALWAYS END UP AS "RIDES"?
OH, YOU NEED THE EXERCISE MORE ANYWAY.

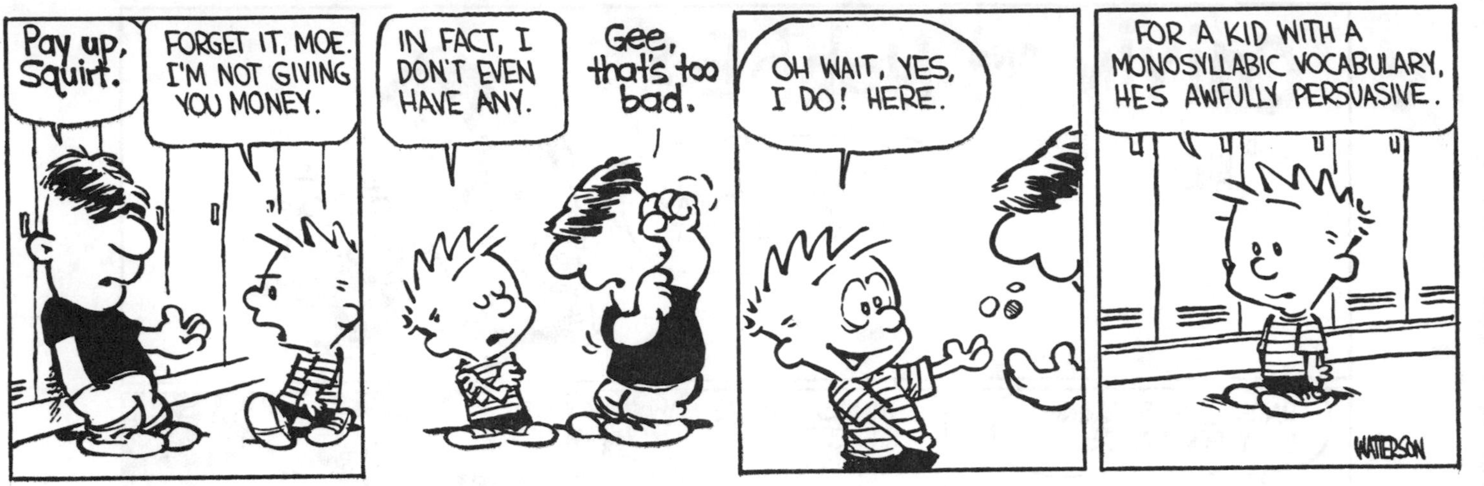
Pay up, Squirt.
FORGET IT, MOE. I'M NOT GIVING YOU MONEY.
IN FACT, I DON'T EVEN HAVE ANY.
Gee, that's too bad.
OH WAIT, YES, I DO! HERE.
FOR A KID WITH A MONOSYLLABIC VOCABULARY, HE'S AWFULLY PERSUASIVE.
WATERSON

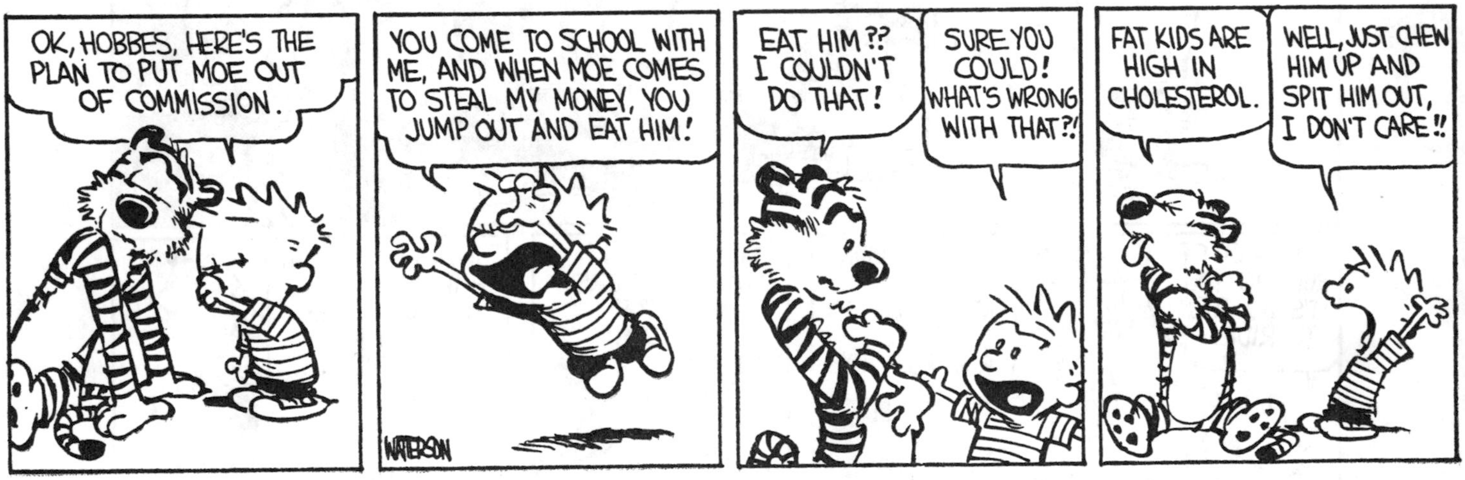
OK, HOBBES, HERE'S THE PLAN TO PUT MOE OUT OF COMMISSION.
YOU COME TO SCHOOL WITH ME, AND WHEN MOE COMES TO STEAL MY MONEY, YOU JUMP OUT AND EAT HIM!
WATERSON
EAT HIM?? I COULDN'T DO THAT!
SURE YOU COULD! WHAT'S WRONG WITH THAT?!
FAT KIDS ARE HIGH IN CHOLESTEROL.
WELL, JUST CHEW HIM UP AND SPIT HIM OUT, I DON'T CARE!!

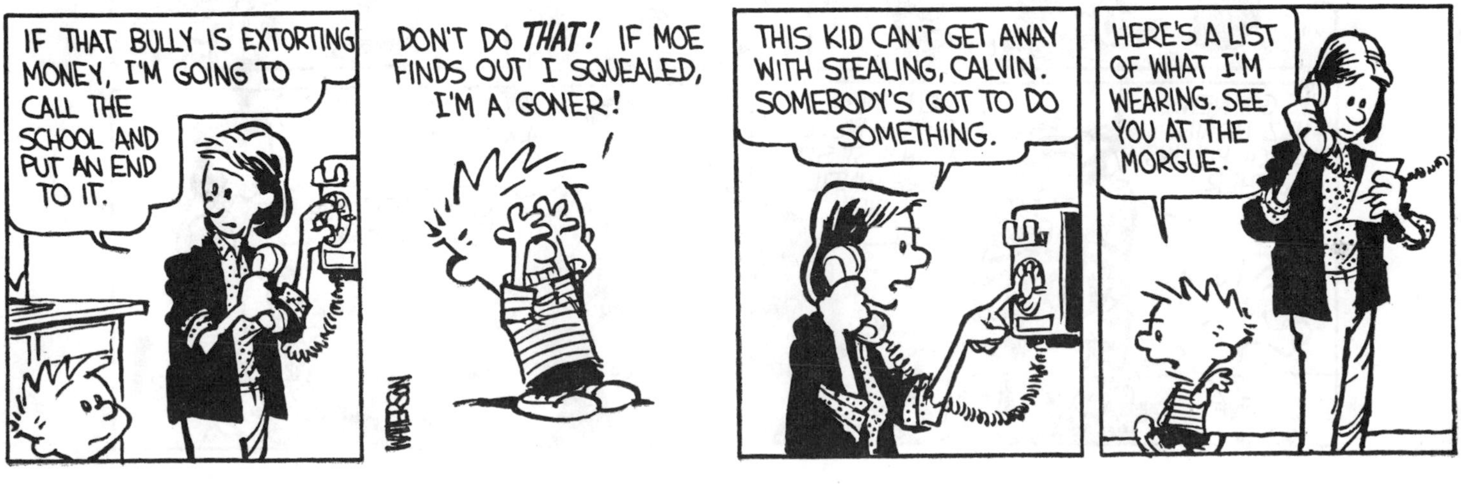
IF THAT BULLY IS EXTORTING MONEY, I'M GOING TO CALL THE SCHOOL AND PUT AN END TO IT.
WATERSON
DON'T DO THAT! IF MOE FINDS OUT I SQUEALED, I'M A GONER!
THIS KID CAN'T GET AWAY WITH STEALING, CALVIN. SOMEBODY'S GOT TO DO SOMETHING.
HERE'S A LIST OF WHAT I'M WEARING. SEE YOU AT THE MORGUE.

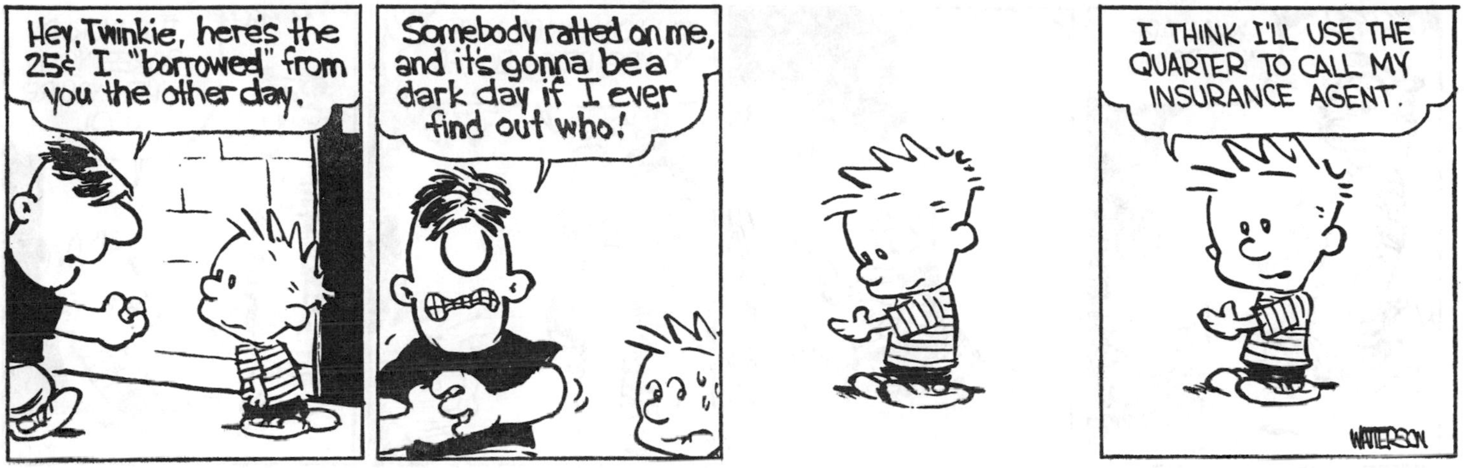
Hey, Twinkie, here's the 25¢ I "borrowed" from you the other day.
Somebody ratted on me, and it's gonna be a dark day if I ever find out who!
I THINK I'LL USE THE QUARTER TO CALL MY INSURANCE AGENT.
WATTERSON

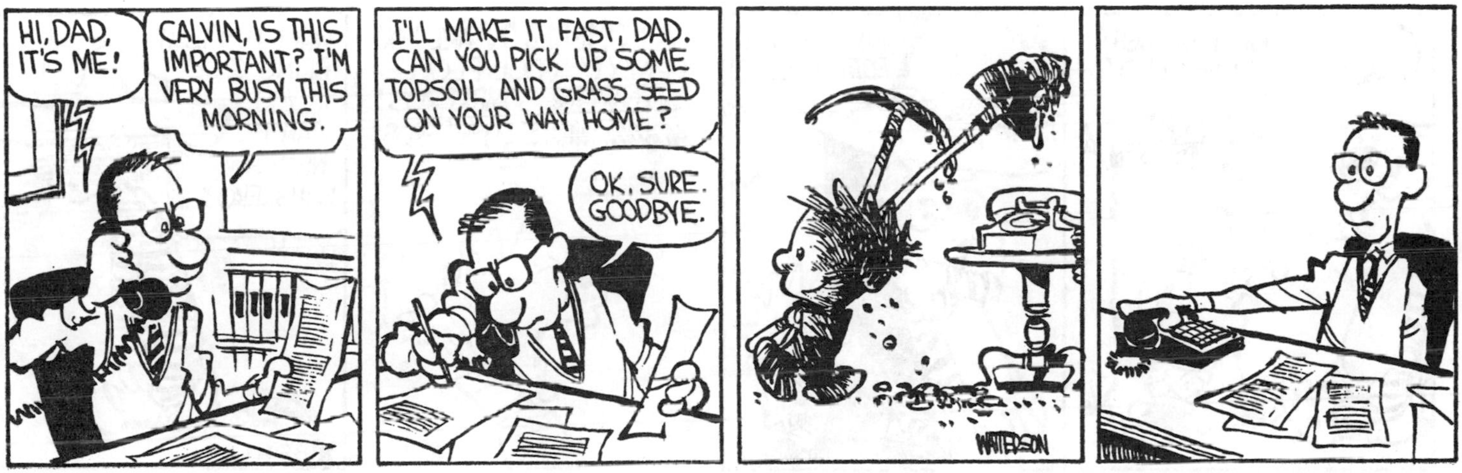
HI, DAD, IT'S ME!
CALVIN, IS THIS IMPORTANT? I'M VERY BUSY THIS MORNING.
I'LL MAKE IT FAST, DAD. CAN YOU PICK UP SOME TOPSOIL AND GRASS SEED ON YOUR WAY HOME?
OK, SURE. GOODBYE.
WATTERSON

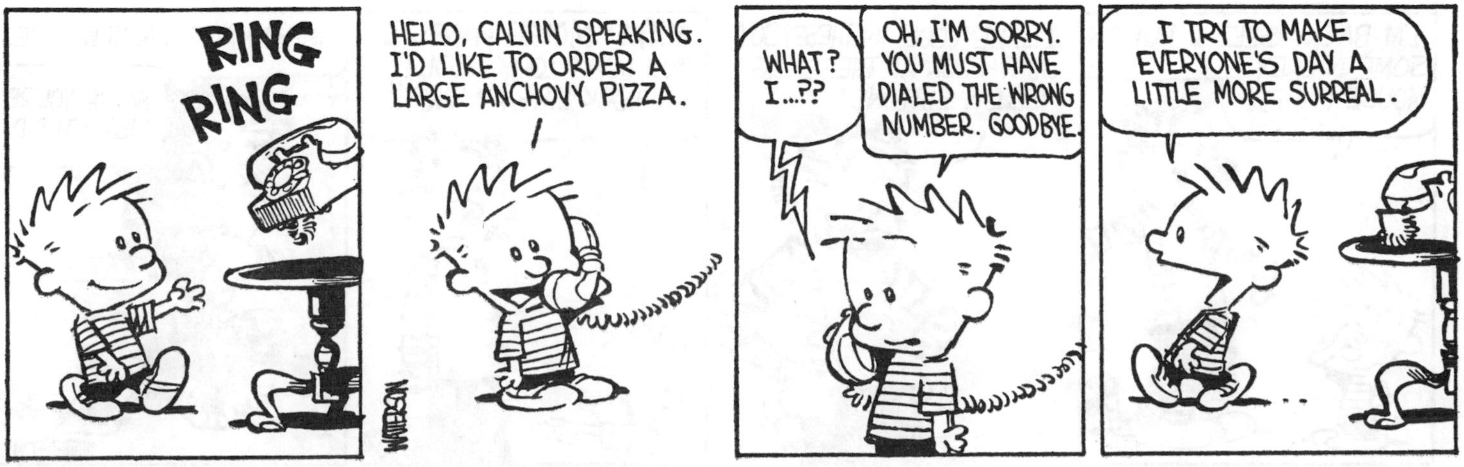
RING
RING
HELLO, CALVIN SPEAKING. I'D LIKE TO ORDER A LARGE ANCHOVY PIZZA.
WATTERSON
WHAT? I...??
OH, I'M SORRY. YOU MUST HAVE DIALED THE WRONG NUMBER. GOODBYE.
I TRY TO MAKE EVERYONE'S DAY A LITTLE MORE SURREAL.

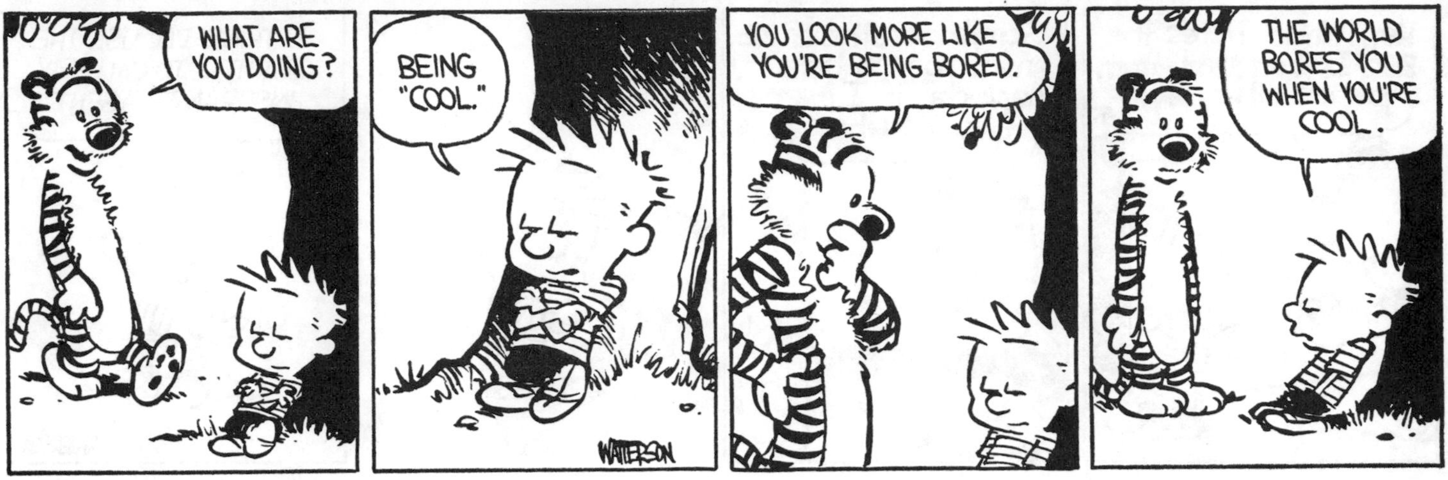
WHAT ARE YOU DOING?
BEING "COOL."
YOU LOOK MORE LIKE YOU'RE BEING BORED.
THE WORLD BORES YOU WHEN YOU'RE COOL.

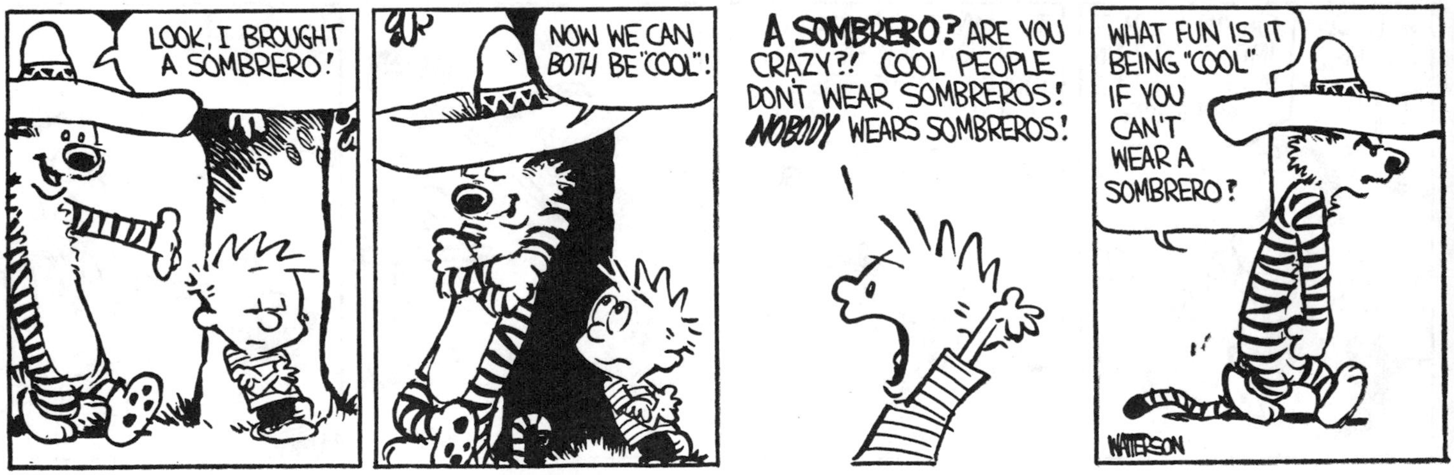
LOOK, I BROUGHT A SOMBRERO!
NOW WE CAN BOTH BE "COOL"!
A SOMBRERO? ARE YOU CRAZY?! COOL PEOPLE DON'T WEAR SOMBREROS! NOBODY WEARS SOMBREROS!
WHAT FUN IS IT BEING "COOL" IF YOU CAN'T WEAR A SOMBRERO?

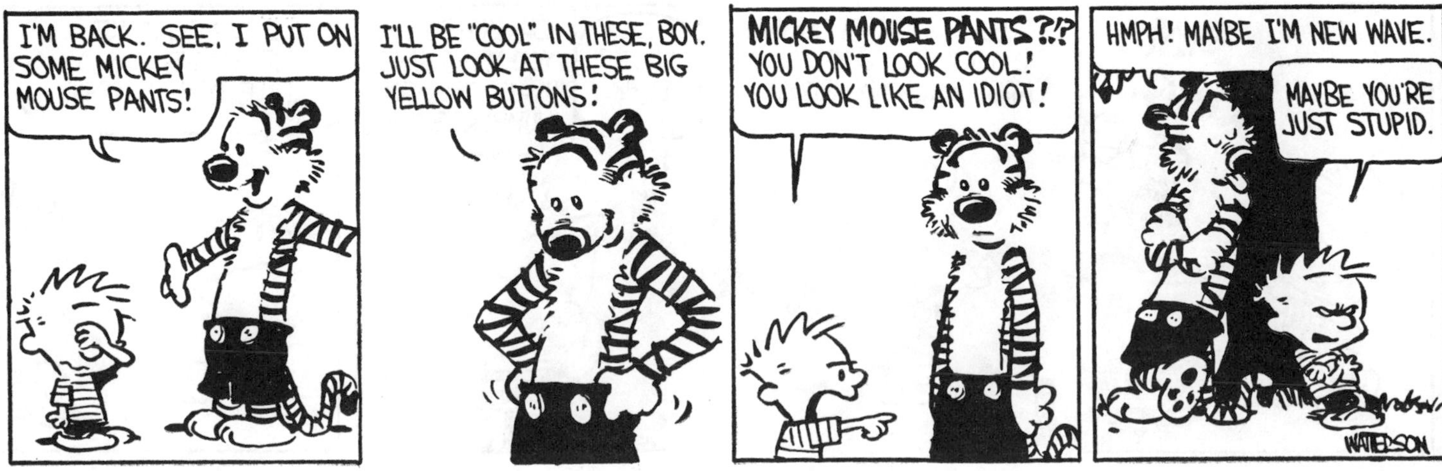
I'M BACK. SEE, I PUT ON SOME MICKEY MOUSE PANTS!
I'LL BE "COOL" IN THESE, BOY. JUST LOOK AT THESE BIG YELLOW BUTTONS!
MICKEY MOUSE PANTS?!? YOU DON'T LOOK COOL! YOU LOOK LIKE AN IDIOT!
HMPH! MAYBE I'M NEW WAVE.
MAYBE YOU'RE JUST STUPID.

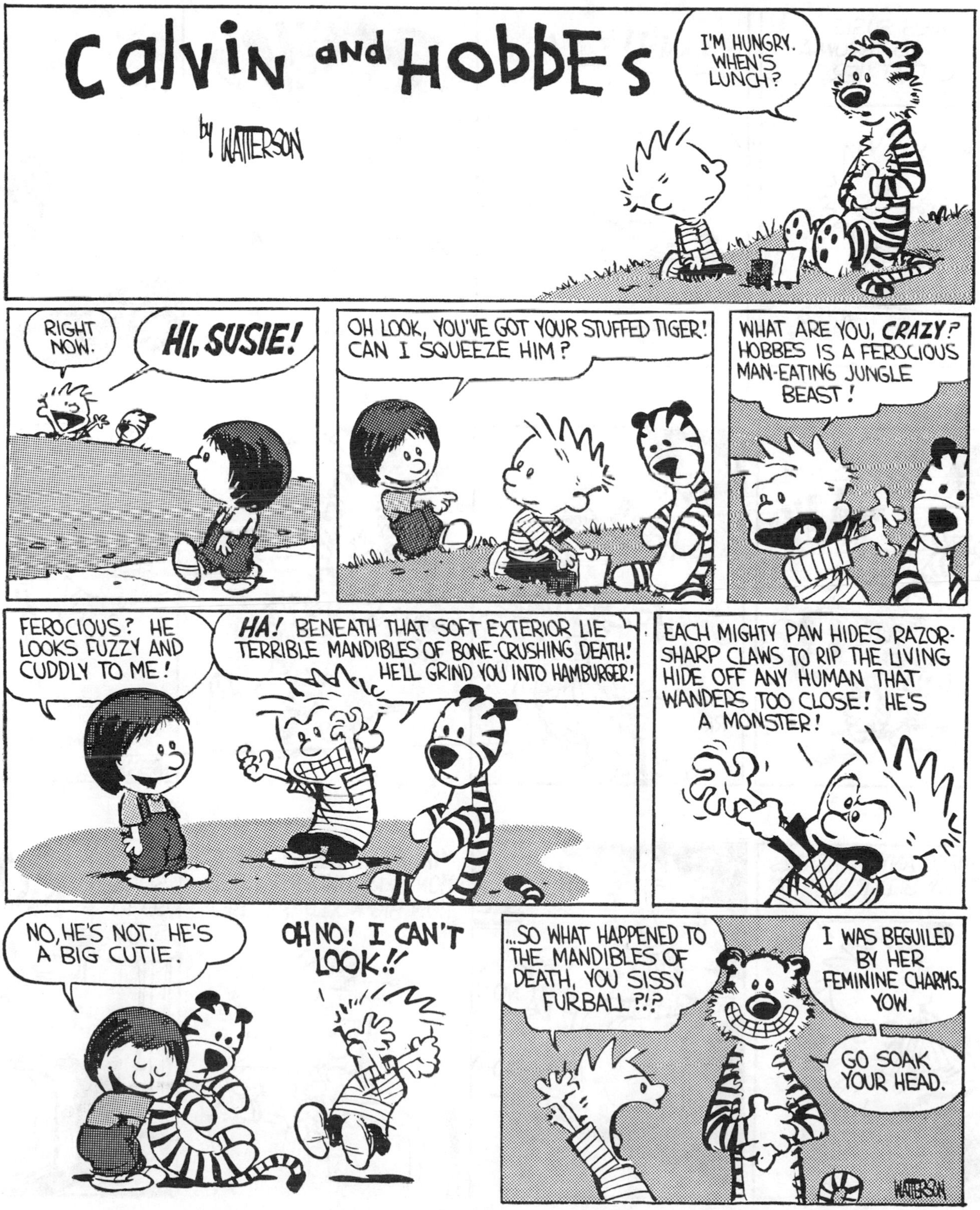
Calvin and HOBBES
by WATTERSON
I'M HUNGRY. WHEN'S LUNCH?
RIGHT NOW.
HI, SUSIE!
OH LOOK, YOU'VE GOT YOUR STUFFED TIGER! CAN I SQUEEZE HIM?
WHAT ARE YOU, CRAZY? HOBBES IS A FEROCIOUS MAN-EATING JUNGLE BEAST!
FEROCIOUS? HE LOOKS FUZZY AND CUDDLY TO ME!
HA! BENEATH THAT SOFT EXTERIOR LIE TERRIBLE MANDIBLES OF BONE-CRUSHING DEATH! HE'LL GRIND YOU INTO HAMBURGER!
EACH MIGHTY PAW HIDES RAZOR-SHARP CLAWS TO RIP THE LIVING HIDE OFF ANY HUMAN THAT WANDERS TOO CLOSE! HE'S A MONSTER!
NO, HE'S NOT. HE'S A BIG CUTIE.
OH NO! I CAN'T LOOK!!
...SO WHAT HAPPENED TO THE MANDIBLES OF DEATH, YOU SISSY FURBALL?!?
I WAS BEGUILED BY HER FEMININE CHARMS. YOW.
GO SOAK YOUR HEAD.
WATTERSON

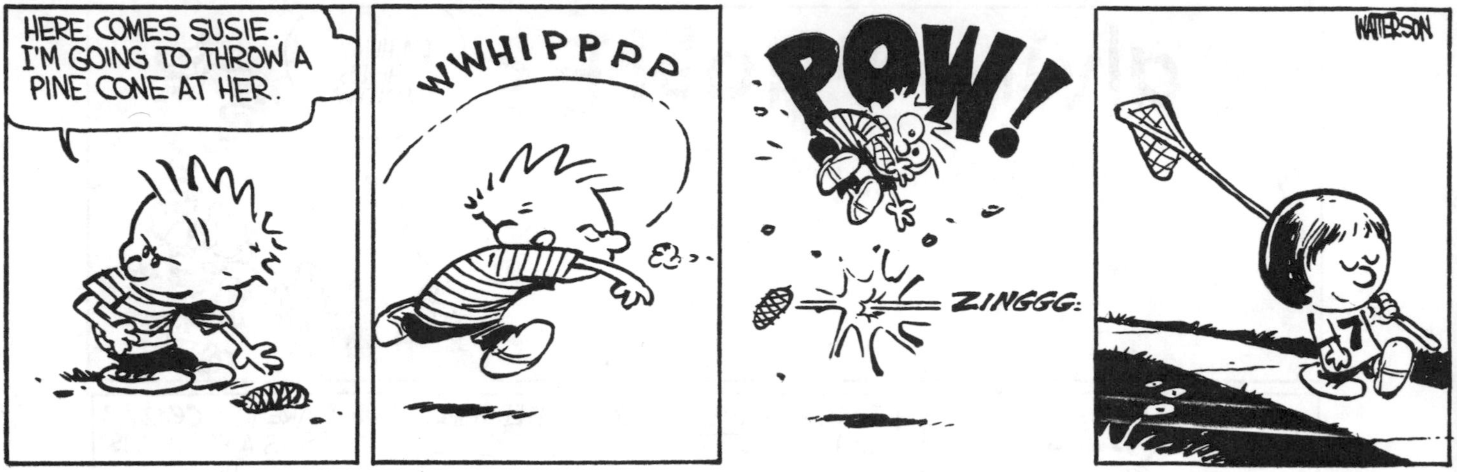
HERE COMES SUSIE. I'M GOING TO THROW A PINE CONE AT HER.
WWHIPPPPP
POW!
ZINGGG
WATTERSON

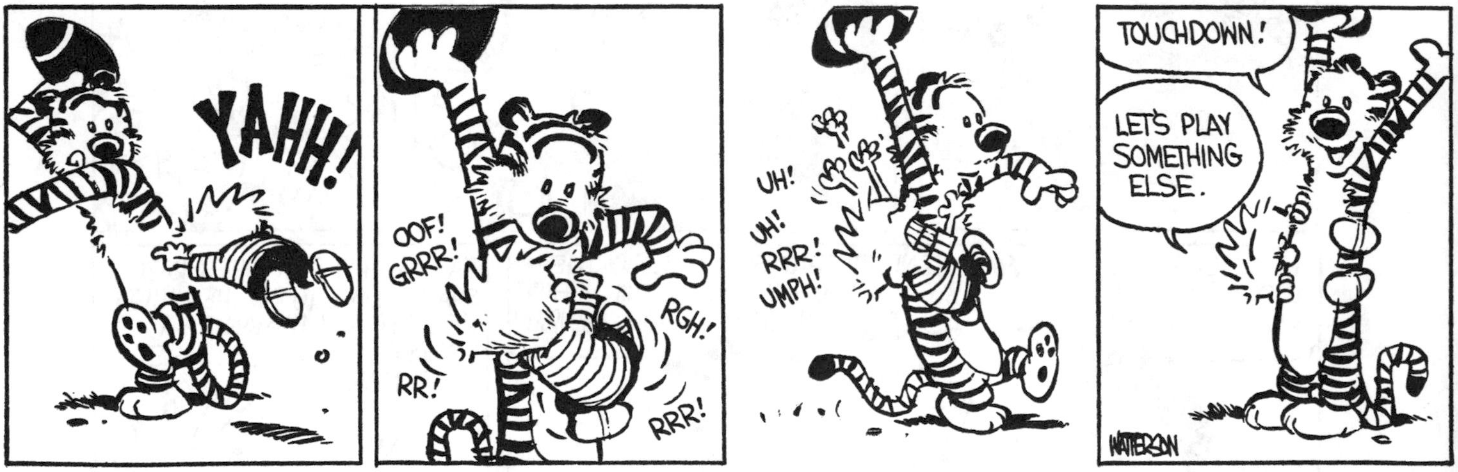
YAHH!
OOF! GRRR!
RGH!
RR!
RRR!
UH!
UH!
RRR!
UMPH!
TOUCHDOWN!
LET'S PLAY SOMETHING ELSE.
WATTERSON

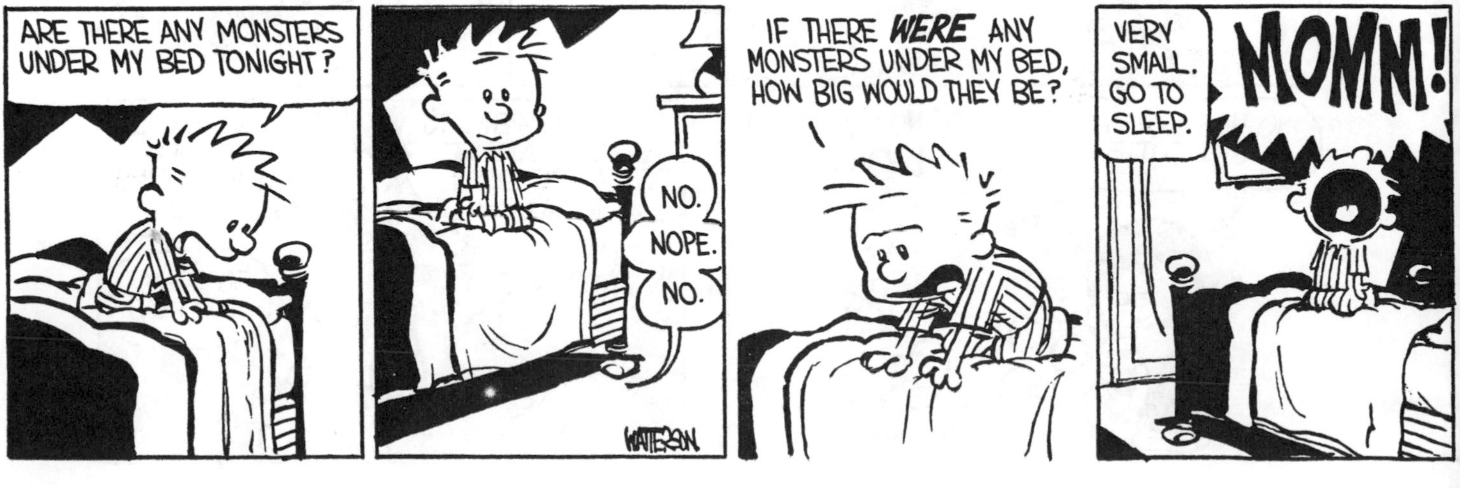
ARE THERE ANY MONSTERS UNDER MY BED TONIGHT?
NO.
NOPE.
NO.
WATTERSON
IF THERE *WERE* ANY MONSTERS UNDER MY BED, HOW BIG WOULD THEY BE?
VERY SMALL. GO TO SLEEP.
MOMM!

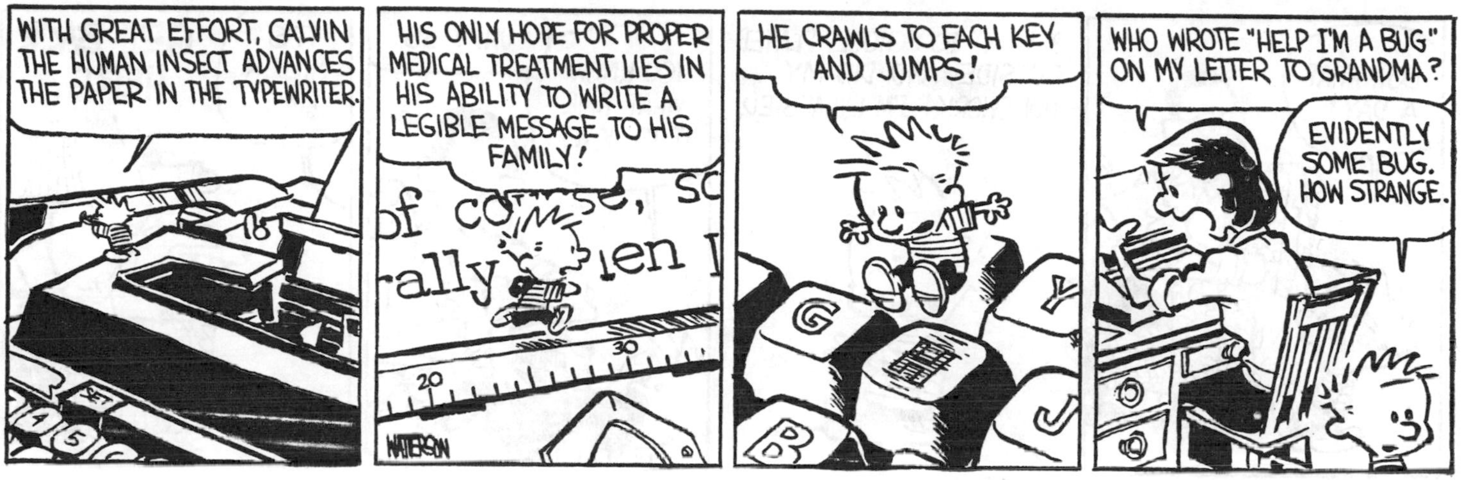
WITH GREAT EFFORT, CALVIN THE HUMAN INSECT ADVANCES THE PAPER IN THE TYPEWRITER.
HIS ONLY HOPE FOR PROPER MEDICAL TREATMENT LIES IN HIS ABILITY TO WRITE A LEGIBLE MESSAGE TO HIS FAMILY!
HE CRAWLS TO EACH KEY AND JUMPS!
WHO WROTE "HELP I'M A BUG" ON MY LETTER TO GRANDMA?
EVIDENTLY SOME BUG. HOW STRANGE.

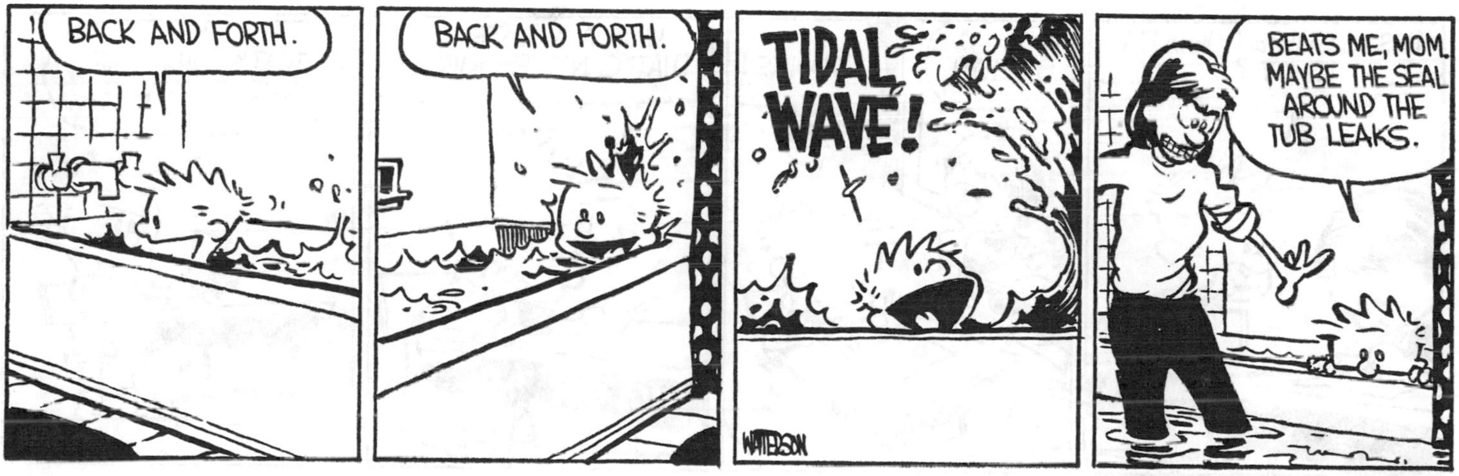
BACK AND FORTH.
BACK AND FORTH.
TIDAL WAVE!
BEATS ME, MOM. MAYBE THE SEAL AROUND THE TUB LEAKS.

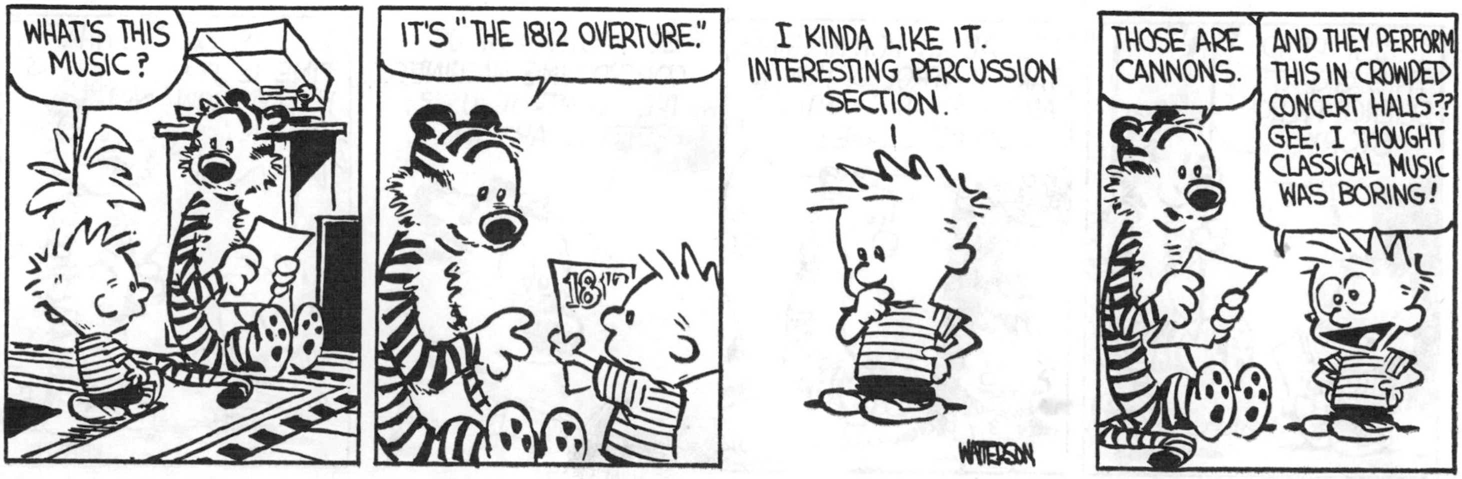
WHAT'S THIS MUSIC?
IT'S "THE 1812 OVERTURE."
I KINDA LIKE IT. INTERESTING PERCUSSION SECTION.
THOSE ARE CANNONS.
AND THEY PERFORM THIS IN CROWDED CONCERT HALLS?? GEE, I THOUGHT CLASSICAL MUSIC WAS BORING!

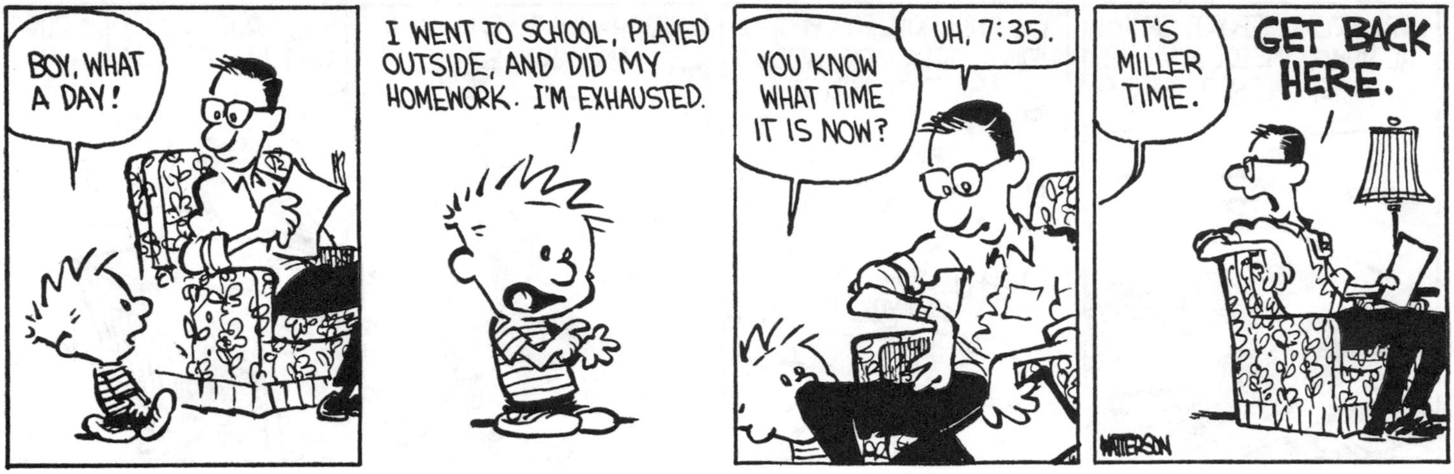
BOY, WHAT A DAY!
I WENT TO SCHOOL, PLAYED OUTSIDE, AND DID MY HOMEWORK. I'M EXHAUSTED.
YOU KNOW WHAT TIME IT IS NOW?
UH, 7:35.
IT'S MILLER TIME.
GET BACK HERE.
WATTERSON

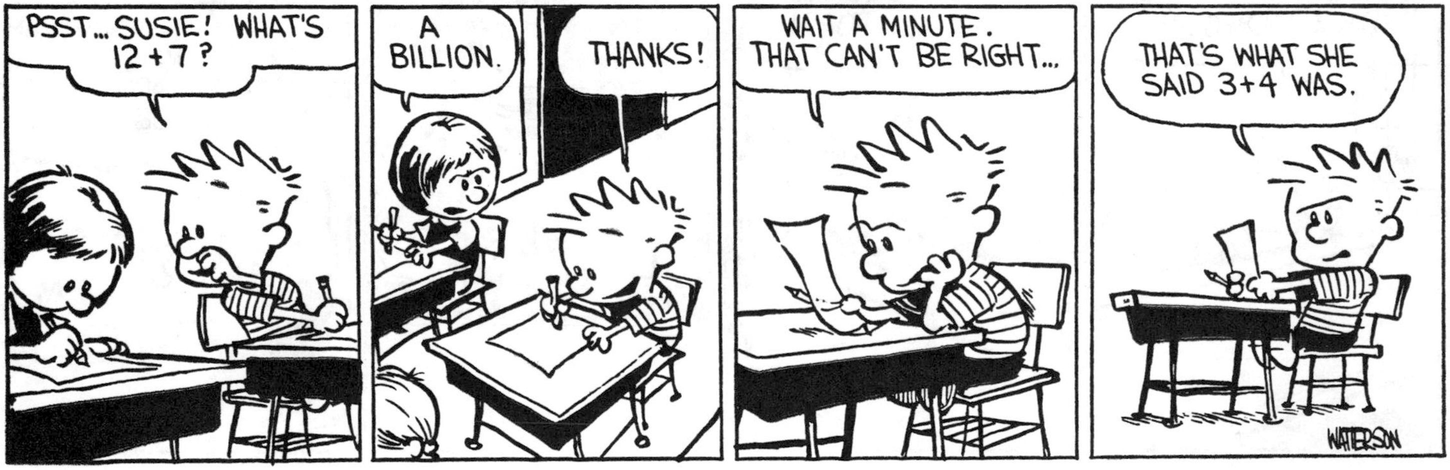
PSST... SUSIE! WHAT'S 12 + 7?
A BILLION.
THANKS!
WAIT A MINUTE. THAT CAN'T BE RIGHT...
THAT'S WHAT SHE SAID 3+4 WAS.
WATTERSON

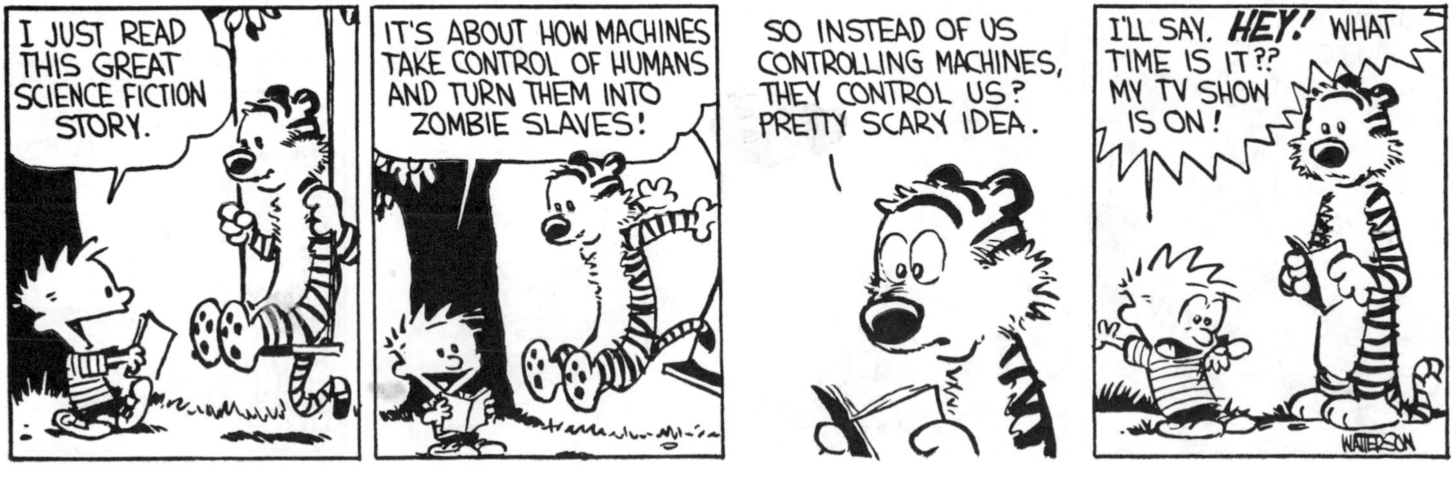
I JUST READ THIS GREAT SCIENCE FICTION STORY.
IT'S ABOUT HOW MACHINES TAKE CONTROL OF HUMANS AND TURN THEM INTO ZOMBIE SLAVES!
SO INSTEAD OF US CONTROLLING MACHINES, THEY CONTROL US? PRETTY SCARY IDEA.
I'LL SAY. HEY! WHAT TIME IS IT?? MY TV SHOW IS ON!
WATTERSON

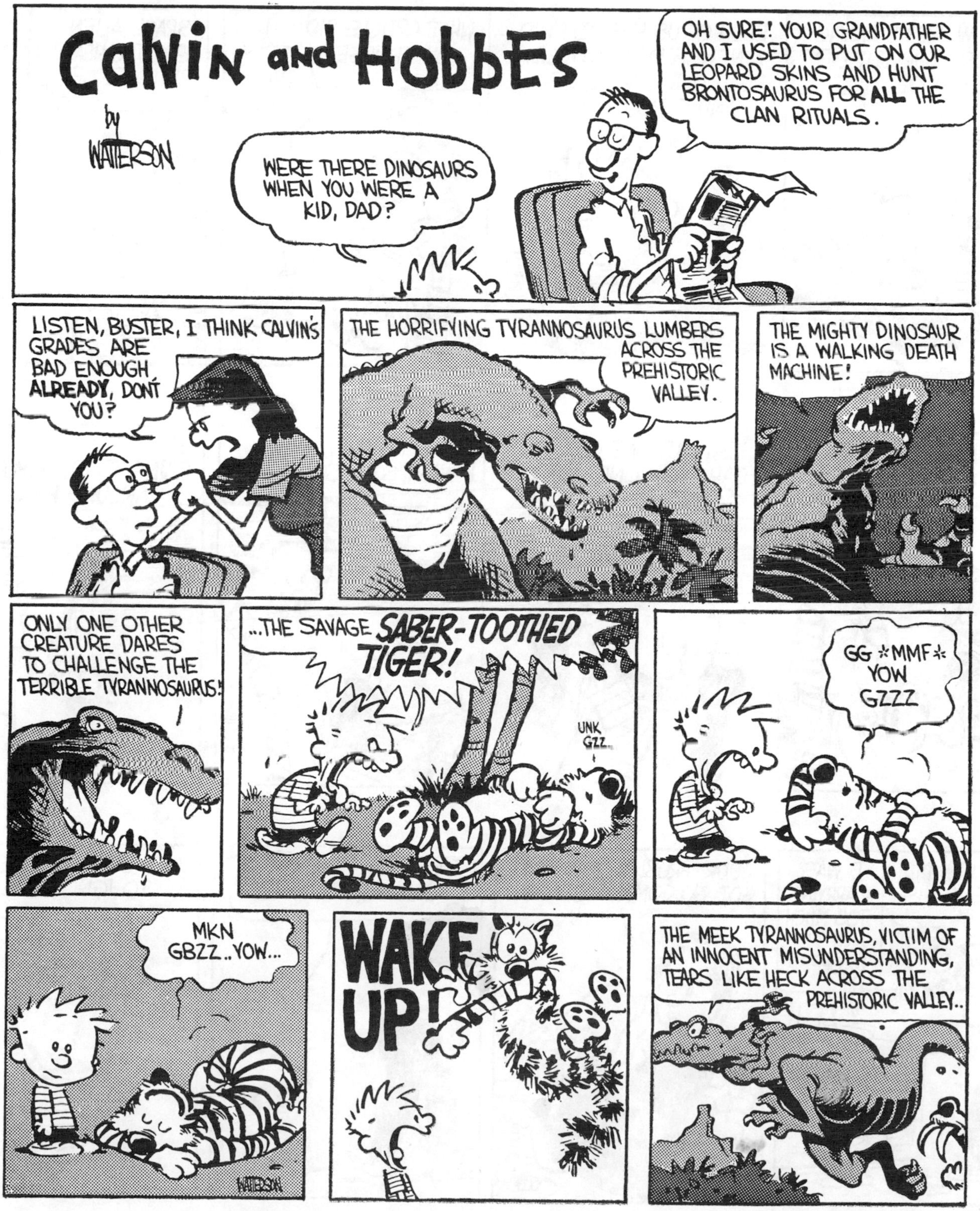
Calvin and Hobbes
by WATTERSON
WERE THERE DINOSAURS WHEN YOU WERE A KID, DAD?
OH SURE! YOUR GRANDFATHER AND I USED TO PUT ON OUR LEOPARD SKINS AND HUNT BRONTOSAURUS FOR ALL THE CLAN RITUALS.
LISTEN, BUSTER, I THINK CALVIN'S GRADES ARE BAD ENOUGH ALREADY, DON'T YOU?
THE HORRIFYING TYRANNOSAURUS LUMBERS ACROSS THE PREHISTORIC VALLEY.
THE MIGHTY DINOSAUR IS A WALKING DEATH MACHINE!
ONLY ONE OTHER CREATURE DARES TO CHALLENGE THE TERRIBLE TYRANNOSAURUS!
...THE SAVAGE SABER-TOOTHED TIGER!
UNK GZZ
GG *MMF* YOW GZZZ
MKN GBZZ..YOW...
WATTERSON
WAKE UP!
THE MEEK TYRANNOSAURUS, VICTIM OF AN INNOCENT MISUNDERSTANDING, TEARS LIKE HECK ACROSS THE PREHISTORIC VALLEY..

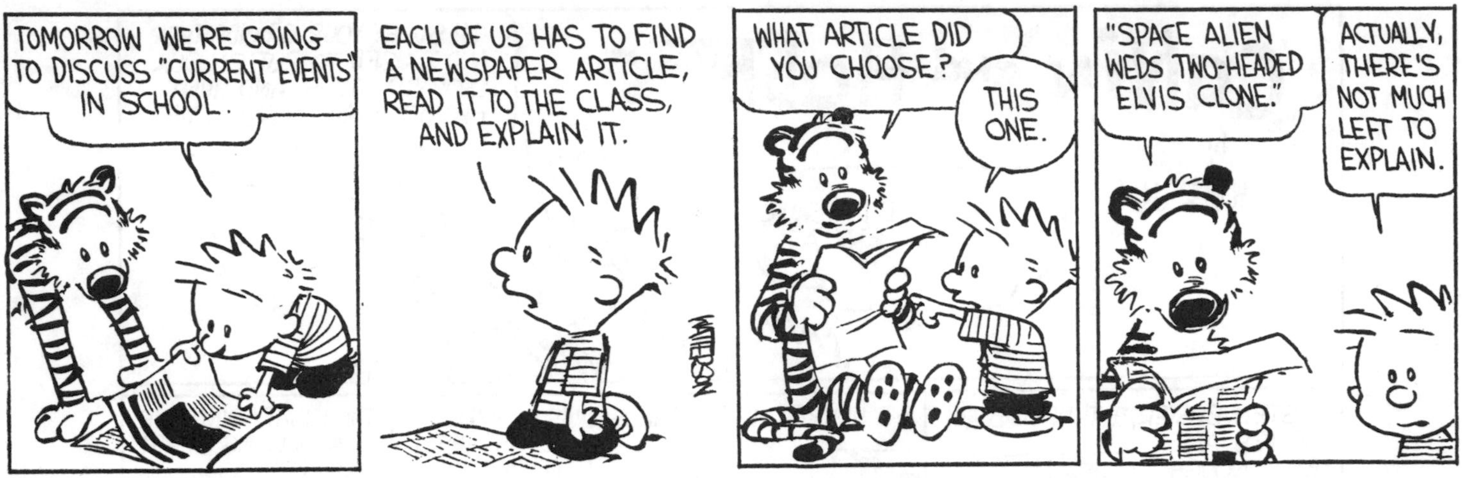
TOMORROW WE'RE GOING TO DISCUSS "CURRENT EVENTS" IN SCHOOL.
EACH OF US HAS TO FIND A NEWSPAPER ARTICLE, READ IT TO THE CLASS, AND EXPLAIN IT.
WATTERSON
WHAT ARTICLE DID YOU CHOOSE?
THIS ONE.
"SPACE ALIEN WEDS TWO-HEADED ELVIS CLONE."
ACTUALLY, THERE'S NOT MUCH LEFT TO EXPLAIN.

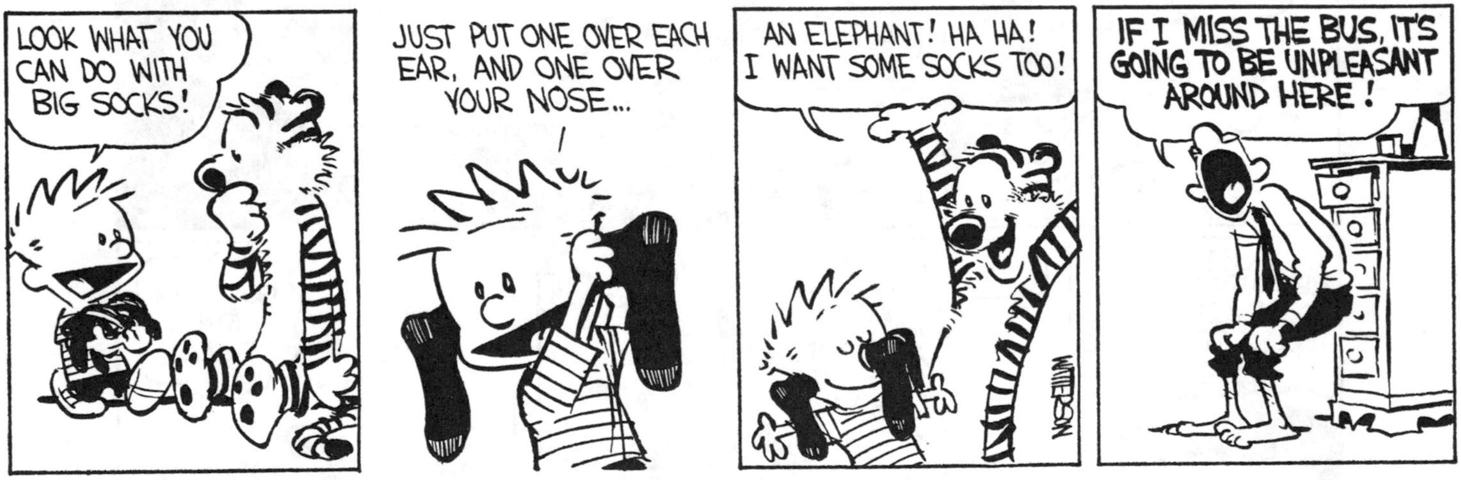
LOOK WHAT YOU CAN DO WITH BIG SOCKS!
JUST PUT ONE OVER EACH EAR, AND ONE OVER YOUR NOSE...
AN ELEPHANT! HA HA! I WANT SOME SOCKS TOO!
WATTERSON
IF I MISS THE BUS, IT'S GOING TO BE UNPLEASANT AROUND HERE!

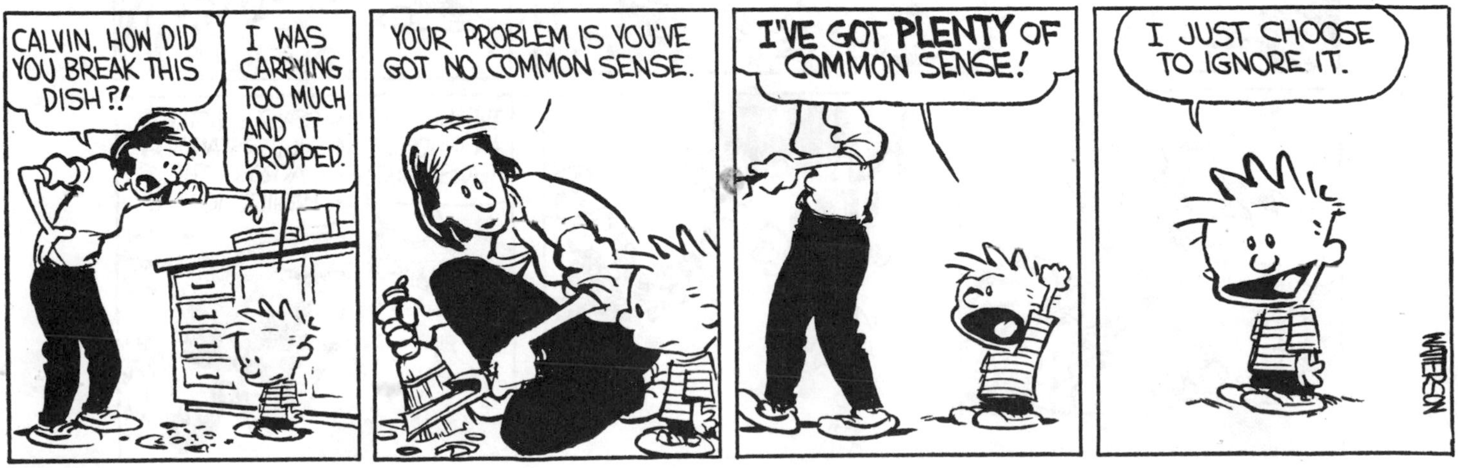
CALVIN, HOW DID YOU BREAK THIS DISH?!
I WAS CARRYING TOO MUCH AND IT DROPPED.
YOUR PROBLEM IS YOU'VE GOT NO COMMON SENSE.
I'VE GOT PLENTY OF COMMON SENSE!
I JUST CHOOSE TO IGNORE IT.
WATTERSON

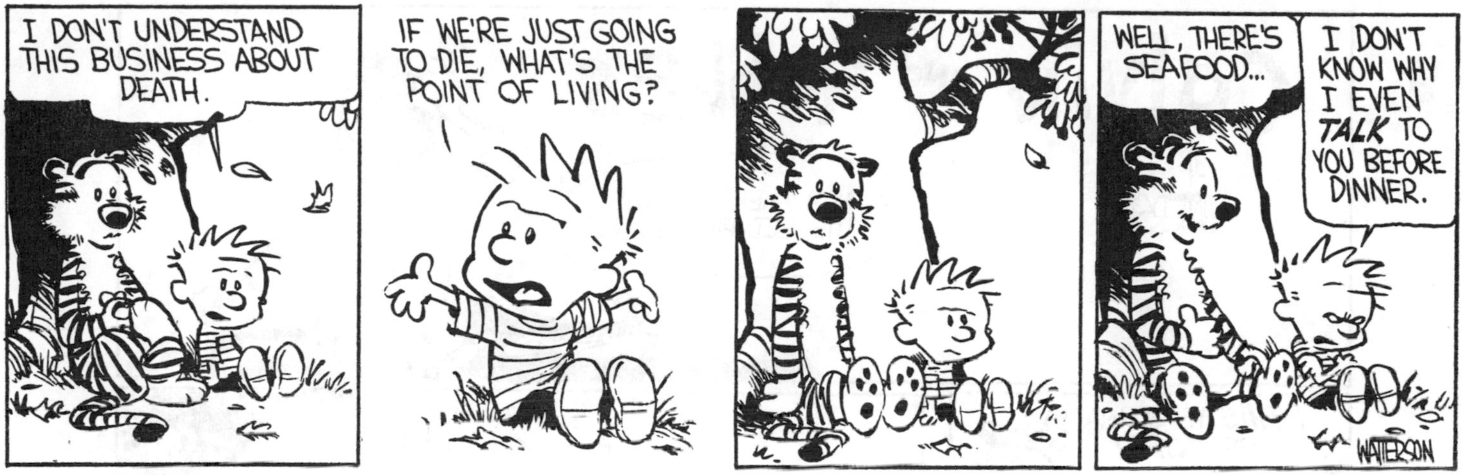
I DON'T UNDERSTAND THIS BUSINESS ABOUT DEATH.
IF WE'RE JUST GOING TO DIE, WHAT'S THE POINT OF LIVING?
WELL, THERE'S SEAFOOD...
I DON'T KNOW WHY I EVEN *TALK* TO YOU BEFORE DINNER.
WATTERSON

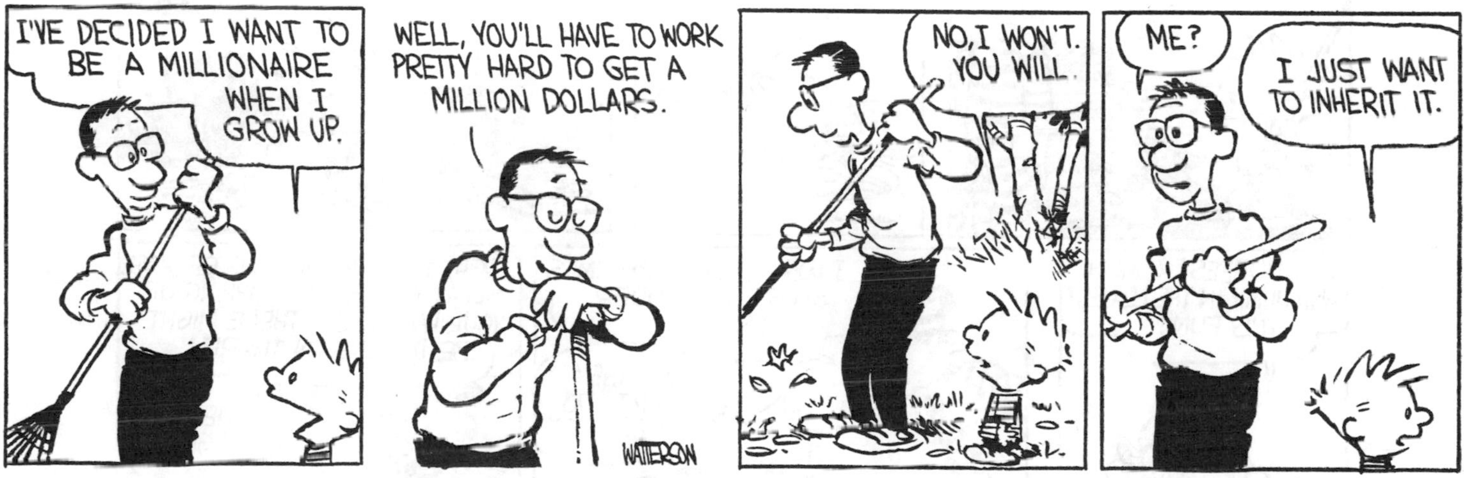
I'VE DECIDED I WANT TO BE A MILLIONAIRE WHEN I GROW UP.
WELL, YOU'LL HAVE TO WORK PRETTY HARD TO GET A MILLION DOLLARS.
WATTERSON
NO, I WON'T. YOU WILL.
ME?
I JUST WANT TO INHERIT IT.

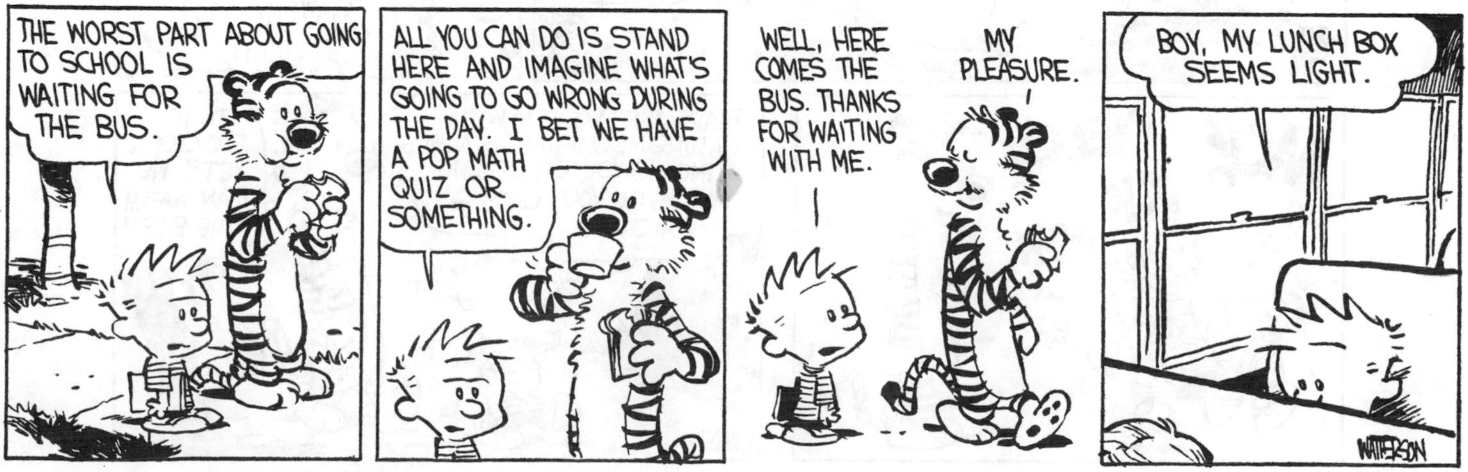
THE WORST PART ABOUT GOING TO SCHOOL IS WAITING FOR THE BUS.
ALL YOU CAN DO IS STAND HERE AND IMAGINE WHAT'S GOING TO GO WRONG DURING THE DAY. I BET WE HAVE A POP MATH QUIZ OR SOMETHING.
WELL, HERE COMES THE BUS. THANKS FOR WAITING WITH ME.
MY PLEASURE.
BOY, MY LUNCH BOX SEEMS LIGHT.
WATTERSON

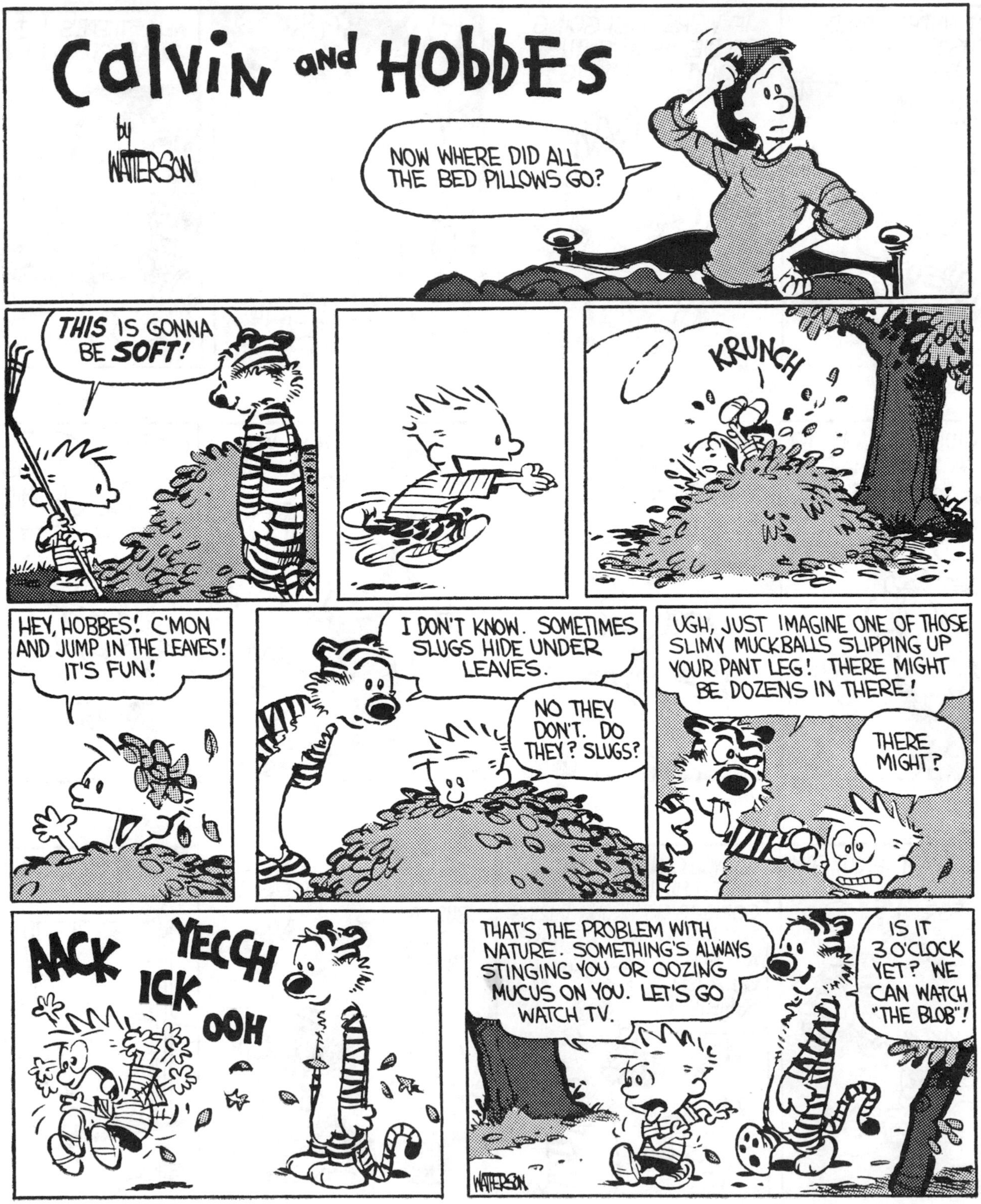
Calvin and HOBBES
by WATTERSON
NOW WHERE DID ALL THE BED PILLOWS GO?
THIS IS GONNA BE SOFT!
KRUNCH
HEY, HOBBES! C'MON AND JUMP IN THE LEAVES! IT'S FUN!
I DON'T KNOW. SOMETIMES SLUGS HIDE UNDER LEAVES.
NO THEY DON'T. DO THEY? SLUGS?
UGH, JUST IMAGINE ONE OF THOSE SLIMY MUCKBALLS SLIPPING UP YOUR PANT LEG! THERE MIGHT BE DOZENS IN THERE!
THERE MIGHT?
AACK
YECCH
ICK
OOH
THAT'S THE PROBLEM WITH NATURE. SOMETHING'S ALWAYS STINGING YOU OR OOZING MUCUS ON YOU. LET'S GO WATCH TV.
IS IT 3 O'CLOCK YET? WE CAN WATCH "THE BLOB"!
WATTERSON

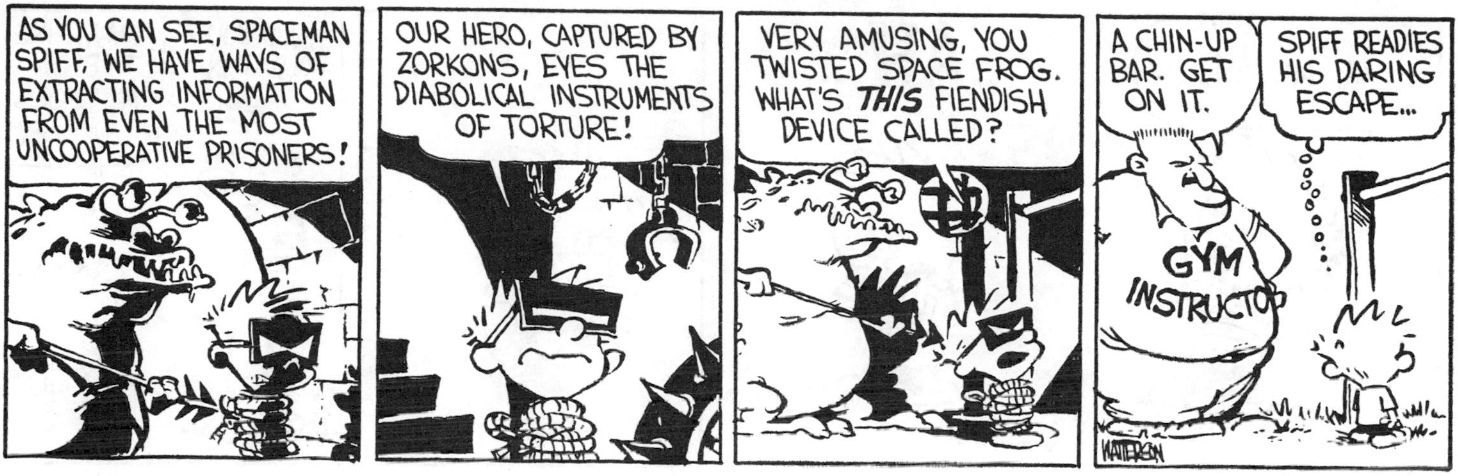

AS YOU CAN SEE, SPACEMAN SPIFF, WE HAVE WAYS OF EXTRACTING INFORMATION FROM EVEN THE MOST UNCOOPERATIVE PRISONERS!
OUR HERO, CAPTURED BY ZORKONS, EYES THE DIABOLICAL INSTRUMENTS OF TORTURE!
VERY AMUSING, YOU TWISTED SPACE FROG. WHAT'S THIS FIENDISH DEVICE CALLED?
A CHIN-UP BAR. GET ON IT.
SPIFF READIES HIS DARING ESCAPE...
GYM INSTRUCTOR
WATTERSON

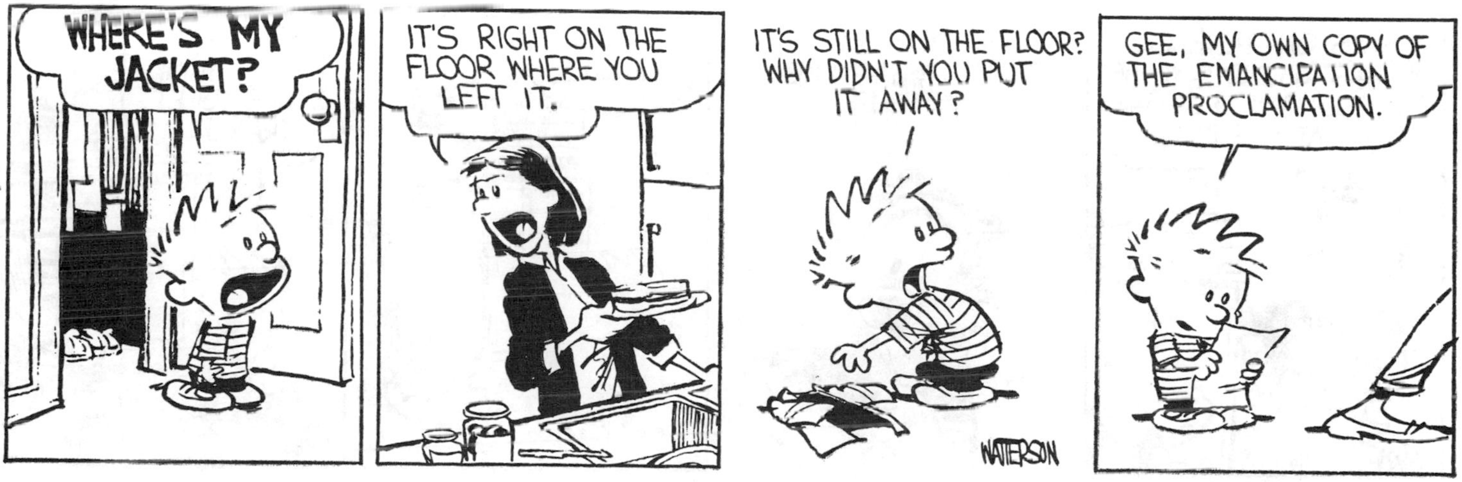

WHERE'S MY JACKET?
IT'S RIGHT ON THE FLOOR WHERE YOU LEFT IT.
IT'S STILL ON THE FLOOR? WHY DIDN'T YOU PUT IT AWAY?
WATTERSON
GEE, MY OWN COPY OF THE EMANCIPATION PROCLAMATION.

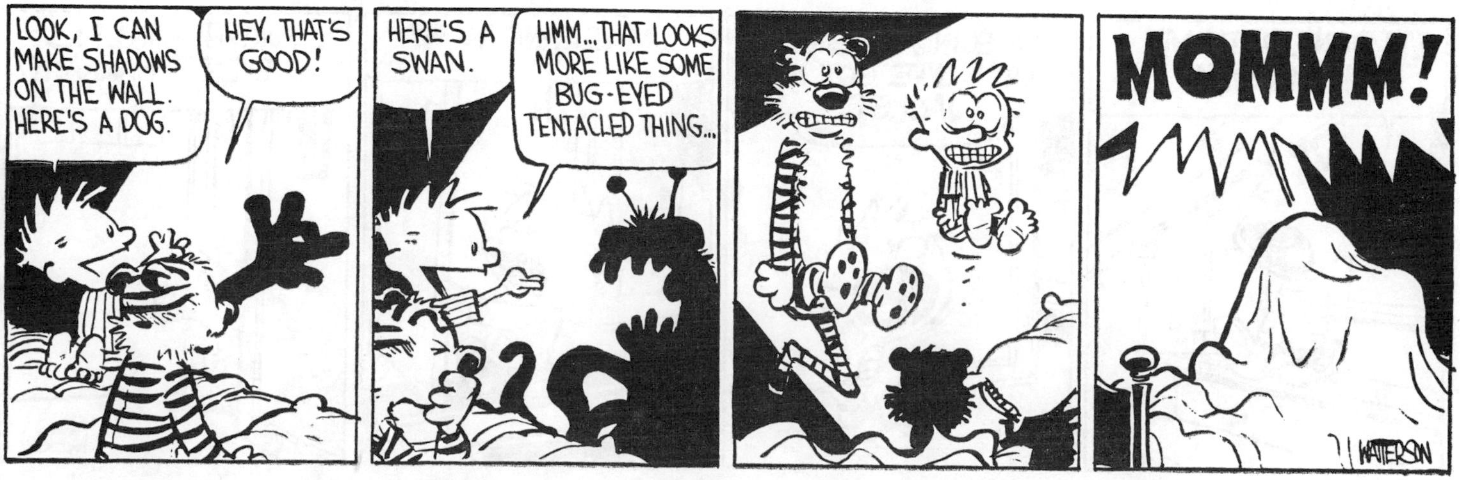

LOOK, I CAN MAKE SHADOWS ON THE WALL. HERE'S A DOG.
HEY, THAT'S GOOD!
HERE'S A SWAN.
HMM... THAT LOOKS MORE LIKE SOME BUG-EYED TENTACLED THING...
MOMMM!
WATTERSON

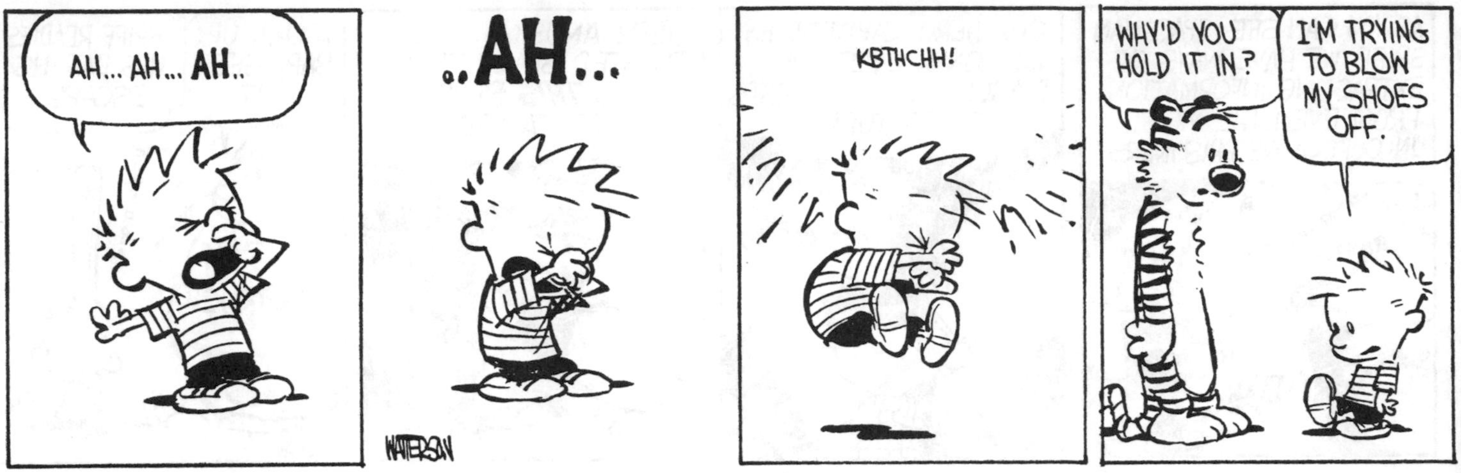
AH... AH... AH..
..AH...
WATTERSON
KBTHCHH!
WHY'D YOU HOLD IT IN?
I'M TRYING TO BLOW MY SHOES OFF.

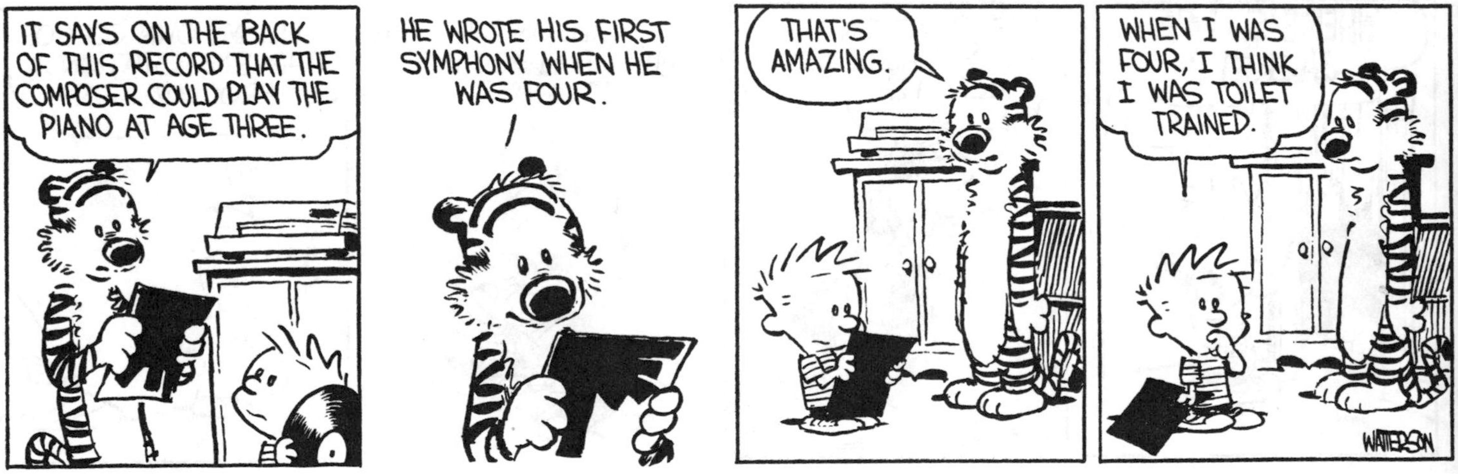
IT SAYS ON THE BACK OF THIS RECORD THAT THE COMPOSER COULD PLAY THE PIANO AT AGE THREE.
HE WROTE HIS FIRST SYMPHONY WHEN HE WAS FOUR.
THAT'S AMAZING.
WHEN I WAS FOUR, I THINK I WAS TOILET TRAINED.
WATTERSON

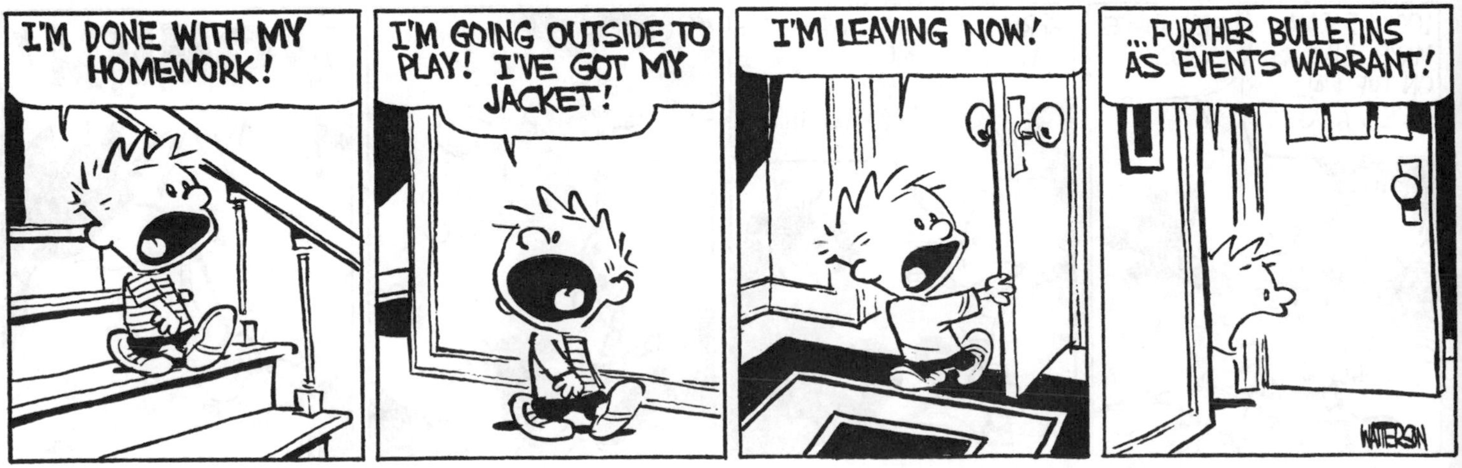
I'M DONE WITH MY HOMEWORK!
I'M GOING OUTSIDE TO PLAY! I'VE GOT MY JACKET!
I'M LEAVING NOW!
...FURTHER BULLETINS AS EVENTS WARRANT!
WATTERSON

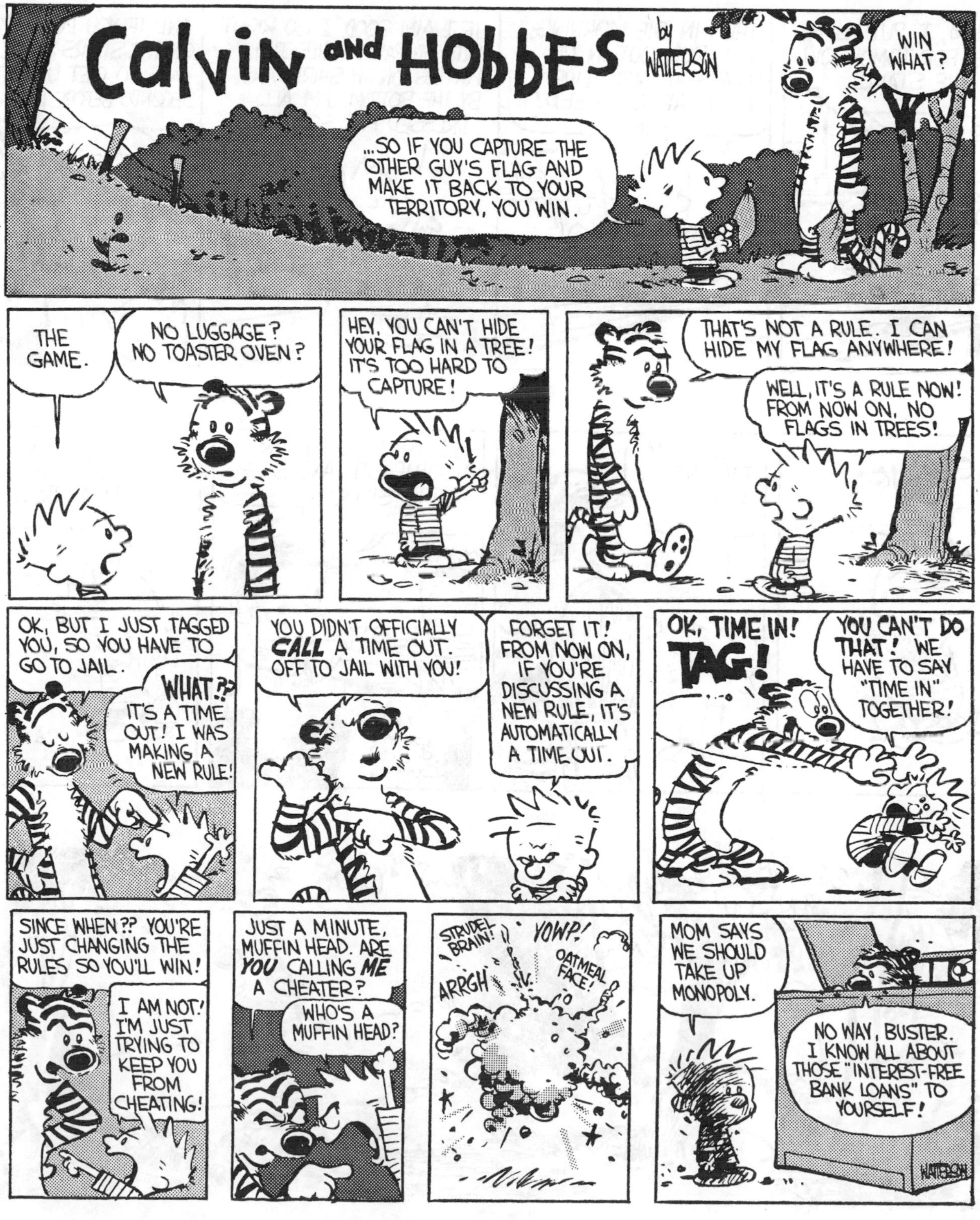
Calvin and HOBBES
by WATTERSON
...SO IF YOU CAPTURE THE OTHER GUY'S FLAG AND MAKE IT BACK TO YOUR TERRITORY, YOU WIN.
WIN WHAT?
THE GAME.
NO LUGGAGE? NO TOASTER OVEN?
HEY, YOU CAN'T HIDE YOUR FLAG IN A TREE! IT'S TOO HARD TO CAPTURE!
THAT'S NOT A RULE. I CAN HIDE MY FLAG ANYWHERE!
WELL, IT'S A RULE NOW! FROM NOW ON, NO FLAGS IN TREES!
OK, BUT I JUST TAGGED YOU, SO YOU HAVE TO GO TO JAIL.
WHAT?? IT'S A TIME OUT! I WAS MAKING A NEW RULE!
YOU DIDN'T OFFICIALLY CALL A TIME OUT. OFF TO JAIL WITH YOU!
FORGET IT! FROM NOW ON, IF YOU'RE DISCUSSING A NEW RULE, IT'S AUTOMATICALLY A TIME OUT.
OK, TIME IN!
TAG!
YOU CAN'T DO THAT! WE HAVE TO SAY "TIME IN" TOGETHER!
SINCE WHEN?? YOU'RE JUST CHANGING THE RULES SO YOU'LL WIN!
I AM NOT! I'M JUST TRYING TO KEEP YOU FROM CHEATING!
JUST A MINUTE, MUFFIN HEAD. ARE YOU CALLING ME A CHEATER?
WHO'S A MUFFIN HEAD?
STRUDEL BRAIN!
YOWP!
OATMEAL FACE!
ARRGH
MOM SAYS WE SHOULD TAKE UP MONOPOLY.
NO WAY, BUSTER. I KNOW ALL ABOUT THOSE "INTEREST-FREE BANK LOANS" TO YOURSELF!
WATTERSON

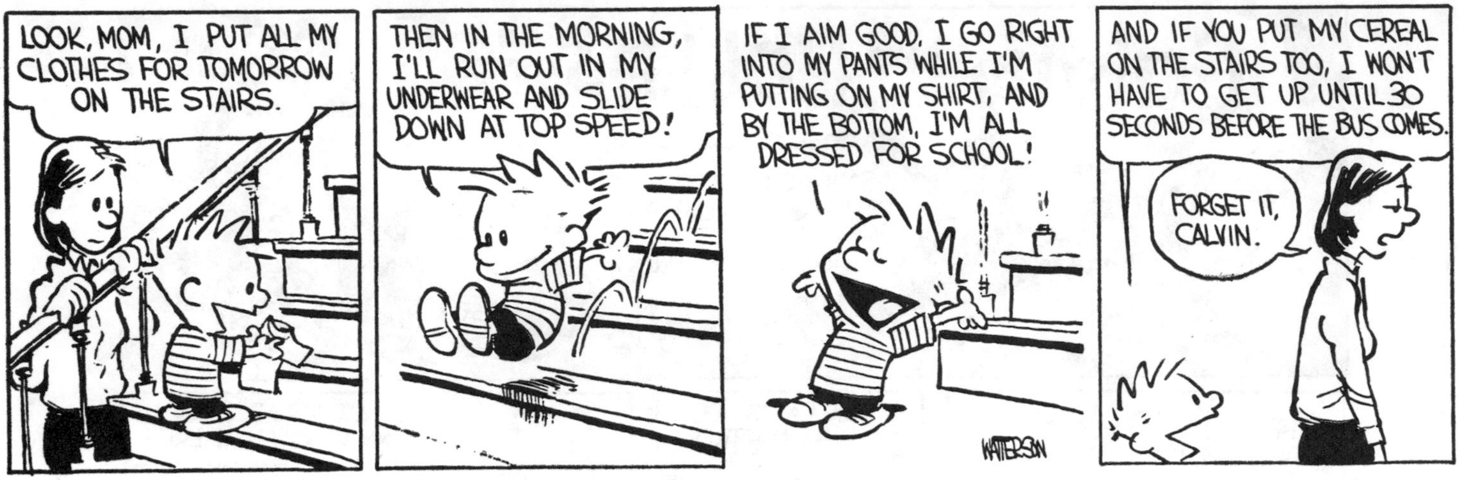
LOOK, MOM, I PUT ALL MY CLOTHES FOR TOMORROW ON THE STAIRS.
THEN IN THE MORNING, I'LL RUN OUT IN MY UNDERWEAR AND SLIDE DOWN AT TOP SPEED!
IF I AIM GOOD, I GO RIGHT INTO MY PANTS WHILE I'M PUTTING ON MY SHIRT, AND BY THE BOTTOM, I'M ALL DRESSED FOR SCHOOL!
WATTERSON
AND IF YOU PUT MY CEREAL ON THE STAIRS TOO, I WON'T HAVE TO GET UP UNTIL 30 SECONDS BEFORE THE BUS COMES.
FORGET IT, CALVIN.

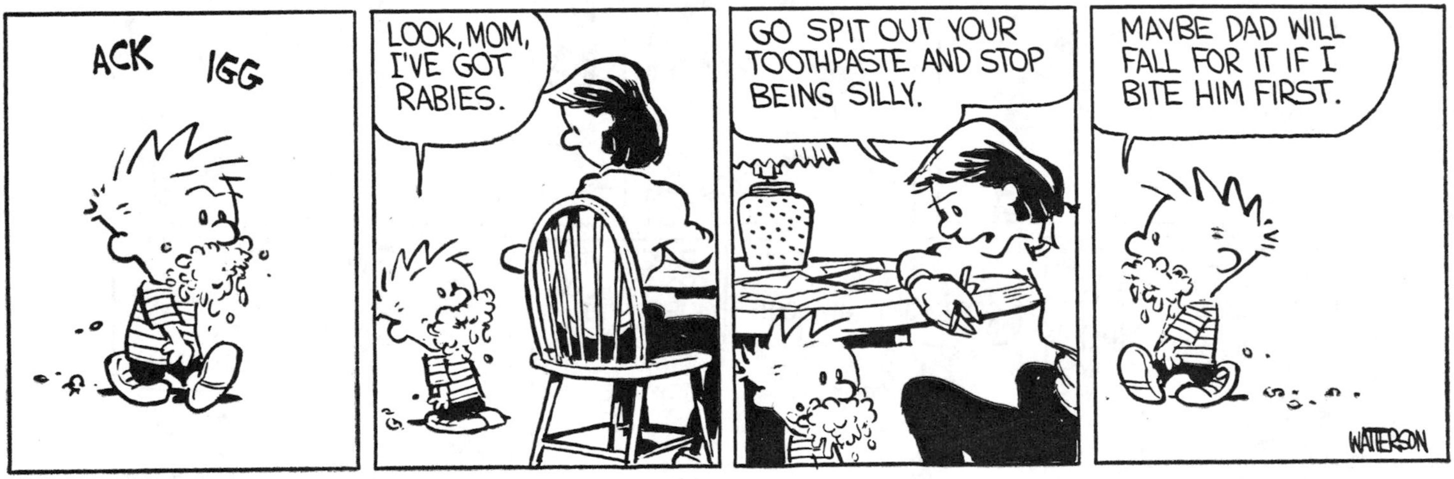
ACK
IGG
LOOK, MOM, I'VE GOT RABIES.
GO SPIT OUT YOUR TOOTHPASTE AND STOP BEING SILLY.
MAYBE DAD WILL FALL FOR IT IF I BITE HIM FIRST.
WATTERSON

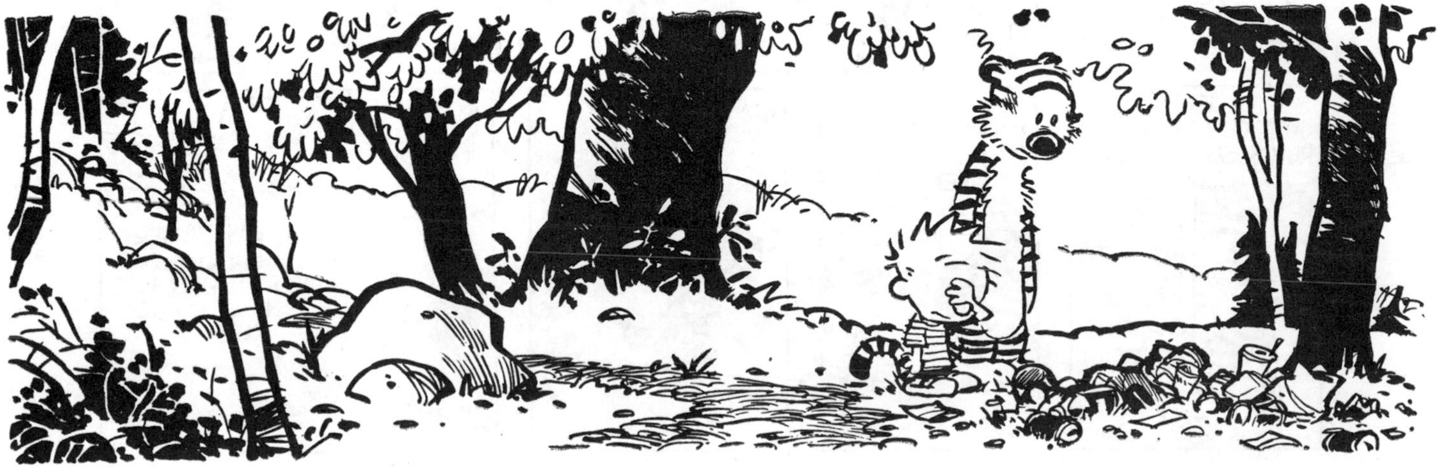

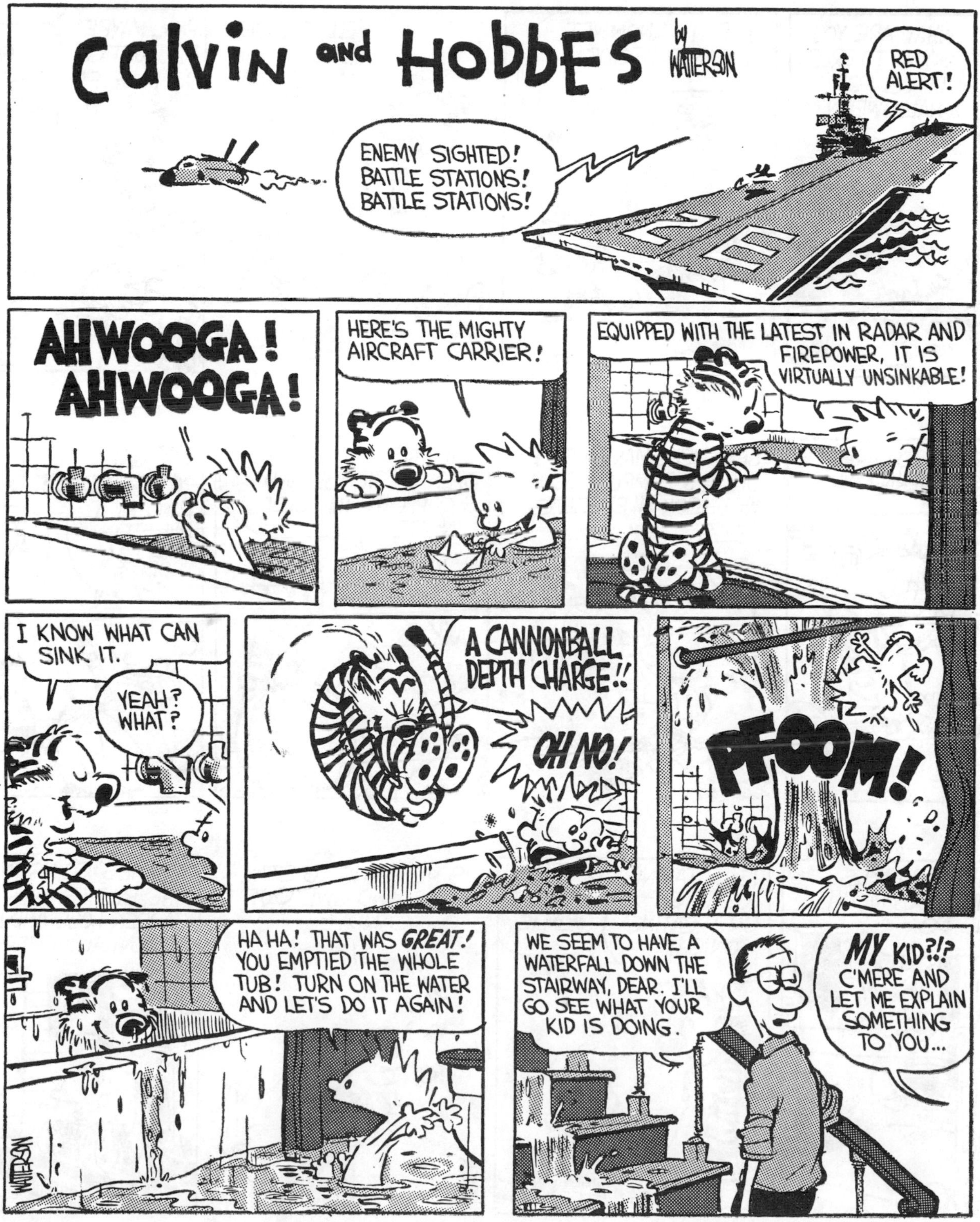
Calvin and HOBBES
by WATTERSON
RED ALERT!
ENEMY SIGHTED! BATTLE STATIONS! BATTLE STATIONS!
AHWOOGA! AHWOOGA!
HERE'S THE MIGHTY AIRCRAFT CARRIER!
EQUIPPED WITH THE LATEST IN RADAR AND FIREPOWER, IT IS VIRTUALLY UNSINKABLE!
I KNOW WHAT CAN SINK IT.
YEAH? WHAT?
A CANNONBALL DEPTH CHARGE!!
OH NO!
PFOOM!
HA HA! THAT WAS GREAT! YOU EMPTIED THE WHOLE TUB! TURN ON THE WATER AND LET'S DO IT AGAIN!
WE SEEM TO HAVE A WATERFALL DOWN THE STAIRWAY, DEAR. I'LL GO SEE WHAT YOUR KID IS DOING.
MY KID?!? C'MERE AND LET ME EXPLAIN SOMETHING TO YOU...

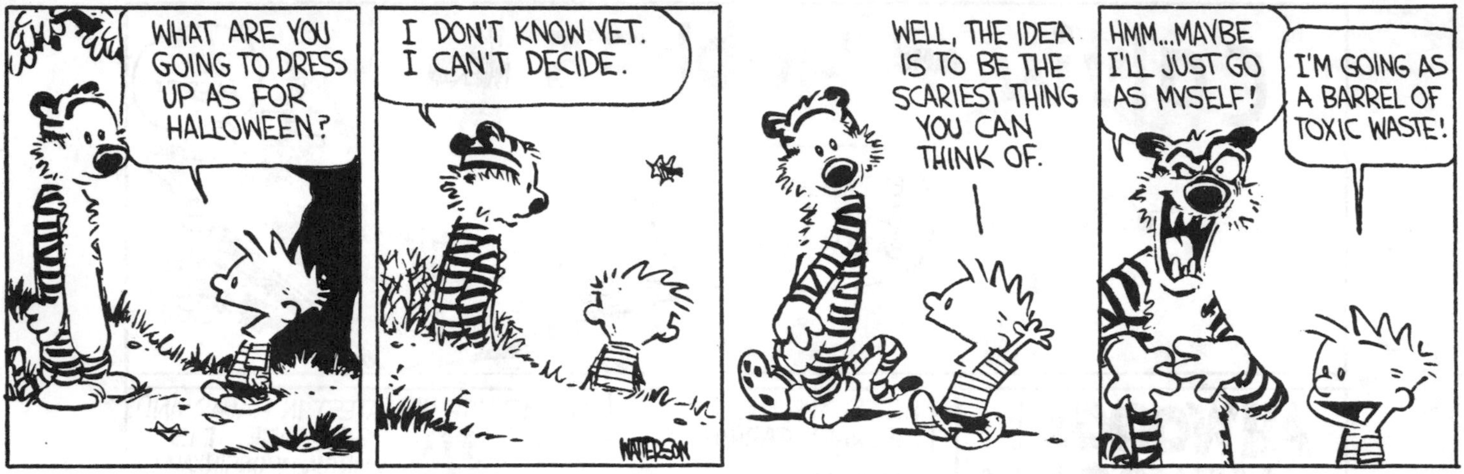
WHAT ARE YOU GOING TO DRESS UP AS FOR HALLOWEEN?
I DON'T KNOW YET. I CAN'T DECIDE.
WATTERSON
WELL, THE IDEA IS TO BE THE SCARIEST THING YOU CAN THINK OF.
HMM...MAYBE I'LL JUST GO AS MYSELF!
I'M GOING AS A BARREL OF TOXIC WASTE!

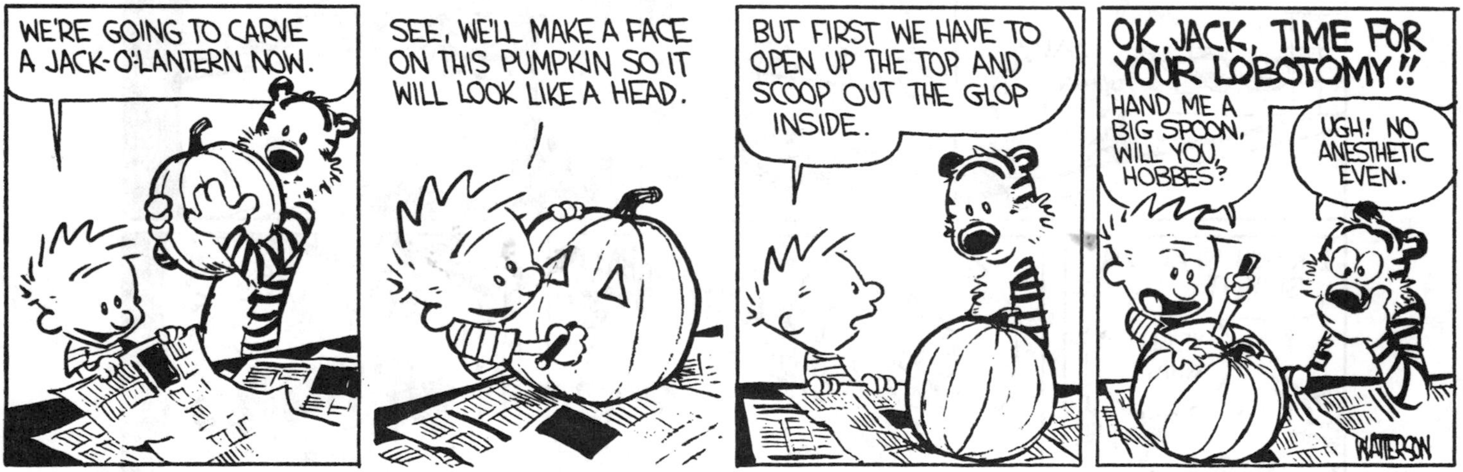
WE'RE GOING TO CARVE A JACK-O'-LANTERN NOW.
SEE, WE'LL MAKE A FACE ON THIS PUMPKIN SO IT WILL LOOK LIKE A HEAD.
BUT FIRST WE HAVE TO OPEN UP THE TOP AND SCOOP OUT THE GLOP INSIDE.
OK, JACK, TIME FOR YOUR LOBOTOMY!!
HAND ME A BIG SPOON, WILL YOU, HOBBES?
UGH! NO ANESTHETIC EVEN.
WATTERSON

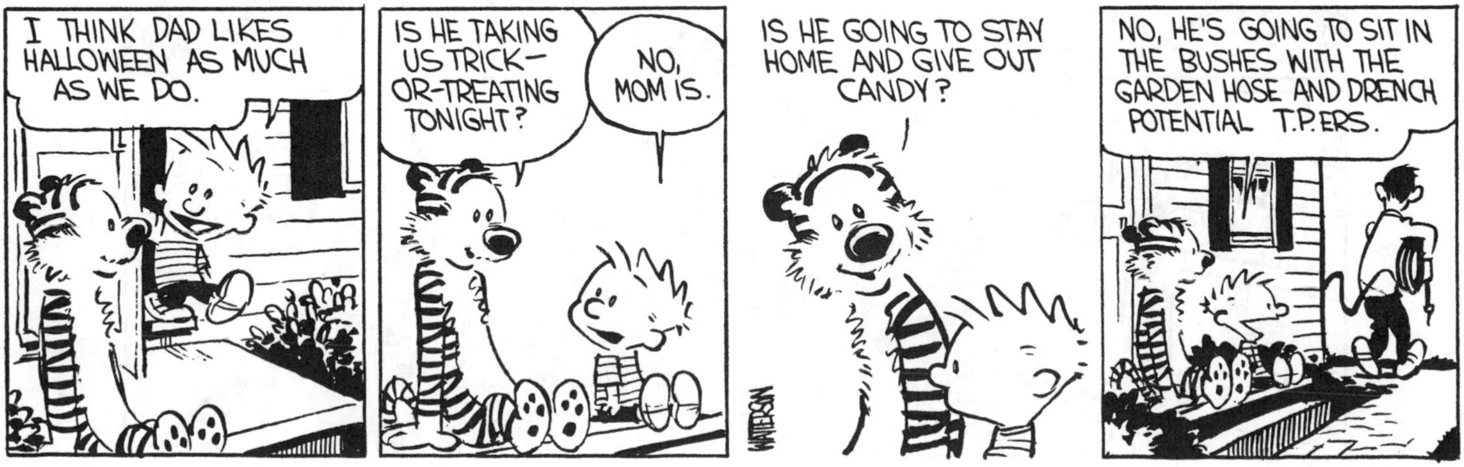
I THINK DAD LIKES HALLOWEEN AS MUCH AS WE DO.
IS HE TAKING US TRICK-OR-TREATING TONIGHT?
NO, MOM IS.
WATTERSON
IS HE GOING TO STAY HOME AND GIVE OUT CANDY?
NO, HE'S GOING TO SIT IN THE BUSHES WITH THE GARDEN HOSE AND DRENCH POTENTIAL T.P.ERS.

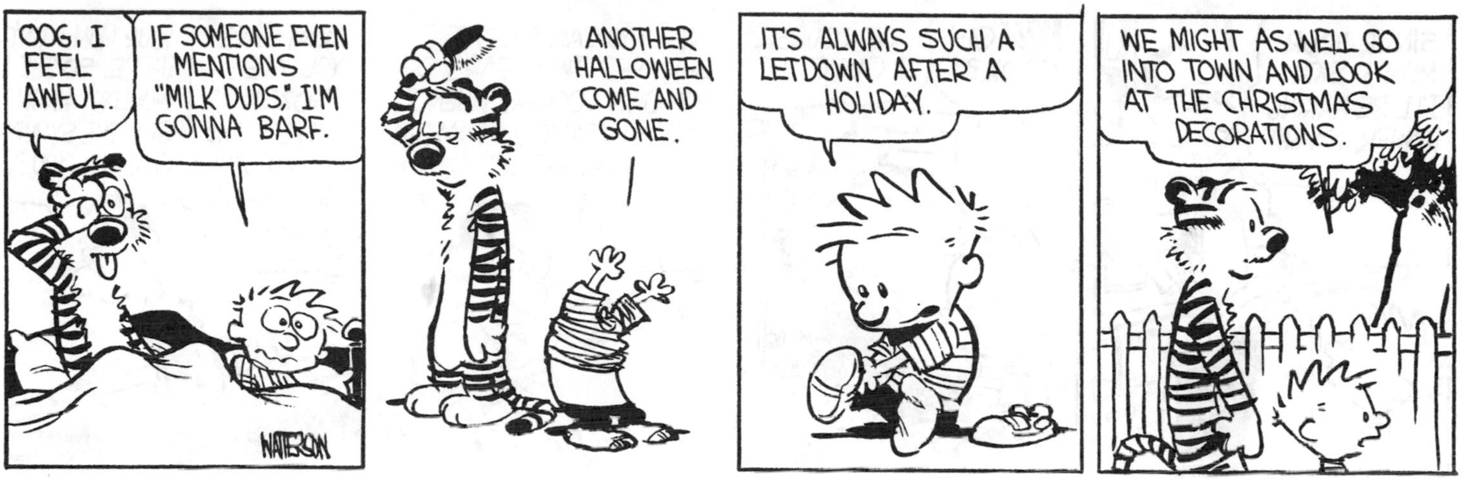
OOG, I FEEL AWFUL.
IF SOMEONE EVEN MENTIONS "MILK DUDS," I'M GONNA BARF.
WATTERSON
ANOTHER HALLOWEEN COME AND GONE.
IT'S ALWAYS SUCH A LETDOWN AFTER A HOLIDAY.
WE MIGHT AS WELL GO INTO TOWN AND LOOK AT THE CHRISTMAS DECORATIONS.

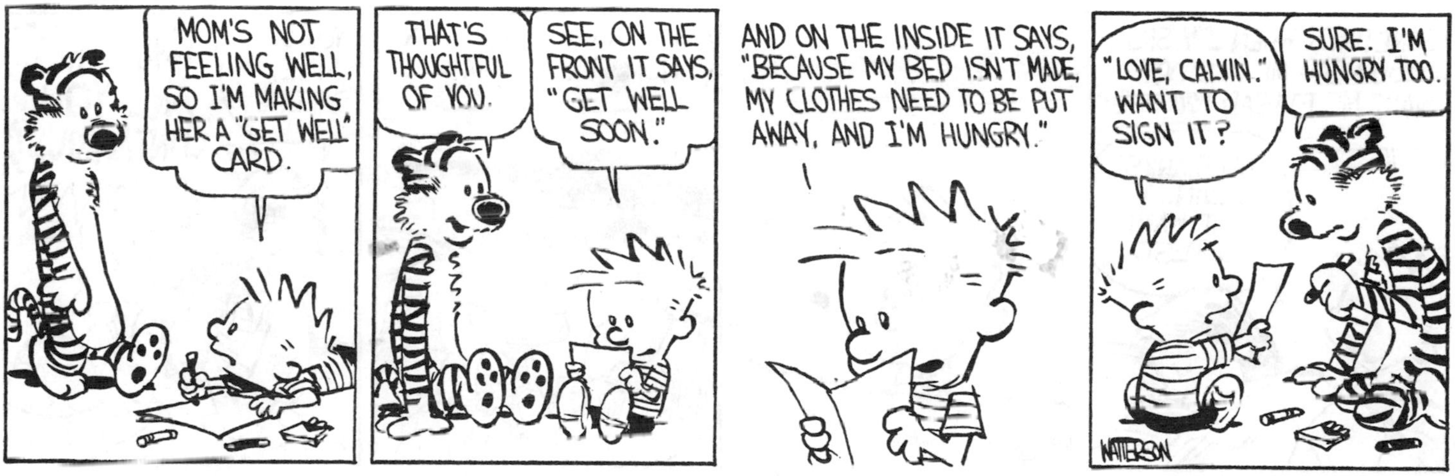
MOM'S NOT FEELING WELL, SO I'M MAKING HER A "GET WELL" CARD.
THAT'S THOUGHTFUL OF YOU.
SEE, ON THE FRONT IT SAYS, "GET WELL SOON."
AND ON THE INSIDE IT SAYS, "BECAUSE MY BED ISN'T MADE, MY CLOTHES NEED TO BE PUT AWAY, AND I'M HUNGRY."
"LOVE, CALVIN." WANT TO SIGN IT?
SURE. I'M HUNGRY TOO.
WATTERSON

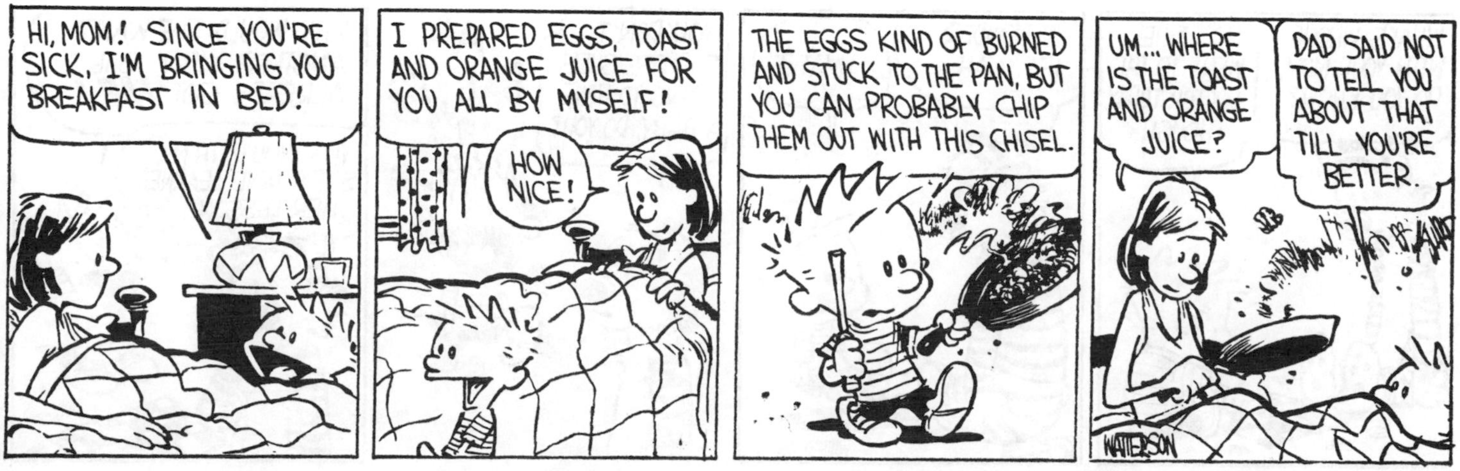
HI, MOM! SINCE YOU'RE SICK, I'M BRINGING YOU BREAKFAST IN BED!
I PREPARED EGGS, TOAST AND ORANGE JUICE FOR YOU ALL BY MYSELF!
HOW NICE!
THE EGGS KIND OF BURNED AND STUCK TO THE PAN, BUT YOU CAN PROBABLY CHIP THEM OUT WITH THIS CHISEL.
UM... WHERE IS THE TOAST AND ORANGE JUICE?
DAD SAID NOT TO TELL YOU ABOUT THAT TILL YOU'RE BETTER.
WATTERSON

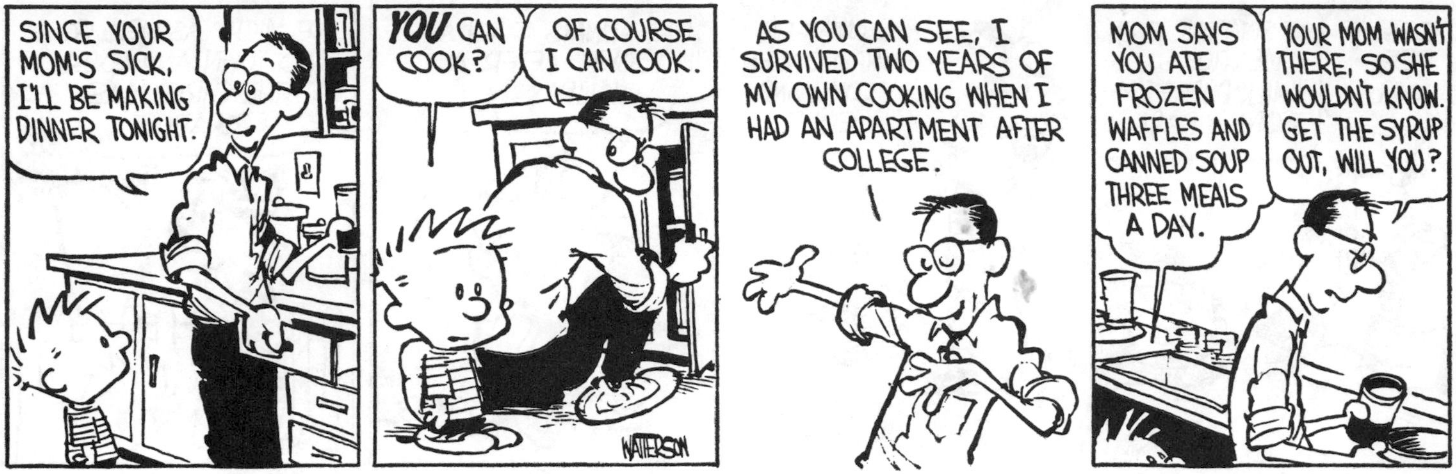
SINCE YOUR MOM'S SICK, I'LL BE MAKING DINNER TONIGHT.
YOU CAN COOK?
OF COURSE I CAN COOK.
WATERSON
AS YOU CAN SEE, I SURVIVED TWO YEARS OF MY OWN COOKING WHEN I HAD AN APARTMENT AFTER COLLEGE.
MOM SAYS YOU ATE FROZEN WAFFLES AND CANNED SOUP THREE MEALS A DAY.
YOUR MOM WASN'T THERE, SO SHE WOULDN'T KNOW. GET THE SYRUP OUT, WILL YOU?

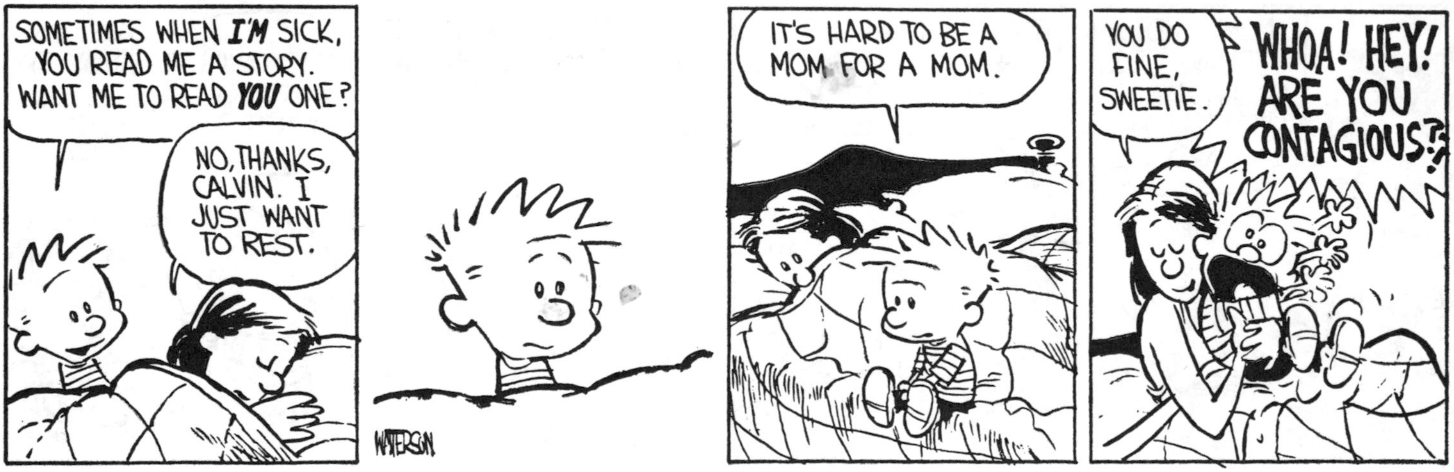
SOMETIMES WHEN I'M SICK, YOU READ ME A STORY. WANT ME TO READ YOU ONE?
NO, THANKS, CALVIN. I JUST WANT TO REST.
WATERSON
IT'S HARD TO BE A MOM FOR A MOM.
YOU DO FINE, SWEETIE.
WHOA! HEY! ARE YOU CONTAGIOUS?!

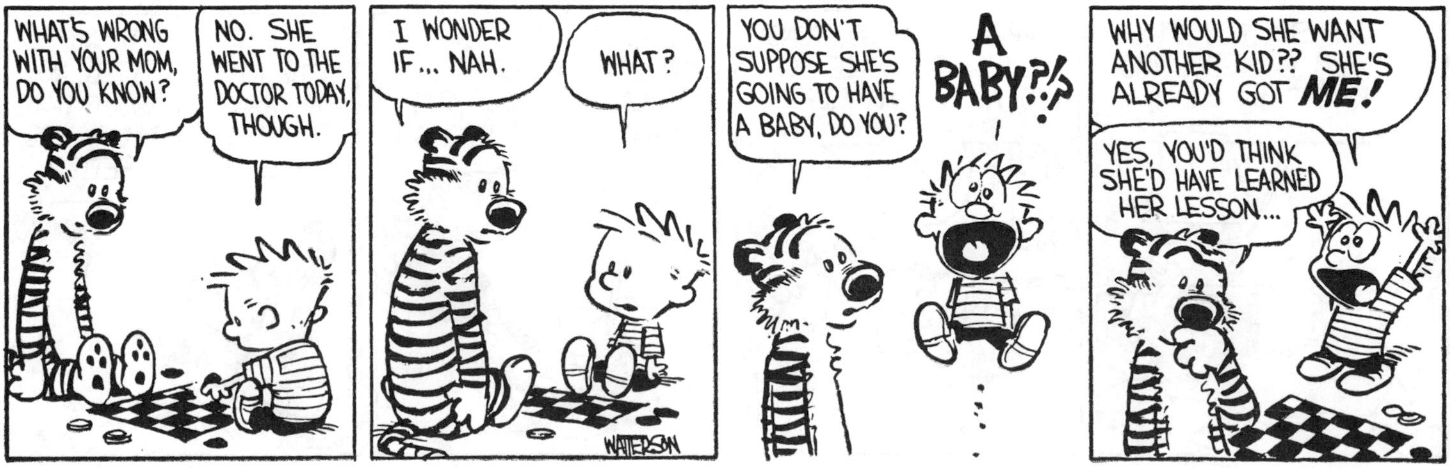
WHAT'S WRONG WITH YOUR MOM, DO YOU KNOW?
NO. SHE WENT TO THE DOCTOR TODAY, THOUGH.
I WONDER IF... NAH.
WHAT?
WATERSON
YOU DON'T SUPPOSE SHE'S GOING TO HAVE A BABY, DO YOU?
A BABY?!
WHY WOULD SHE WANT ANOTHER KID?? SHE'S ALREADY GOT ME!
YES, YOU'D THINK SHE'D HAVE LEARNED HER LESSON...

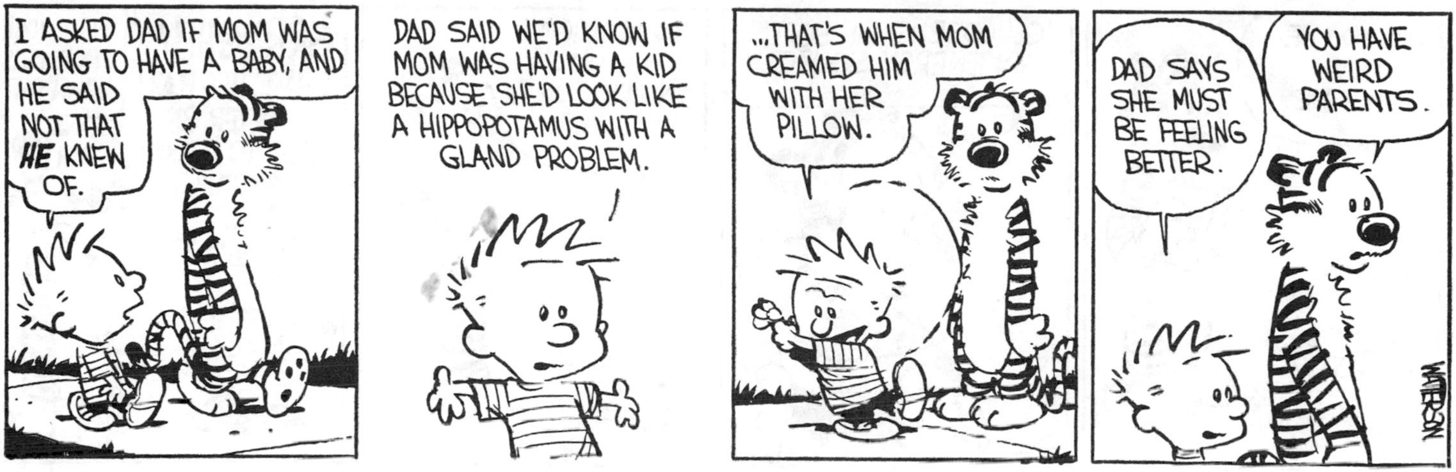
I ASKED DAD IF MOM WAS GOING TO HAVE A BABY, AND HE SAID NOT THAT **HE** KNEW OF.
DAD SAID WE'D KNOW IF MOM WAS HAVING A KID BECAUSE SHE'D LOOK LIKE A HIPPOPOTAMUS WITH A GLAND PROBLEM.
...THAT'S WHEN MOM CREAMED HIM WITH HER PILLOW.
DAD SAYS SHE MUST BE FEELING BETTER.
YOU HAVE WEIRD PARENTS.

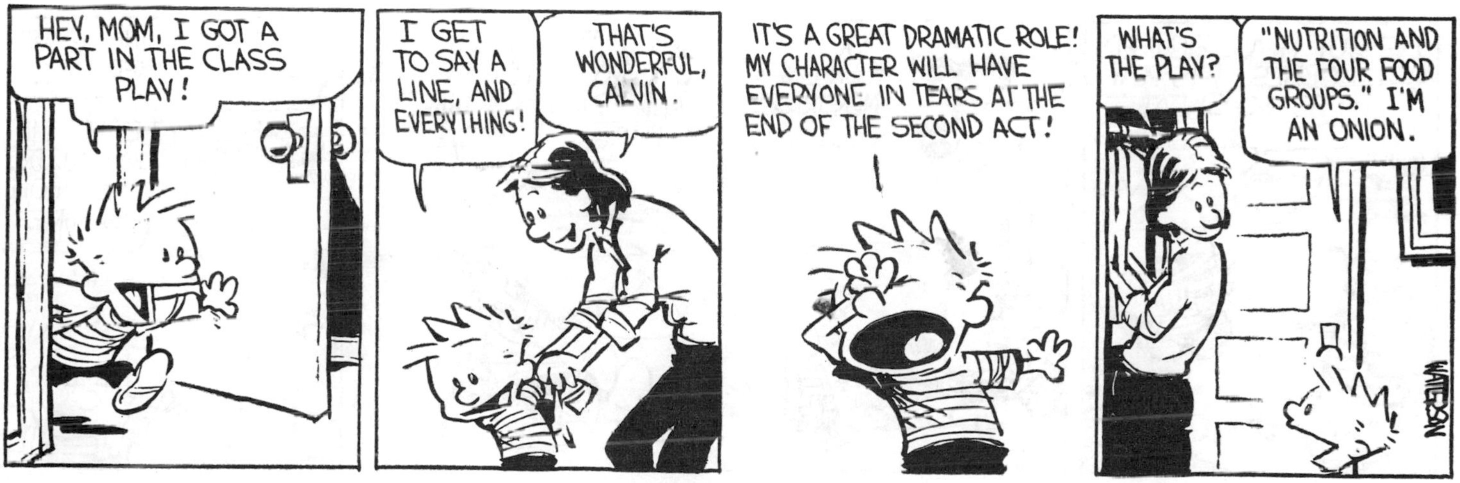
HEY, MOM, I GOT A PART IN THE CLASS PLAY!
I GET TO SAY A LINE, AND EVERYTHING!
THAT'S WONDERFUL, CALVIN.
IT'S A GREAT DRAMATIC ROLE! MY CHARACTER WILL HAVE EVERYONE IN TEARS AT THE END OF THE SECOND ACT!
WHAT'S THE PLAY?
"NUTRITION AND THE FOUR FOOD GROUPS." I'M AN ONION.

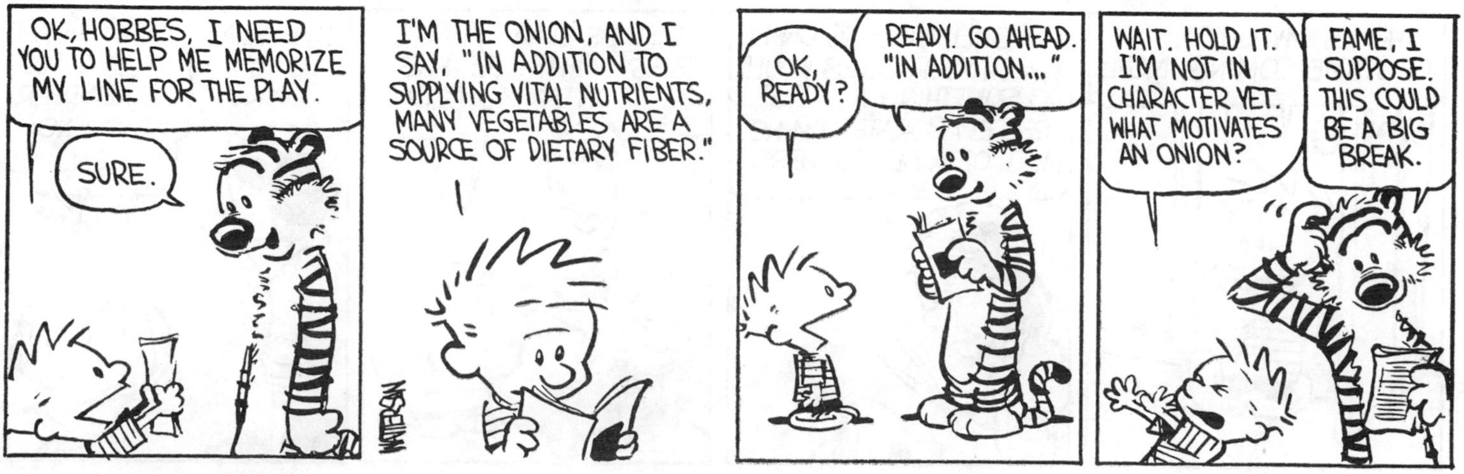
OK, HOBBES, I NEED YOU TO HELP ME MEMORIZE MY LINE FOR THE PLAY.
SURE.
I'M THE ONION, AND I SAY, "IN ADDITION TO SUPPLYING VITAL NUTRIENTS, MANY VEGETABLES ARE A SOURCE OF DIETARY FIBER."
OK, READY?
READY. GO AHEAD. "IN ADDITION..."
WAIT. HOLD IT. I'M NOT IN CHARACTER YET. WHAT MOTIVATES AN ONION?
FAME, I SUPPOSE. THIS COULD BE A BIG BREAK.

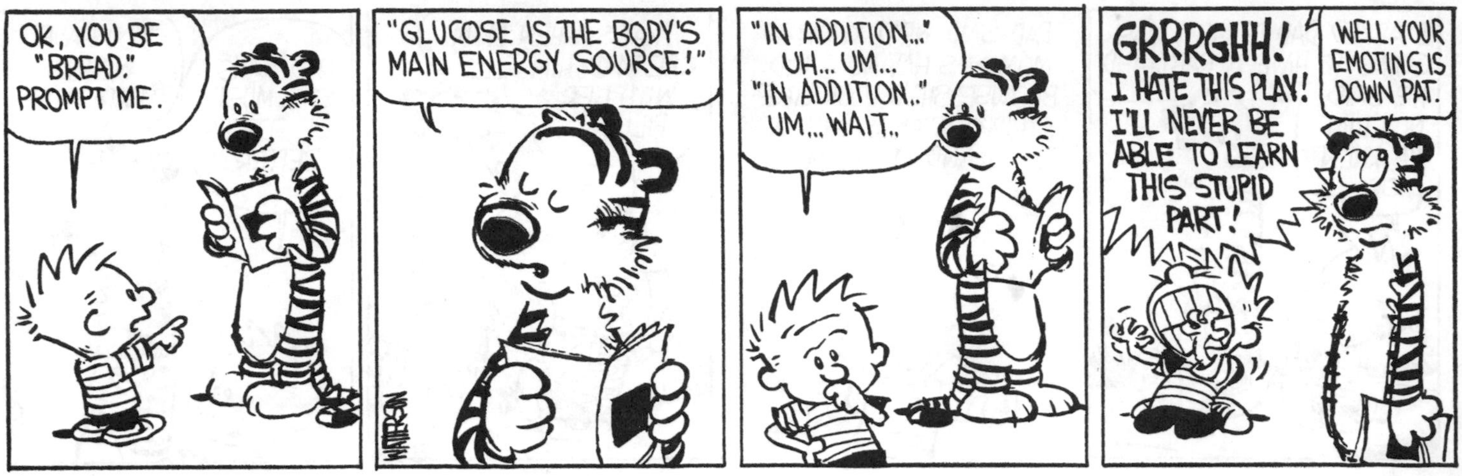
OK, YOU BE "BREAD." PROMPT ME.
"GLUCOSE IS THE BODY'S MAIN ENERGY SOURCE!"
"IN ADDITION..." UH... UM... "IN ADDITION.." UM... WAIT..
GRRRGHH! I HATE THIS PLAY! I'LL NEVER BE ABLE TO LEARN THIS STUPID PART!
WELL, YOUR EMOTING IS DOWN PAT.
WATTERSON

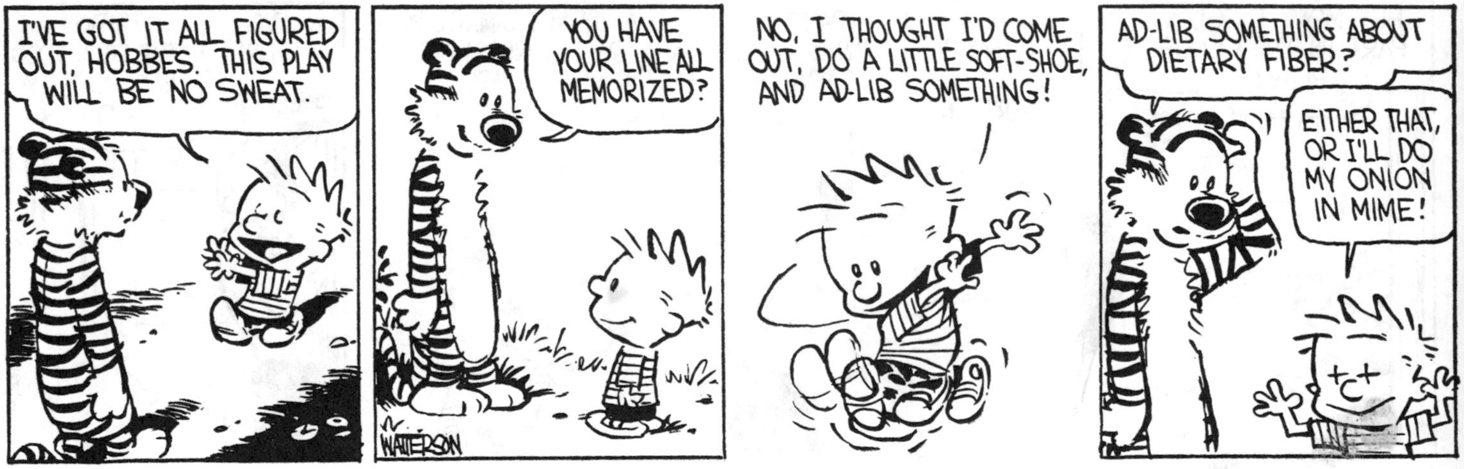
I'VE GOT IT ALL FIGURED OUT, HOBBES. THIS PLAY WILL BE NO SWEAT.
YOU HAVE YOUR LINE ALL MEMORIZED?
NO, I THOUGHT I'D COME OUT, DO A LITTLE SOFT-SHOE, AND AD-LIB SOMETHING!
AD-LIB SOMETHING ABOUT DIETARY FIBER?
EITHER THAT, OR I'LL DO MY ONION IN MIME!
WATTERSON

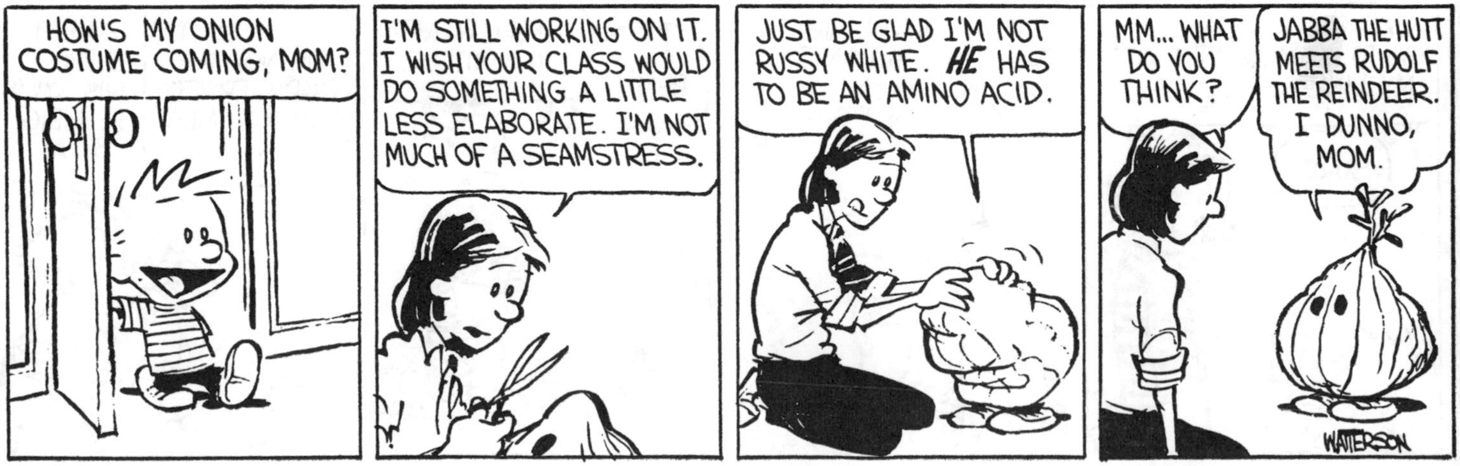
HOW'S MY ONION COSTUME COMING, MOM?
I'M STILL WORKING ON IT. I WISH YOUR CLASS WOULD DO SOMETHING A LITTLE LESS ELABORATE. I'M NOT MUCH OF A SEAMSTRESS.
JUST BE GLAD I'M NOT RUSSY WHITE. HE HAS TO BE AN AMINO ACID.
MM... WHAT DO YOU THINK?
JABBA THE HUTT MEETS RUDOLF THE REINDEER. I DUNNO, MOM.
WATTERSON

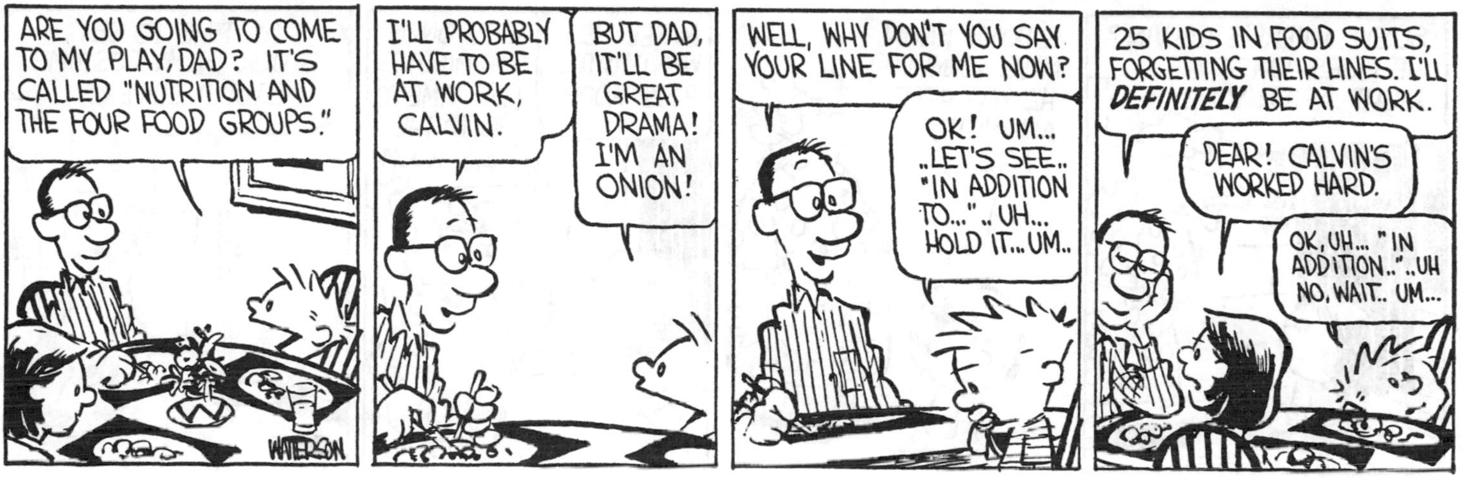
ARE YOU GOING TO COME TO MY PLAY, DAD? IT'S CALLED "NUTRITION AND THE FOUR FOOD GROUPS."
WATTERSON
I'LL PROBABLY HAVE TO BE AT WORK, CALVIN.
BUT DAD, IT'LL BE GREAT DRAMA! I'M AN ONION!
WELL, WHY DON'T YOU SAY YOUR LINE FOR ME NOW?
OK! UM... ..LET'S SEE.. "IN ADDITION TO..." .. UH... HOLD IT... UM..
25 KIDS IN FOOD SUITS, FORGETTING THEIR LINES. I'LL *DEFINITELY* BE AT WORK.
DEAR! CALVIN'S WORKED HARD.
OK, UH... "IN ADDITION.." ..UH NO. WAIT.. UM...

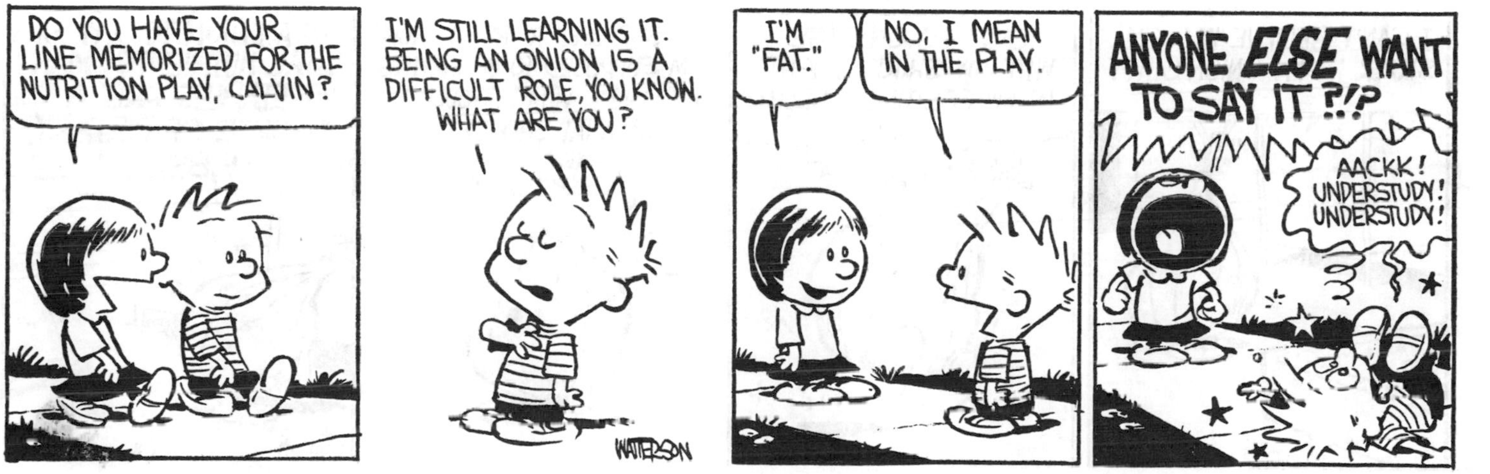
DO YOU HAVE YOUR LINE MEMORIZED FOR THE NUTRITION PLAY, CALVIN?
I'M STILL LEARNING IT. BEING AN ONION IS A DIFFICULT ROLE, YOU KNOW. WHAT ARE YOU?
WATTERSON
I'M "FAT."
NO, I MEAN IN THE PLAY.
ANYONE *ELSE* WANT TO SAY IT ?!?
AACKK! UNDERSTUDY! UNDERSTUDY!

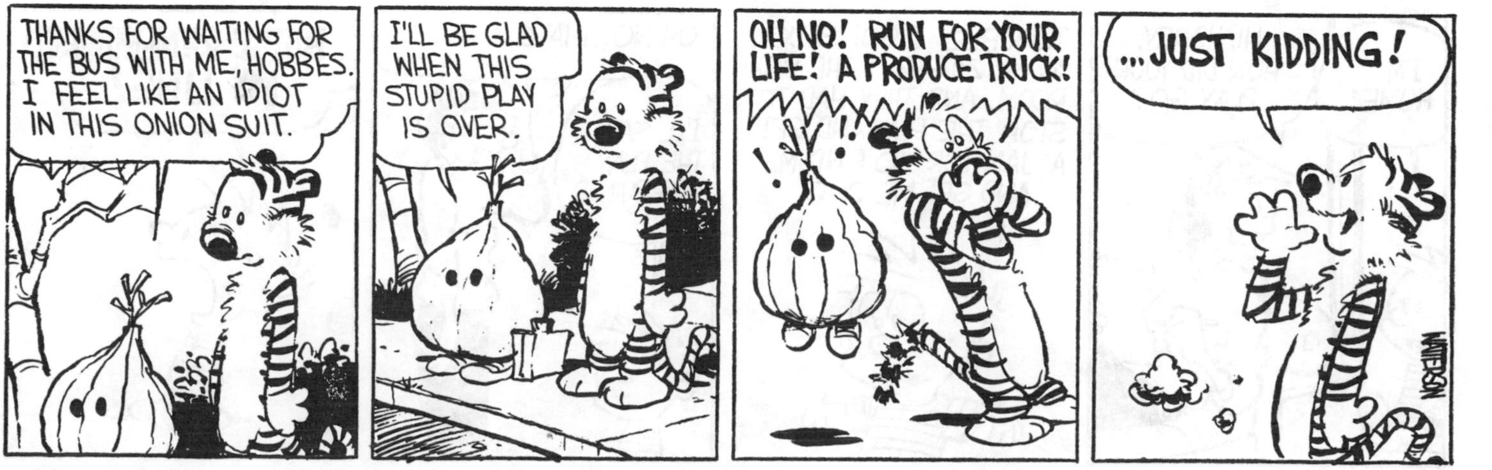
THANKS FOR WAITING FOR THE BUS WITH ME, HOBBES. I FEEL LIKE AN IDIOT IN THIS ONION SUIT.
I'LL BE GLAD WHEN THIS STUPID PLAY IS OVER.
OH NO! RUN FOR YOUR LIFE! A PRODUCE TRUCK!
...JUST KIDDING!
WATTERSON

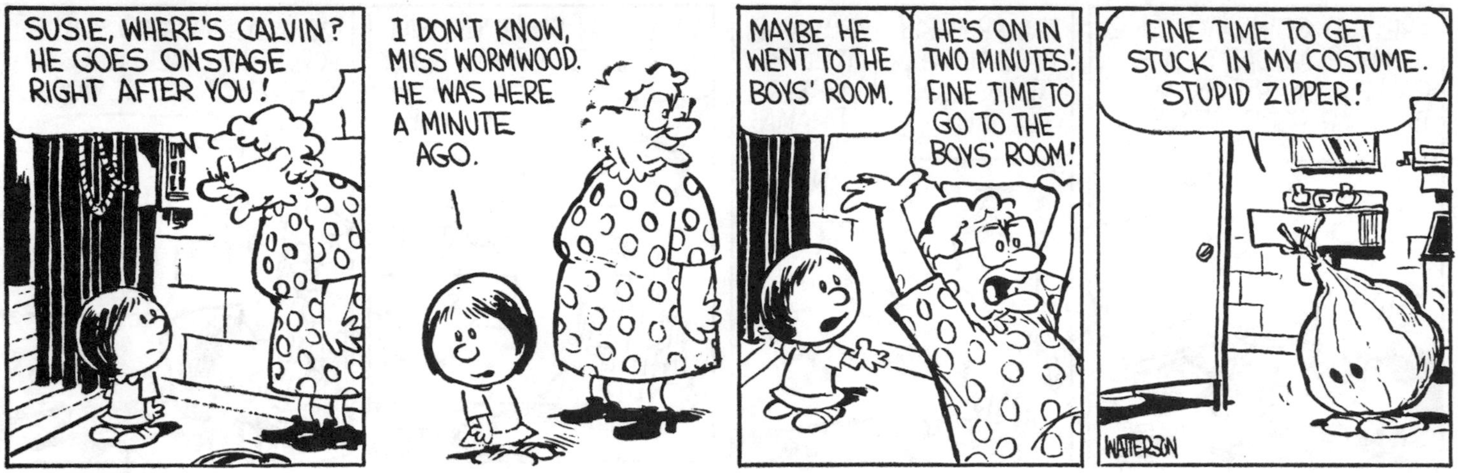
SUSIE, WHERE'S CALVIN? HE GOES ONSTAGE RIGHT AFTER YOU!
I DON'T KNOW, MISS WORMWOOD. HE WAS HERE A MINUTE AGO.
MAYBE HE WENT TO THE BOYS' ROOM.
HE'S ON IN TWO MINUTES! FINE TIME TO GO TO THE BOYS' ROOM!
FINE TIME TO GET STUCK IN MY COSTUME. STUPID ZIPPER!
WATTERSON

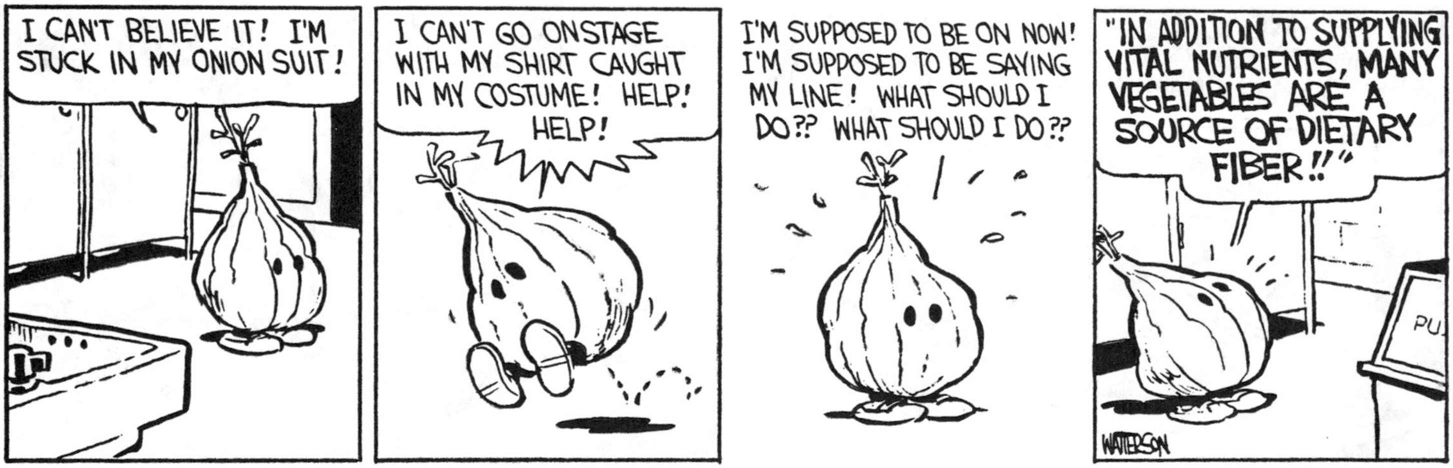
I CAN'T BELIEVE IT! I'M STUCK IN MY ONION SUIT!
I CAN'T GO ONSTAGE WITH MY SHIRT CAUGHT IN MY COSTUME! HELP! HELP!
I'M SUPPOSED TO BE ON NOW! I'M SUPPOSED TO BE SAYING MY LINE! WHAT SHOULD I DO?? WHAT SHOULD I DO??
"IN ADDITION TO SUPPLYING VITAL NUTRIENTS, MANY VEGETABLES ARE A SOURCE OF DIETARY FIBER!!"
PU
WATTERSON

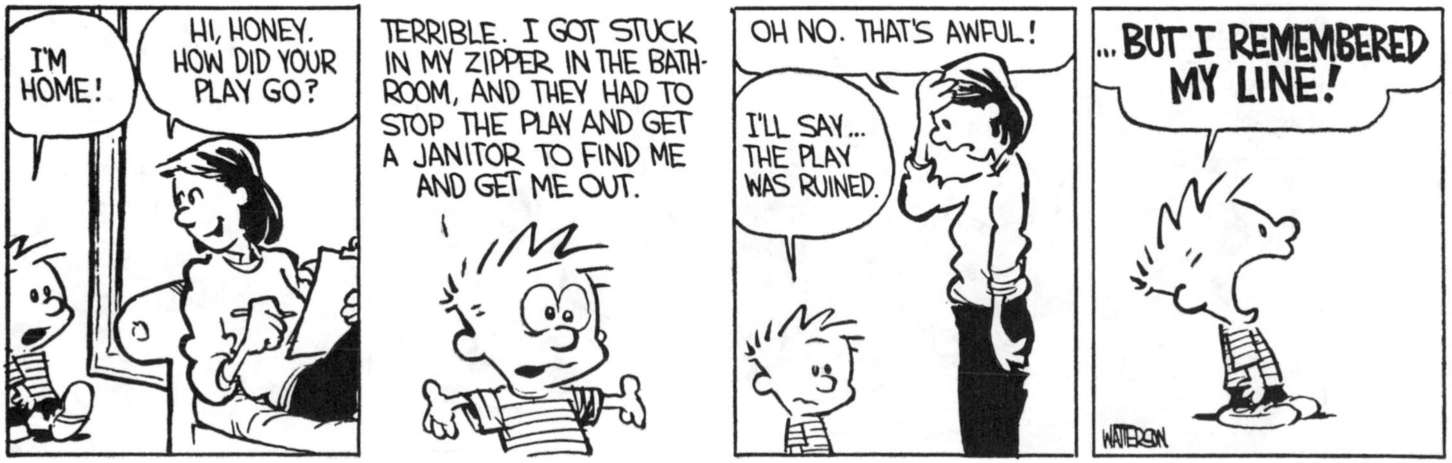
I'M HOME!
HI, HONEY. HOW DID YOUR PLAY GO?
TERRIBLE. I GOT STUCK IN MY ZIPPER IN THE BATHROOM, AND THEY HAD TO STOP THE PLAY AND GET A JANITOR TO FIND ME AND GET ME OUT.
OH NO. THAT'S AWFUL!
I'LL SAY... THE PLAY WAS RUINED.
...BUT I REMEMBERED MY LINE!
WATTERSON

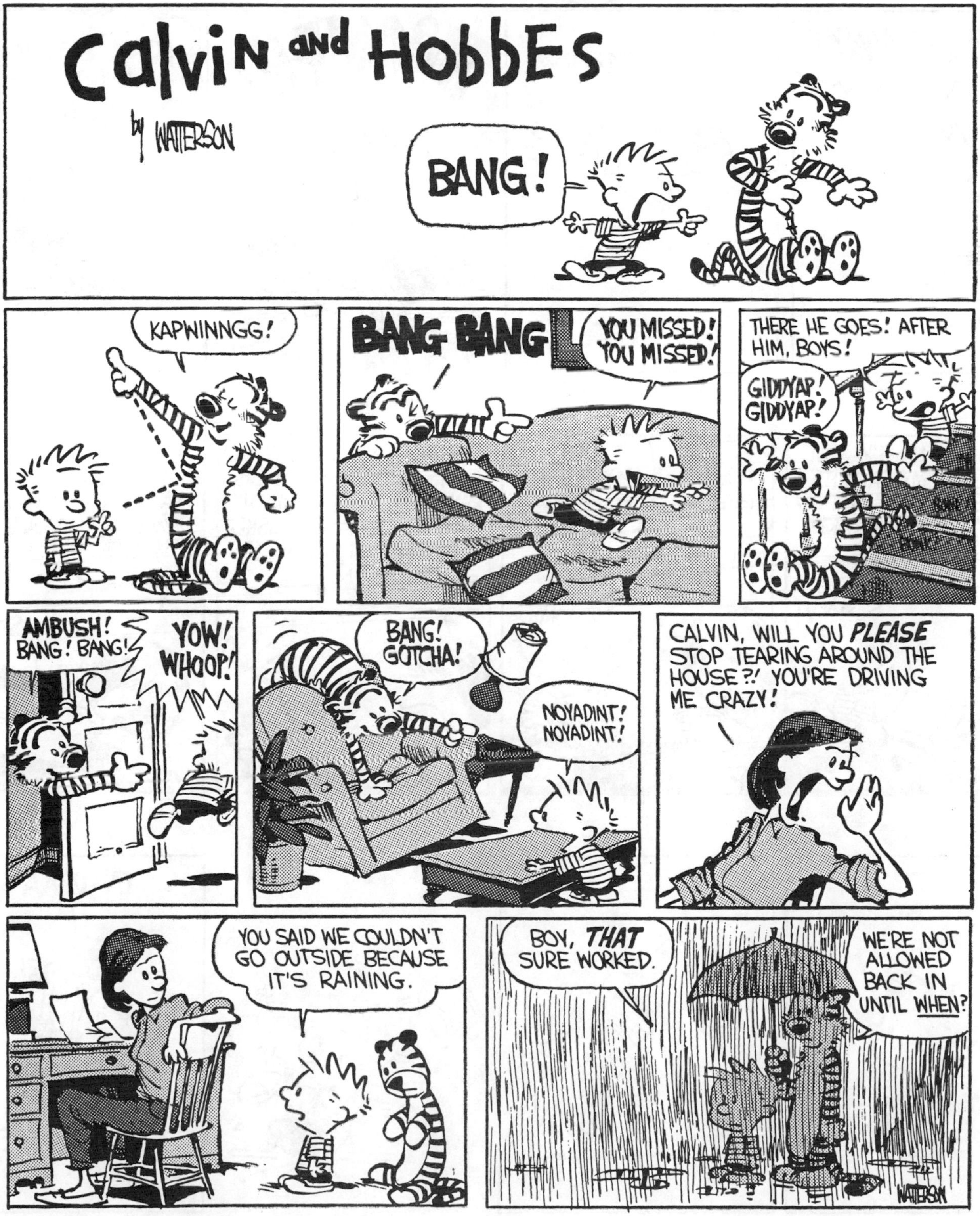
Calvin and Hobbes
by WATTERSON
BANG!
KAPWINNGG!
BANG BANG
YOU MISSED! YOU MISSED!
THERE HE GOES! AFTER HIM, BOYS!
GIDDYAP! GIDDYAP!
AMBUSH! BANG! BANG!
YOW! WHOOP!
BANG! GOTCHA!
NOYADINT! NOYADINT!
CALVIN, WILL YOU PLEASE STOP TEARING AROUND THE HOUSE?! YOU'RE DRIVING ME CRAZY!
YOU SAID WE COULDN'T GO OUTSIDE BECAUSE IT'S RAINING.
BOY, THAT SURE WORKED.
WE'RE NOT ALLOWED BACK IN UNTIL WHEN?
WATTERSON

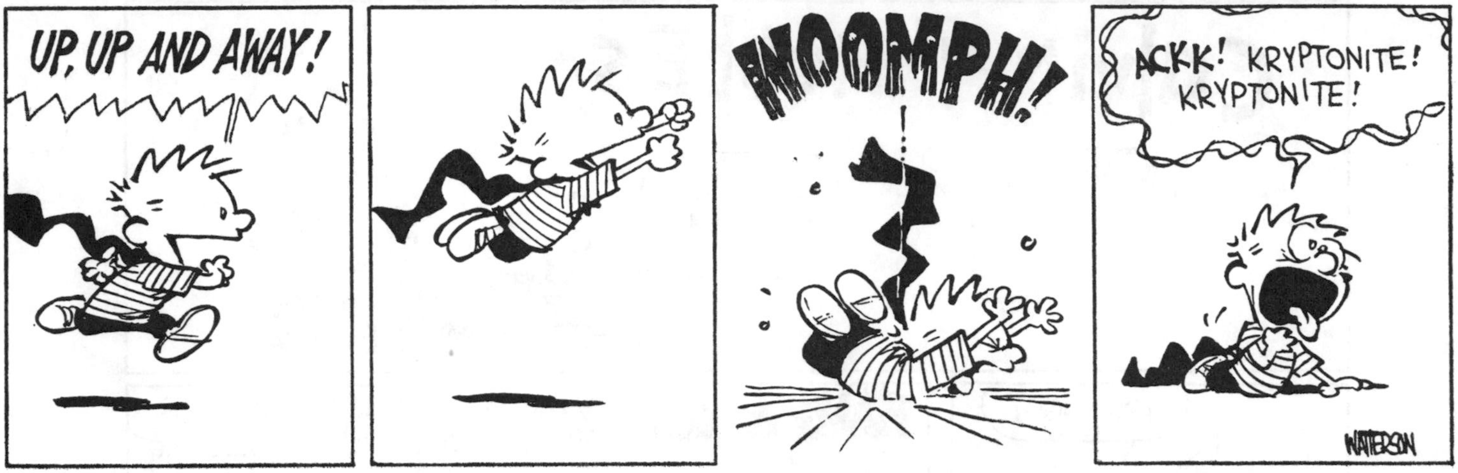
UP, UP AND AWAY!
WOOMPH!
ACKK! KRYPTONITE! KRYPTONITE!
WATTERSON

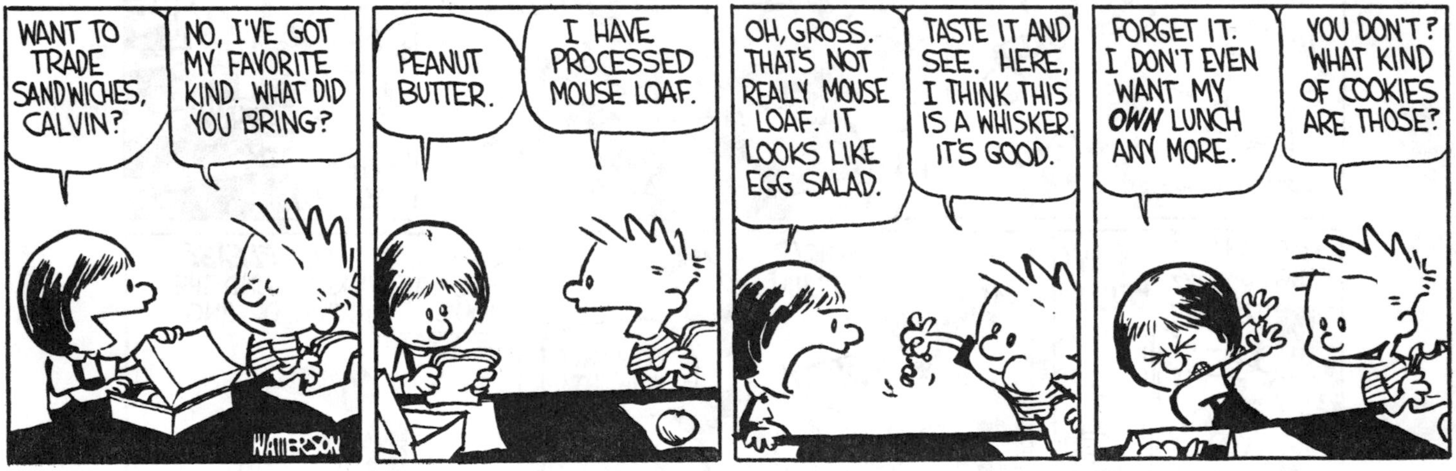
WANT TO TRADE SANDWICHES, CALVIN?
NO, I'VE GOT MY FAVORITE KIND. WHAT DID YOU BRING?
WATTERSON
PEANUT BUTTER.
I HAVE PROCESSED MOUSE LOAF.
OH, GROSS. THAT'S NOT REALLY MOUSE LOAF. IT LOOKS LIKE EGG SALAD.
TASTE IT AND SEE. HERE, I THINK THIS IS A WHISKER. IT'S GOOD.
FORGET IT. I DON'T EVEN WANT MY OWN LUNCH ANY MORE.
YOU DON'T? WHAT KIND OF COOKIES ARE THOSE?

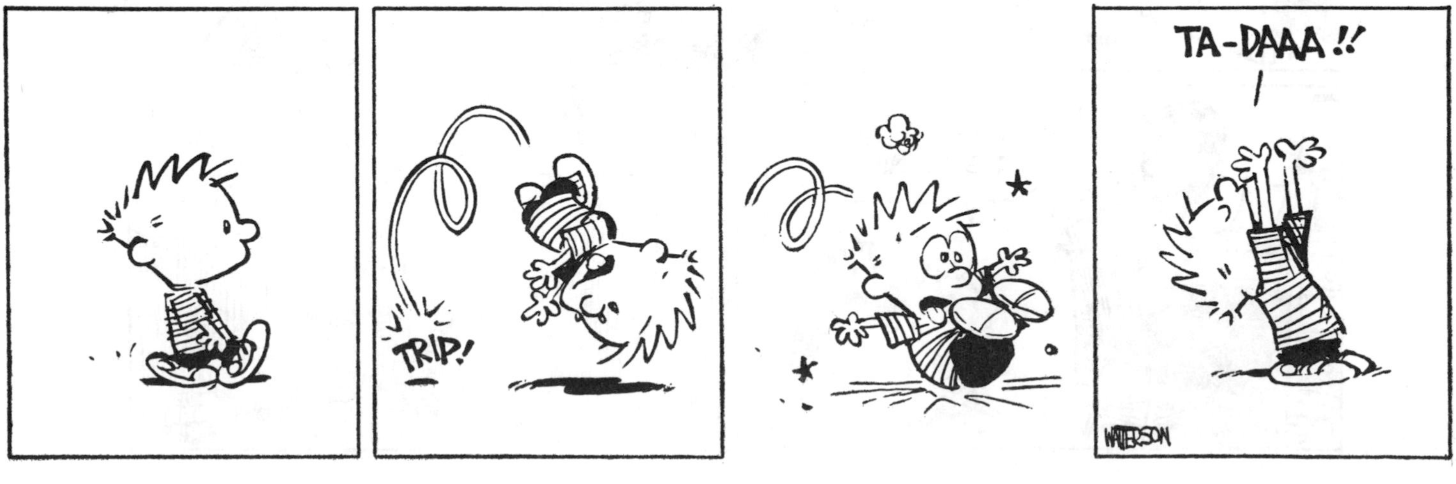
TRIP!
TA-DAAA!!
WATTERSON

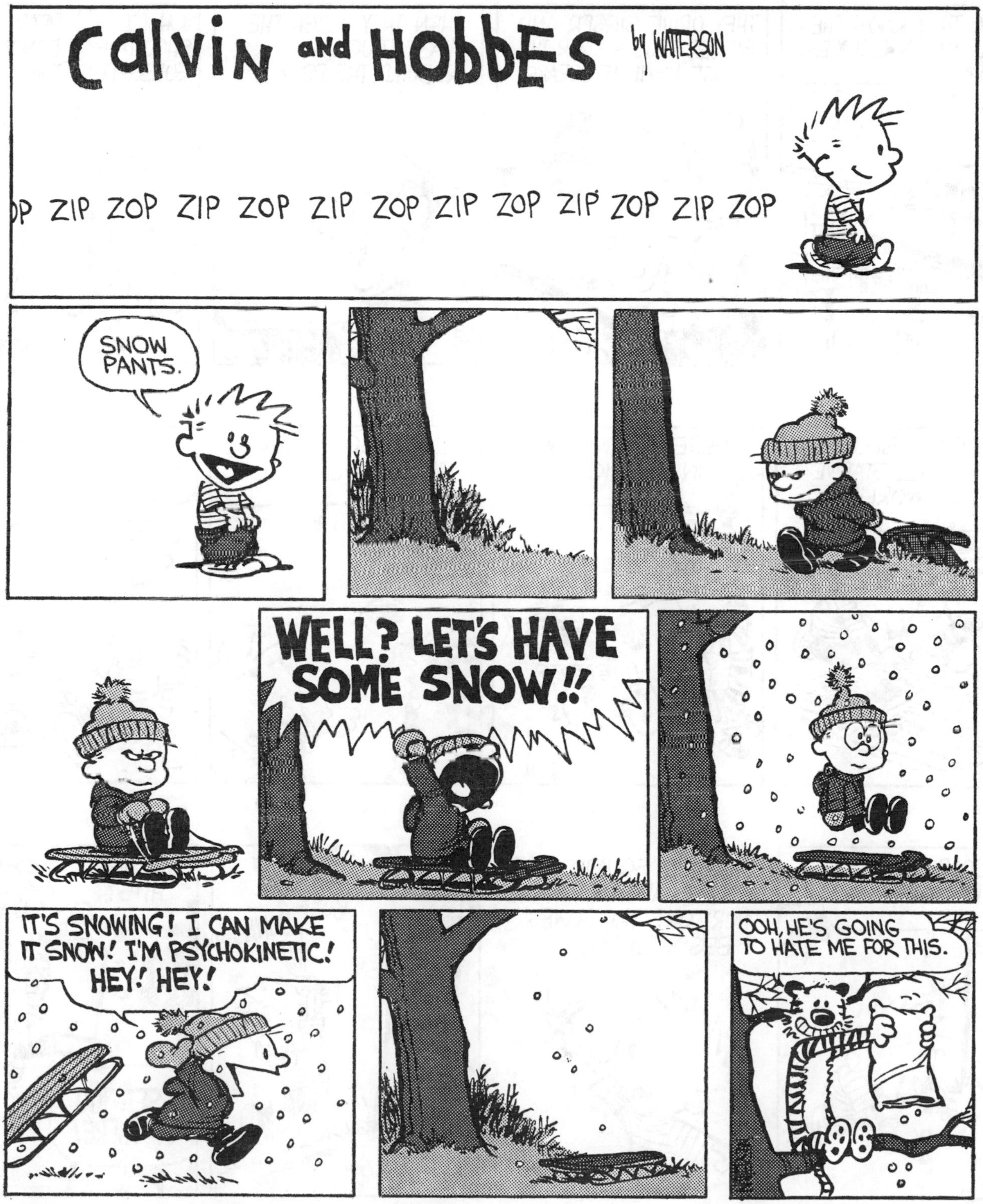
Calvin and HOBBES by WATTERSON
OP ZIP ZOP ZIP ZOP ZIP ZOP ZIP ZOP ZIP ZOP ZIP ZOP
SNOW PANTS.
WELL? LET'S HAVE SOME SNOW!!
IT'S SNOWING! I CAN MAKE IT SNOW! I'M PSYCHOKINETIC! HEY! HEY!
OOH, HE'S GOING TO HATE ME FOR THIS.

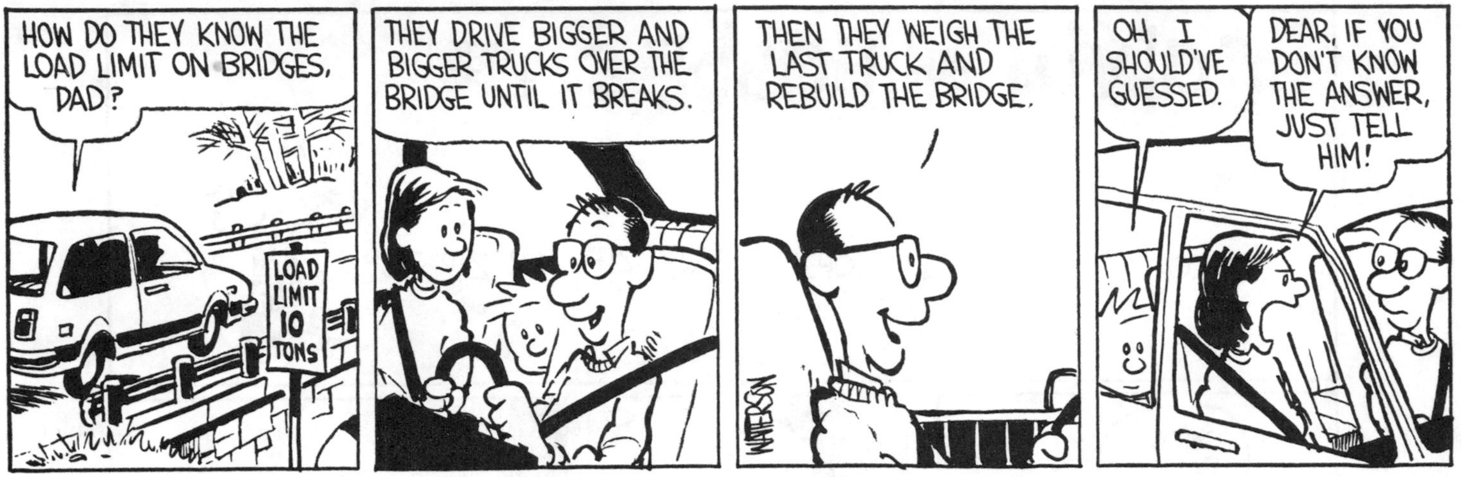
HOW DO THEY KNOW THE LOAD LIMIT ON BRIDGES, DAD?
LOAD LIMIT 10 TONS
THEY DRIVE BIGGER AND BIGGER TRUCKS OVER THE BRIDGE UNTIL IT BREAKS.
THEN THEY WEIGH THE LAST TRUCK AND REBUILD THE BRIDGE.
WATTERSON
OH. I SHOULD'VE GUESSED.
DEAR, IF YOU DON'T KNOW THE ANSWER, JUST TELL HIM!

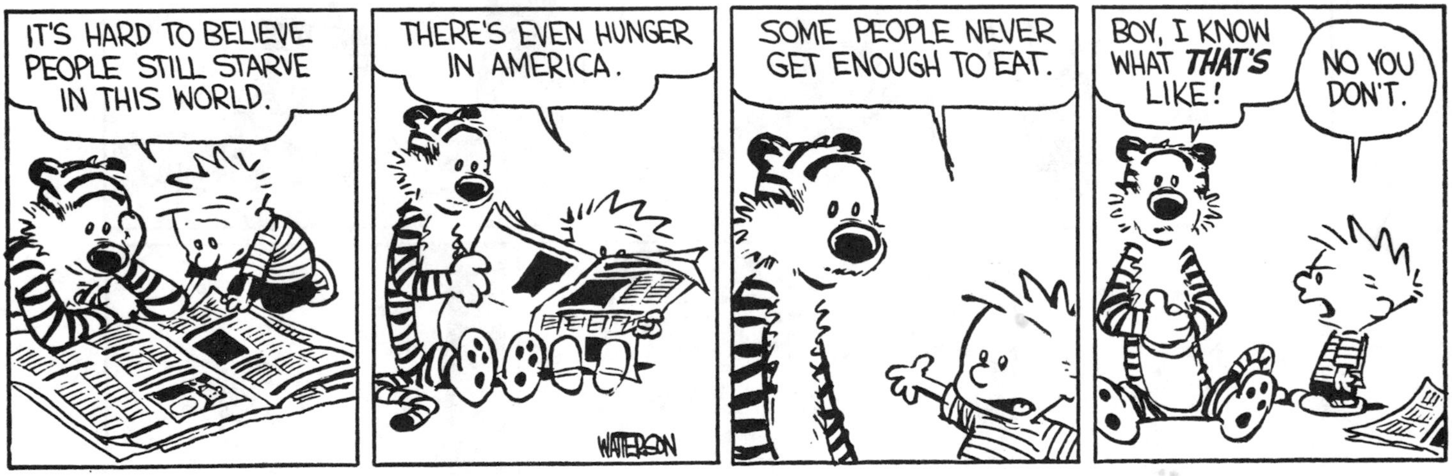
IT'S HARD TO BELIEVE PEOPLE STILL STARVE IN THIS WORLD.
THERE'S EVEN HUNGER IN AMERICA.
WATTERSON
SOME PEOPLE NEVER GET ENOUGH TO EAT.
BOY, I KNOW WHAT THAT'S LIKE!
NO YOU DON'T.

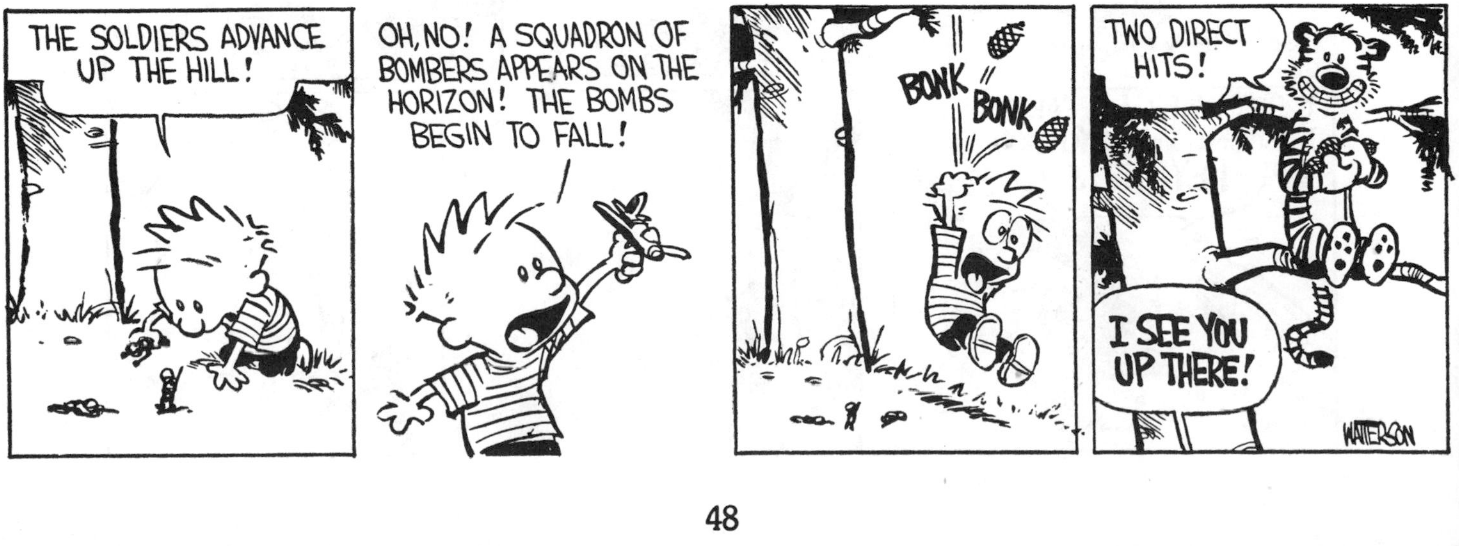
THE SOLDIERS ADVANCE UP THE HILL!
OH, NO! A SQUADRON OF BOMBERS APPEARS ON THE HORIZON! THE BOMBS BEGIN TO FALL!
BONK
BONK
TWO DIRECT HITS!
I SEE YOU UP THERE!
WATTERSON

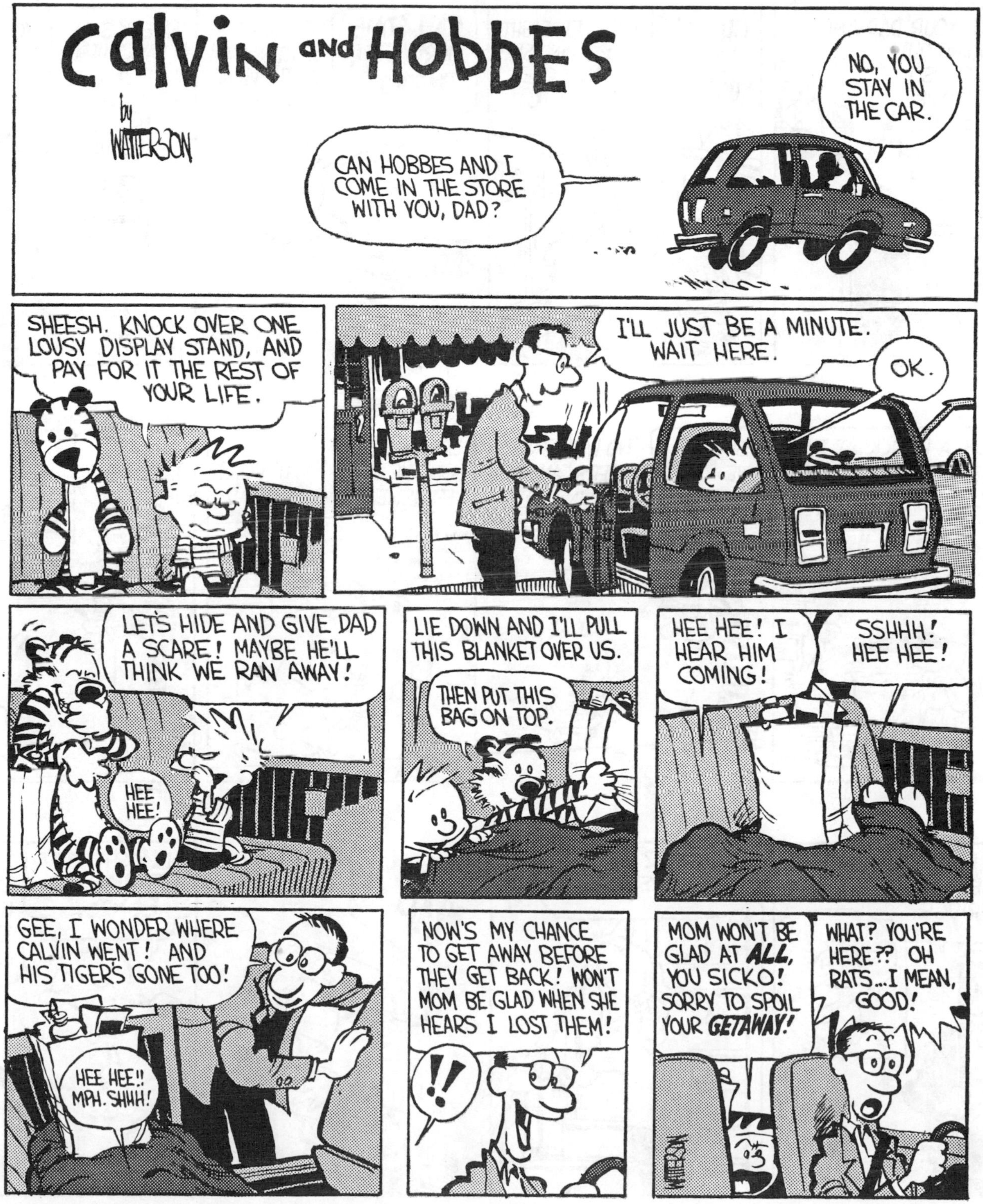
Calvin and HOBBES
by WATTERSON
CAN HOBBES AND I COME IN THE STORE WITH YOU, DAD?
NO, YOU STAY IN THE CAR.
SHEESH. KNOCK OVER ONE LOUSY DISPLAY STAND, AND PAY FOR IT THE REST OF YOUR LIFE.
I'LL JUST BE A MINUTE. WAIT HERE.
OK.
LET'S HIDE AND GIVE DAD A SCARE! MAYBE HE'LL THINK WE RAN AWAY!
HEE HEE!
LIE DOWN AND I'LL PULL THIS BLANKET OVER US.
THEN PUT THIS BAG ON TOP.
HEE HEE! I HEAR HIM COMING!
SSHHH! HEE HEE!
GEE, I WONDER WHERE CALVIN WENT! AND HIS TIGER'S GONE TOO!
HEE HEE!! MPH. SHHH!
NOW'S MY CHANCE TO GET AWAY BEFORE THEY GET BACK! WON'T MOM BE GLAD WHEN SHE HEARS I LOST THEM!
!!
MOM WON'T BE GLAD AT ALL, YOU SICKO! SORRY TO SPOIL YOUR GETAWAY!
WHAT? YOU'RE HERE?? OH RATS...I MEAN, GOOD!

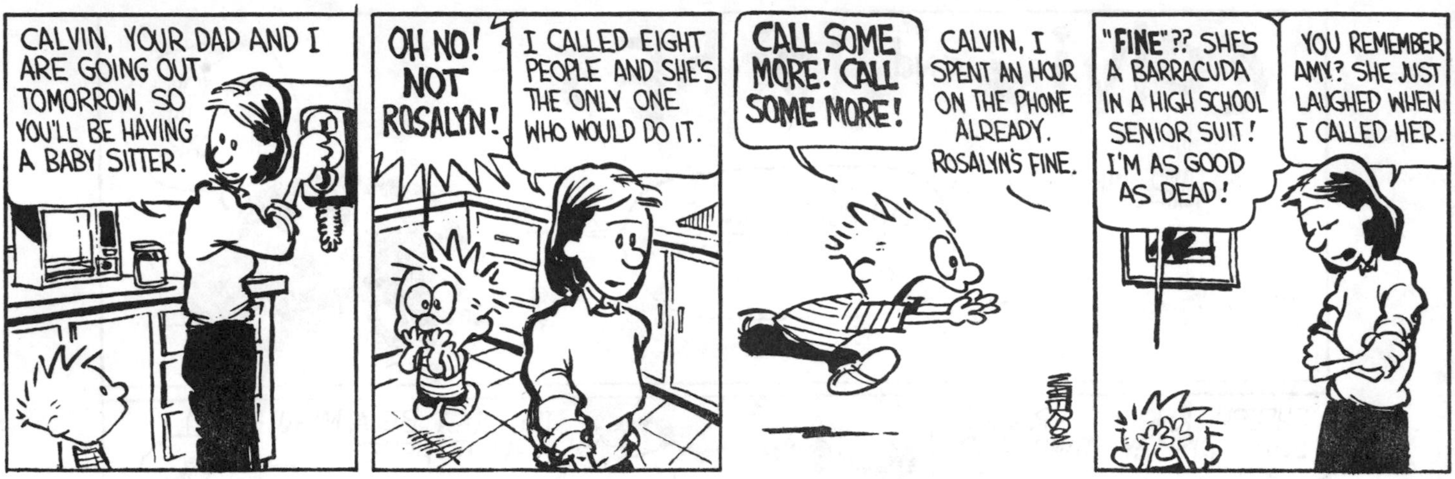
CALVIN, YOUR DAD AND I ARE GOING OUT TOMORROW, SO YOU'LL BE HAVING A BABY SITTER.
OH NO! NOT ROSALYN!
I CALLED EIGHT PEOPLE AND SHE'S THE ONLY ONE WHO WOULD DO IT.
CALL SOME MORE! CALL SOME MORE!
CALVIN, I SPENT AN HOUR ON THE PHONE ALREADY. ROSALYN'S FINE.
"FINE"?? SHE'S A BARRACUDA IN A HIGH SCHOOL SENIOR SUIT! I'M AS GOOD AS DEAD!
YOU REMEMBER AMY? SHE JUST LAUGHED WHEN I CALLED HER.
WATTERSON

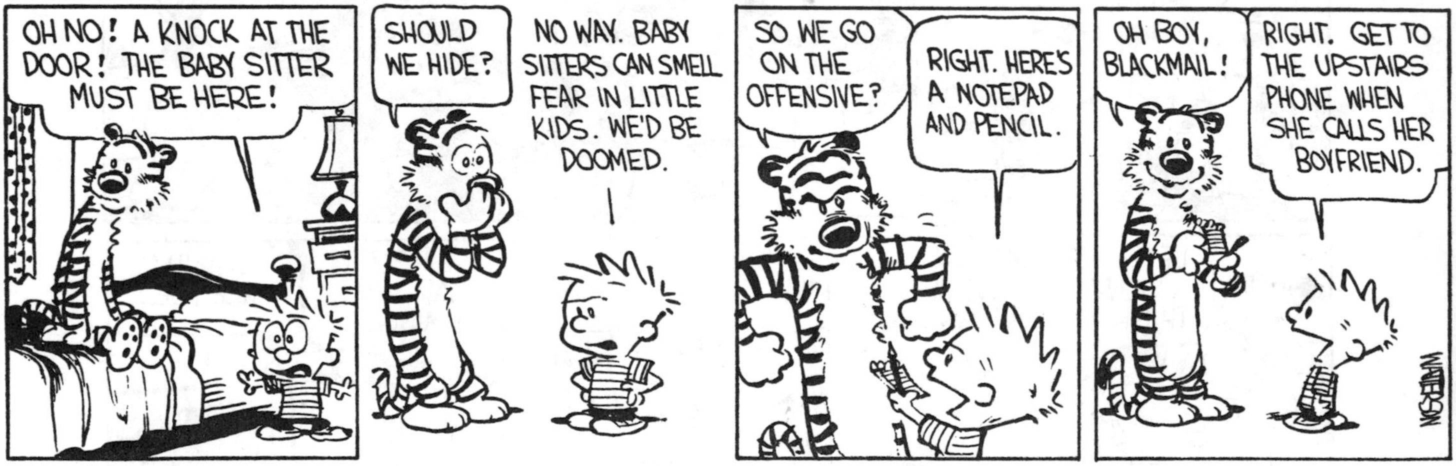
OH NO! A KNOCK AT THE DOOR! THE BABY SITTER MUST BE HERE!
SHOULD WE HIDE?
NO WAY. BABY SITTERS CAN SMELL FEAR IN LITTLE KIDS. WE'D BE DOOMED.
SO WE GO ON THE OFFENSIVE?
RIGHT. HERE'S A NOTEPAD AND PENCIL.
OH BOY, BLACKMAIL!
RIGHT. GET TO THE UPSTAIRS PHONE WHEN SHE CALLS HER BOYFRIEND.
WATTERSON

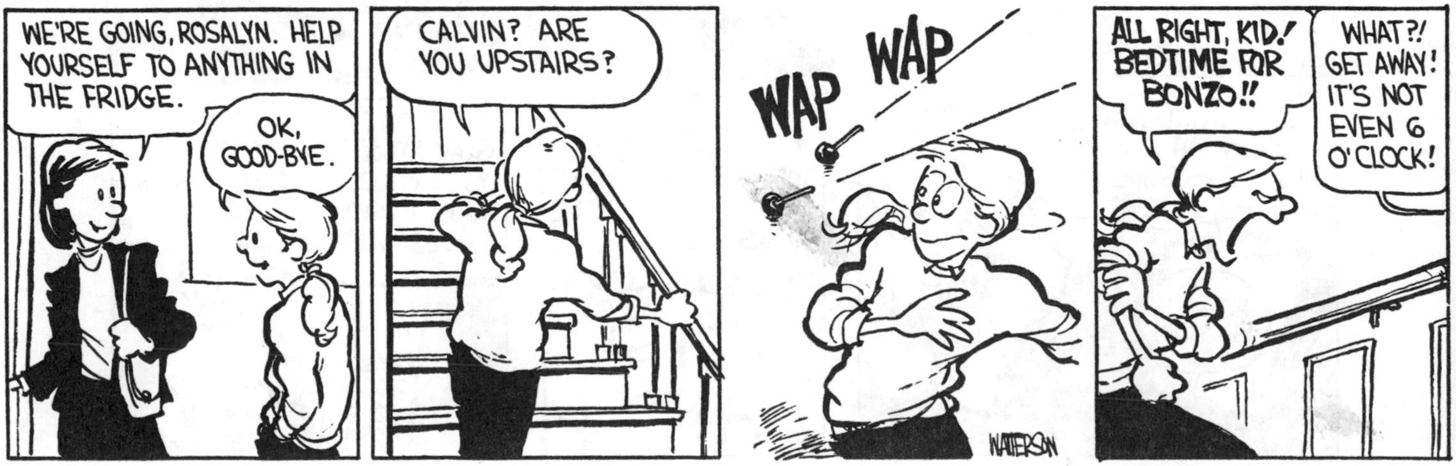
WE'RE GOING, ROSALYN. HELP YOURSELF TO ANYTHING IN THE FRIDGE.
OK, GOOD-BYE.
CALVIN? ARE YOU UPSTAIRS?
WAP
WAP
ALL RIGHT, KID! BEDTIME FOR BONZO!!
WHAT?! GET AWAY! IT'S NOT EVEN 6 O'CLOCK!
WATTERSON

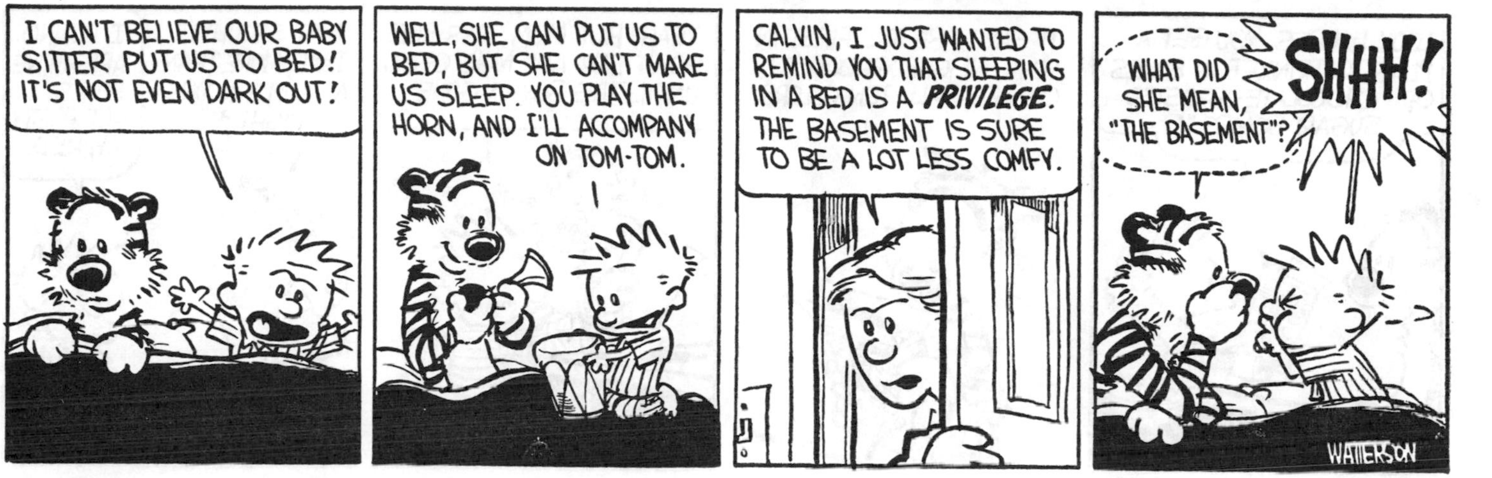
I CAN'T BELIEVE OUR BABY SITTER PUT US TO BED! IT'S NOT EVEN DARK OUT!
WELL, SHE CAN PUT US TO BED, BUT SHE CAN'T MAKE US SLEEP. YOU PLAY THE HORN, AND I'LL ACCOMPANY ON TOM-TOM.
CALVIN, I JUST WANTED TO REMIND YOU THAT SLEEPING IN A BED IS A PRIVILEGE. THE BASEMENT IS SURE TO BE A LOT LESS COMFY.
WHAT DID SHE MEAN, "THE BASEMENT"?
SHHH!
WATTERSON

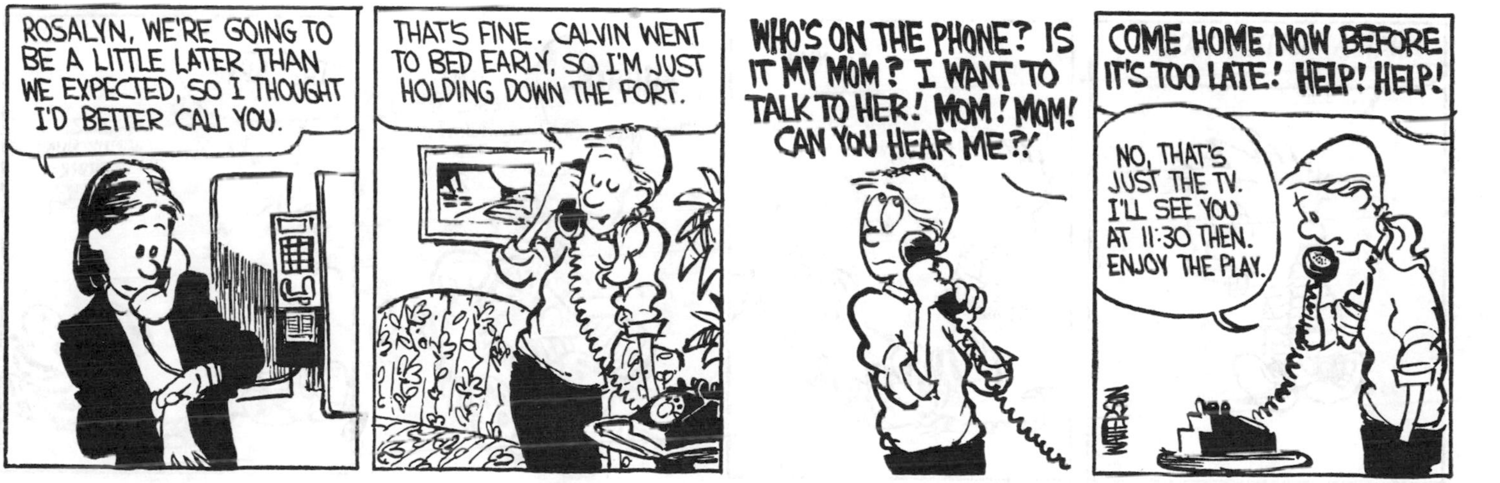
ROSALYN, WE'RE GOING TO BE A LITTLE LATER THAN WE EXPECTED, SO I THOUGHT I'D BETTER CALL YOU.
THAT'S FINE. CALVIN WENT TO BED EARLY, SO I'M JUST HOLDING DOWN THE FORT.
WHO'S ON THE PHONE? IS IT MY MOM? I WANT TO TALK TO HER! MOM! MOM! CAN YOU HEAR ME?!
COME HOME NOW BEFORE IT'S TOO LATE! HELP! HELP!
NO, THAT'S JUST THE TV. I'LL SEE YOU AT 11:30 THEN. ENJOY THE PLAY.
WATTERSON

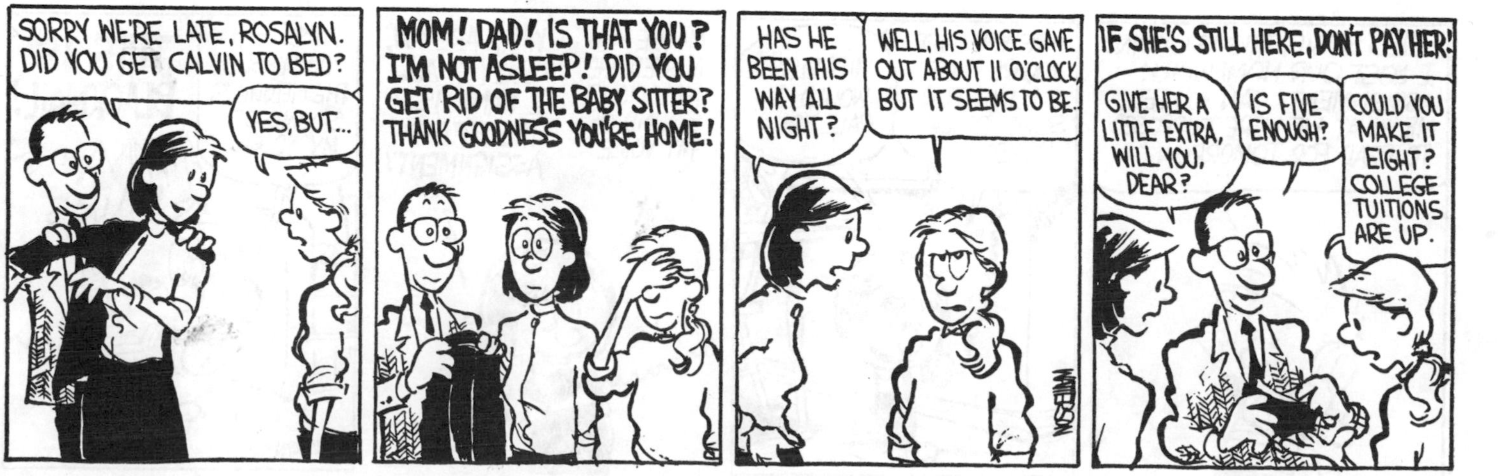
SORRY WE'RE LATE, ROSALYN. DID YOU GET CALVIN TO BED?
YES, BUT...
MOM! DAD! IS THAT YOU? I'M NOT ASLEEP! DID YOU GET RID OF THE BABY SITTER? THANK GOODNESS YOU'RE HOME!
HAS HE BEEN THIS WAY ALL NIGHT?
WELL, HIS VOICE GAVE OUT ABOUT 11 O'CLOCK, BUT IT SEEMS TO BE...
WATTERSON
IF SHE'S STILL HERE, DON'T PAY HER!
GIVE HER A LITTLE EXTRA, WILL YOU, DEAR?
IS FIVE ENOUGH?
COULD YOU MAKE IT EIGHT? COLLEGE TUITIONS ARE UP.

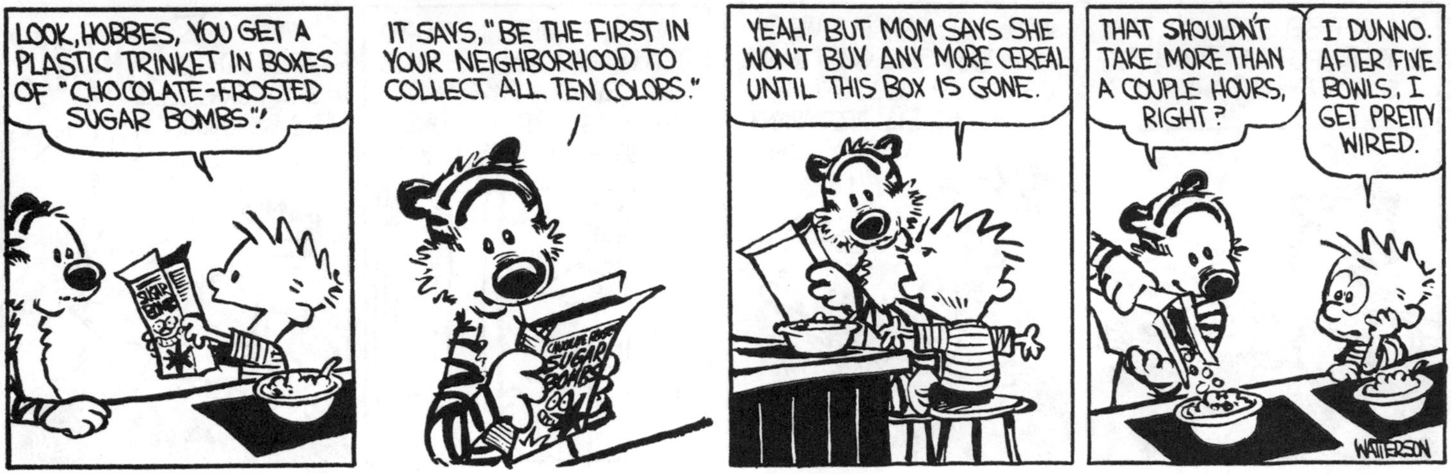
LOOK, HOBBES, YOU GET A PLASTIC TRINKET IN BOXES OF "CHOCOLATE-FROSTED SUGAR BOMBS"!
IT SAYS, "BE THE FIRST IN YOUR NEIGHBORHOOD TO COLLECT ALL TEN COLORS."
SUGAR BOMBS
YEAH, BUT MOM SAYS SHE WON'T BUY ANY MORE CEREAL UNTIL THIS BOX IS GONE.
THAT SHOULDN'T TAKE MORE THAN A COUPLE HOURS, RIGHT?
I DUNNO. AFTER FIVE BOWLS, I GET PRETTY WIRED.
WATTERSON

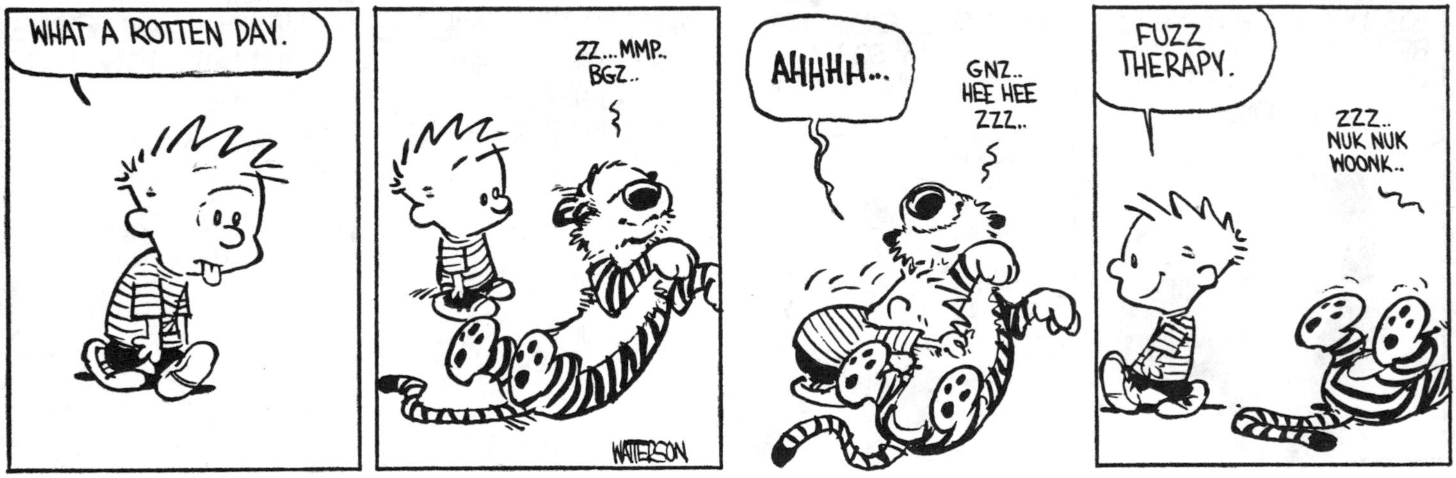
WHAT A ROTTEN DAY.
ZZ...MMP.. BGZ..
WATTERSON
AHHHH...
GNZ.. HEE HEE ZZZ..
FUZZ THERAPY.
ZZZ.. NUK NUK WOONK..

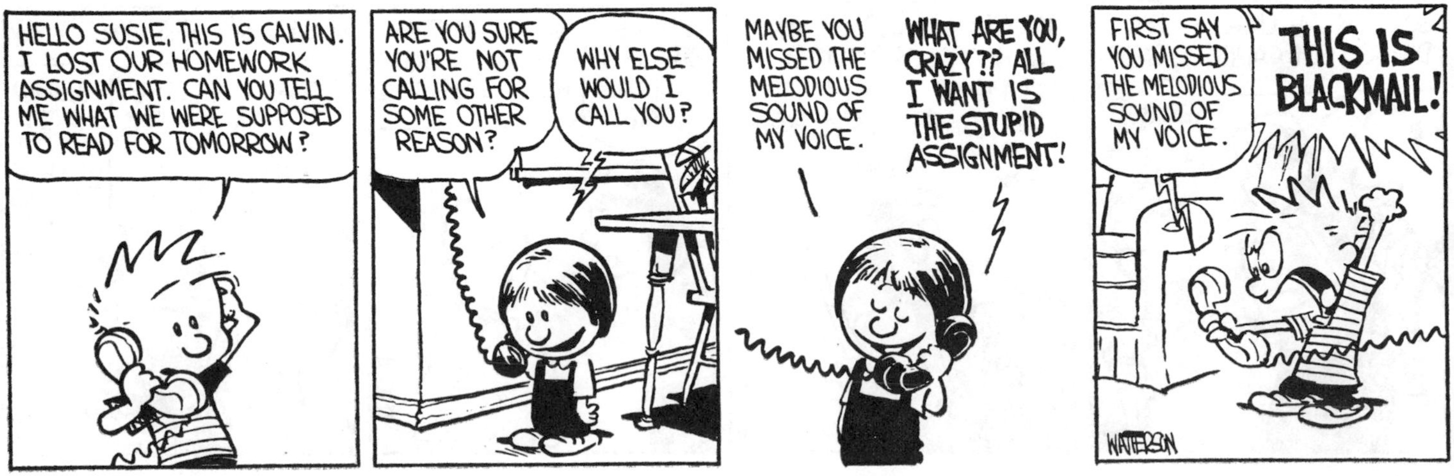
HELLO SUSIE, THIS IS CALVIN. I LOST OUR HOMEWORK ASSIGNMENT. CAN YOU TELL ME WHAT WE WERE SUPPOSED TO READ FOR TOMORROW?
ARE YOU SURE YOU'RE NOT CALLING FOR SOME OTHER REASON?
WHY ELSE WOULD I CALL YOU?
MAYBE YOU MISSED THE MELODIOUS SOUND OF MY VOICE.
WHAT ARE YOU, CRAZY?? ALL I WANT IS THE STUPID ASSIGNMENT!
FIRST SAY YOU MISSED THE MELODIOUS SOUND OF MY VOICE.
THIS IS BLACKMAIL!
WATTERSON

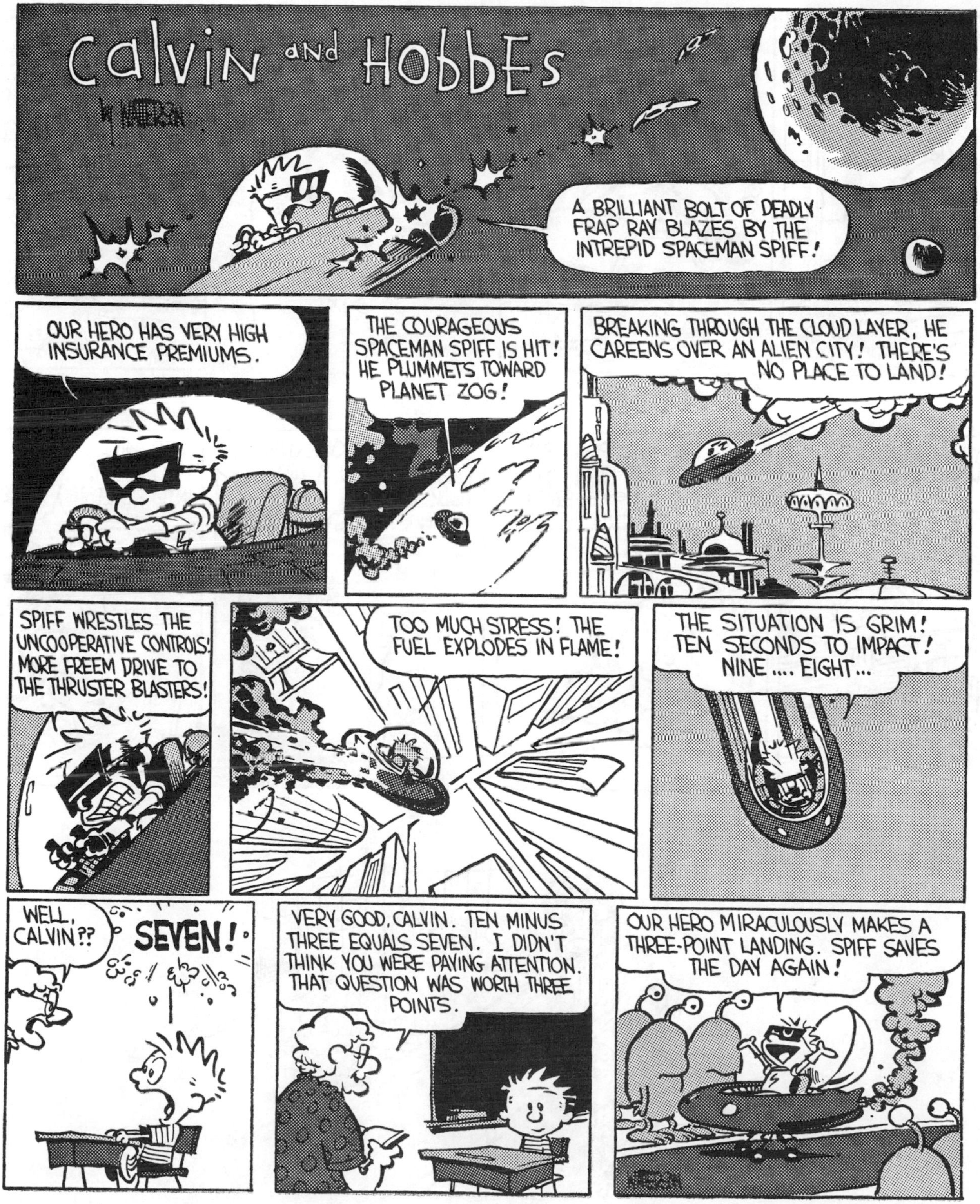
Calvin and HOBBES
by WATTERSON
A BRILLIANT BOLT OF DEADLY FRAP RAY BLAZES BY THE INTREPID SPACEMAN SPIFF!
OUR HERO HAS VERY HIGH INSURANCE PREMIUMS.
THE COURAGEOUS SPACEMAN SPIFF IS HIT! HE PLUMMETS TOWARD PLANET ZOG!
BREAKING THROUGH THE CLOUD LAYER, HE CAREENS OVER AN ALIEN CITY! THERE'S NO PLACE TO LAND!
SPIFF WRESTLES THE UNCOOPERATIVE CONTROLS! MORE FREEM DRIVE TO THE THRUSTER BLASTERS!
TOO MUCH STRESS! THE FUEL EXPLODES IN FLAME!
THE SITUATION IS GRIM! TEN SECONDS TO IMPACT! NINE .... EIGHT...
WELL, CALVIN??
SEVEN!
VERY GOOD, CALVIN. TEN MINUS THREE EQUALS SEVEN. I DIDN'T THINK YOU WERE PAYING ATTENTION. THAT QUESTION WAS WORTH THREE POINTS.
OUR HERO MIRACULOUSLY MAKES A THREE-POINT LANDING. SPIFF SAVES THE DAY AGAIN!
WATTERSON

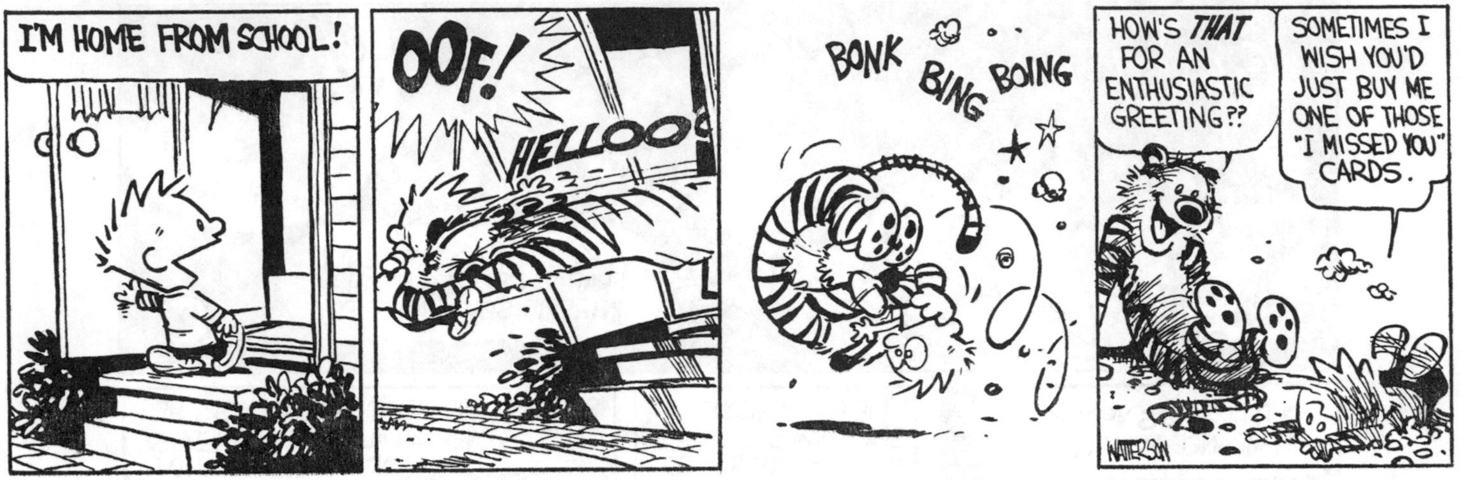
I'M HOME FROM SCHOOL!
OOF!
HELLOO
BONK
BING
BOING
HOW'S THAT FOR AN ENTHUSIASTIC GREETING??
SOMETIMES I WISH YOU'D JUST BUY ME ONE OF THOSE "I MISSED YOU" CARDS.
WATTERSON

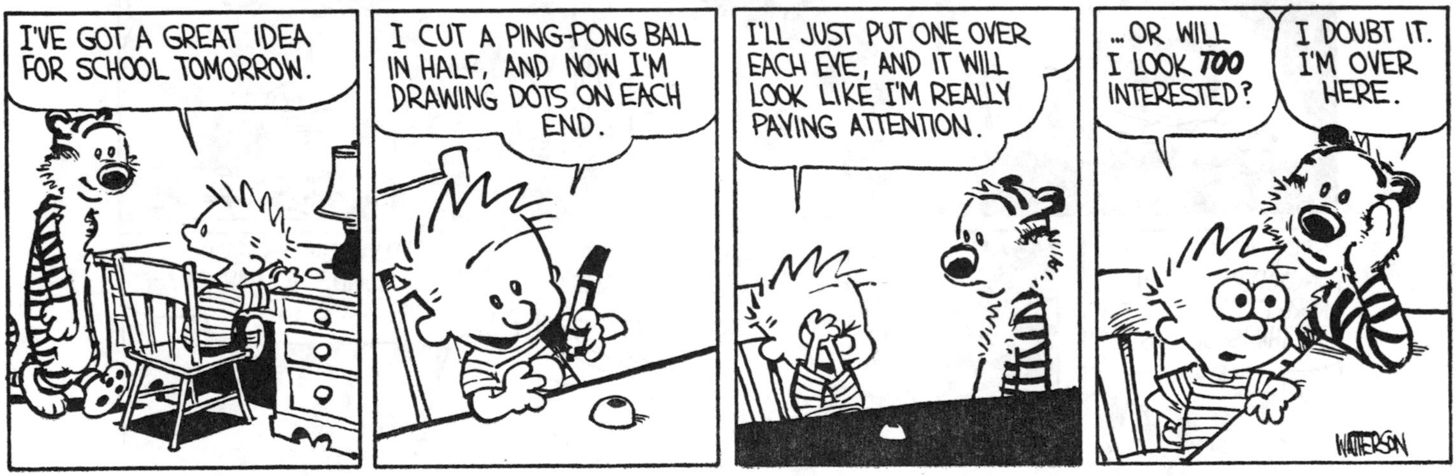
I'VE GOT A GREAT IDEA FOR SCHOOL TOMORROW.
I CUT A PING-PONG BALL IN HALF, AND NOW I'M DRAWING DOTS ON EACH END.
I'LL JUST PUT ONE OVER EACH EYE, AND IT WILL LOOK LIKE I'M REALLY PAYING ATTENTION.
...OR WILL I LOOK TOO INTERESTED?
I DOUBT IT. I'M OVER HERE.
WATTERSON

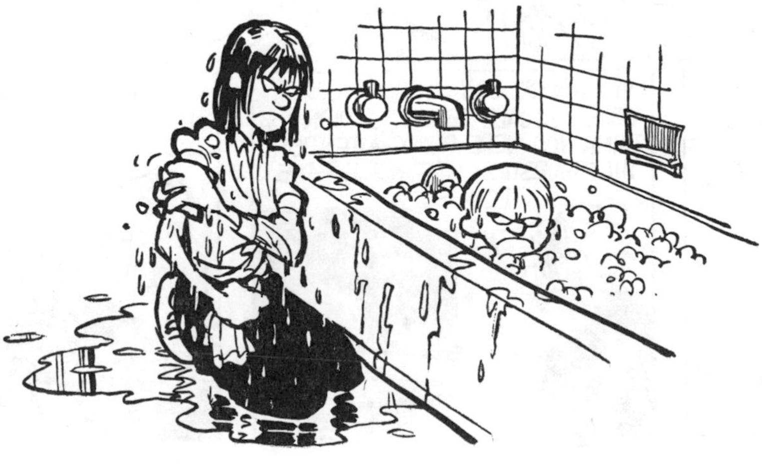

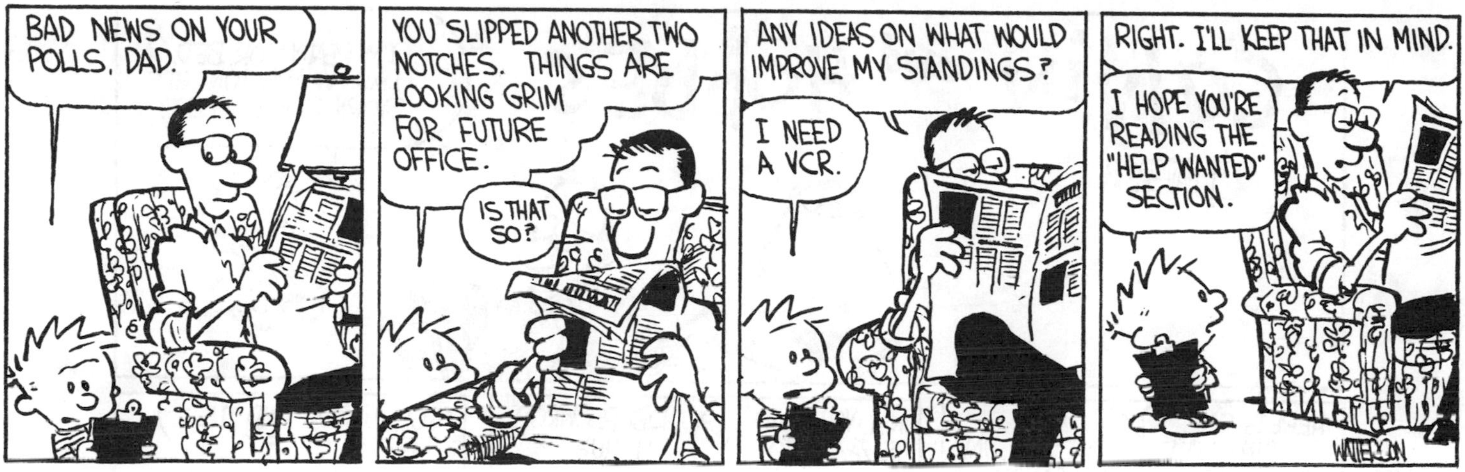
BAD NEWS ON YOUR POLLS, DAD.
YOU SLIPPED ANOTHER TWO NOTCHES. THINGS ARE LOOKING GRIM FOR FUTURE OFFICE.
IS THAT SO?
ANY IDEAS ON WHAT WOULD IMPROVE MY STANDINGS?
I NEED A VCR.
RIGHT. I'LL KEEP THAT IN MIND.
I HOPE YOU'RE READING THE "HELP WANTED" SECTION.
WATTERSON

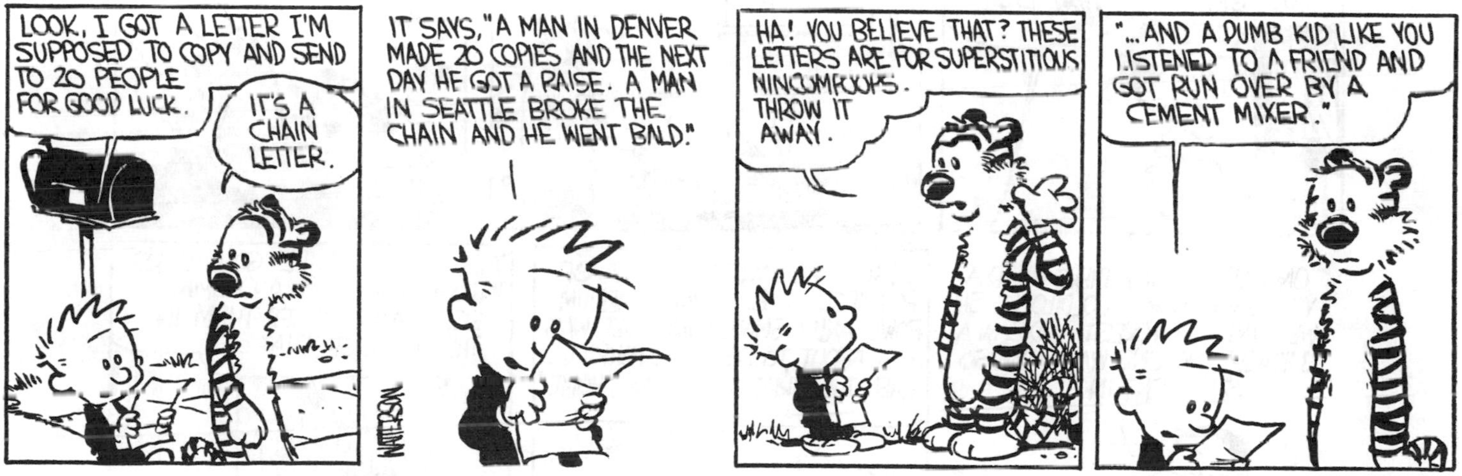
LOOK, I GOT A LETTER I'M SUPPOSED TO COPY AND SEND TO 20 PEOPLE FOR GOOD LUCK.
IT'S A CHAIN LETTER.
WATTERSON
IT SAYS, "A MAN IN DENVER MADE 20 COPIES AND THE NEXT DAY HE GOT A RAISE. A MAN IN SEATTLE BROKE THE CHAIN AND HE WENT BALD."
HA! YOU BELIEVE THAT? THESE LETTERS ARE FOR SUPERSTITIOUS NINCOMPOOPS. THROW IT AWAY.
"...AND A DUMB KID LIKE YOU LISTENED TO A FRIEND AND GOT RUN OVER BY A CEMENT MIXER."

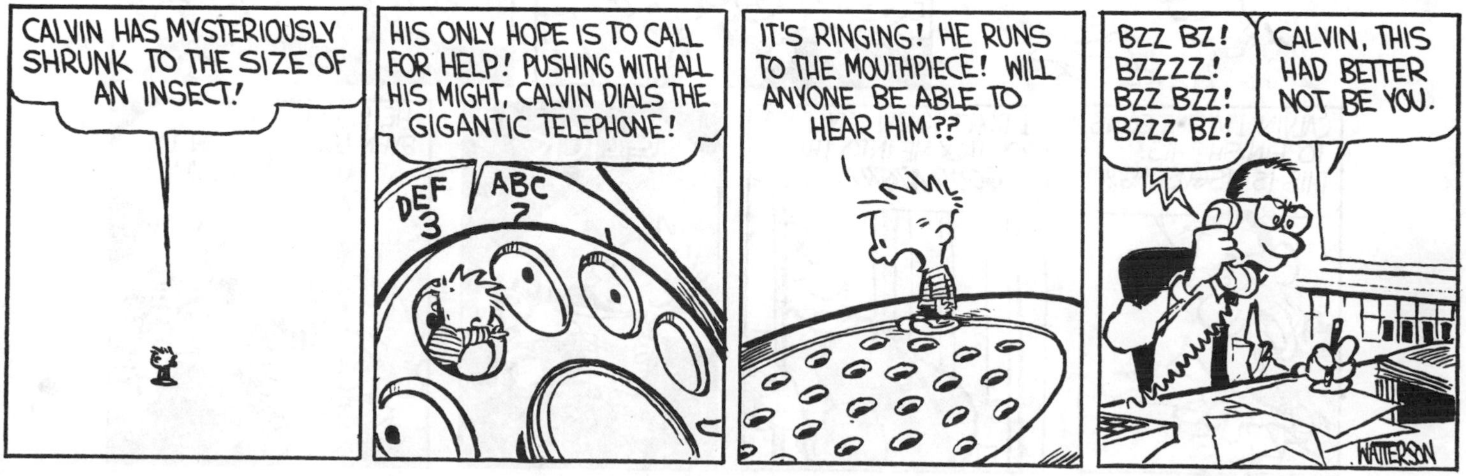
CALVIN HAS MYSTERIOUSLY SHRUNK TO THE SIZE OF AN INSECT!
HIS ONLY HOPE IS TO CALL FOR HELP! PUSHING WITH ALL HIS MIGHT, CALVIN DIALS THE GIGANTIC TELEPHONE!
DEF 3
ABC 2
IT'S RINGING! HE RUNS TO THE MOUTHPIECE! WILL ANYONE BE ABLE TO HEAR HIM??
BZZ BZ! BZZZZ! BZZ BZZ! BZZZ BZ!
CALVIN, THIS HAD BETTER NOT BE YOU.
WATTERSON

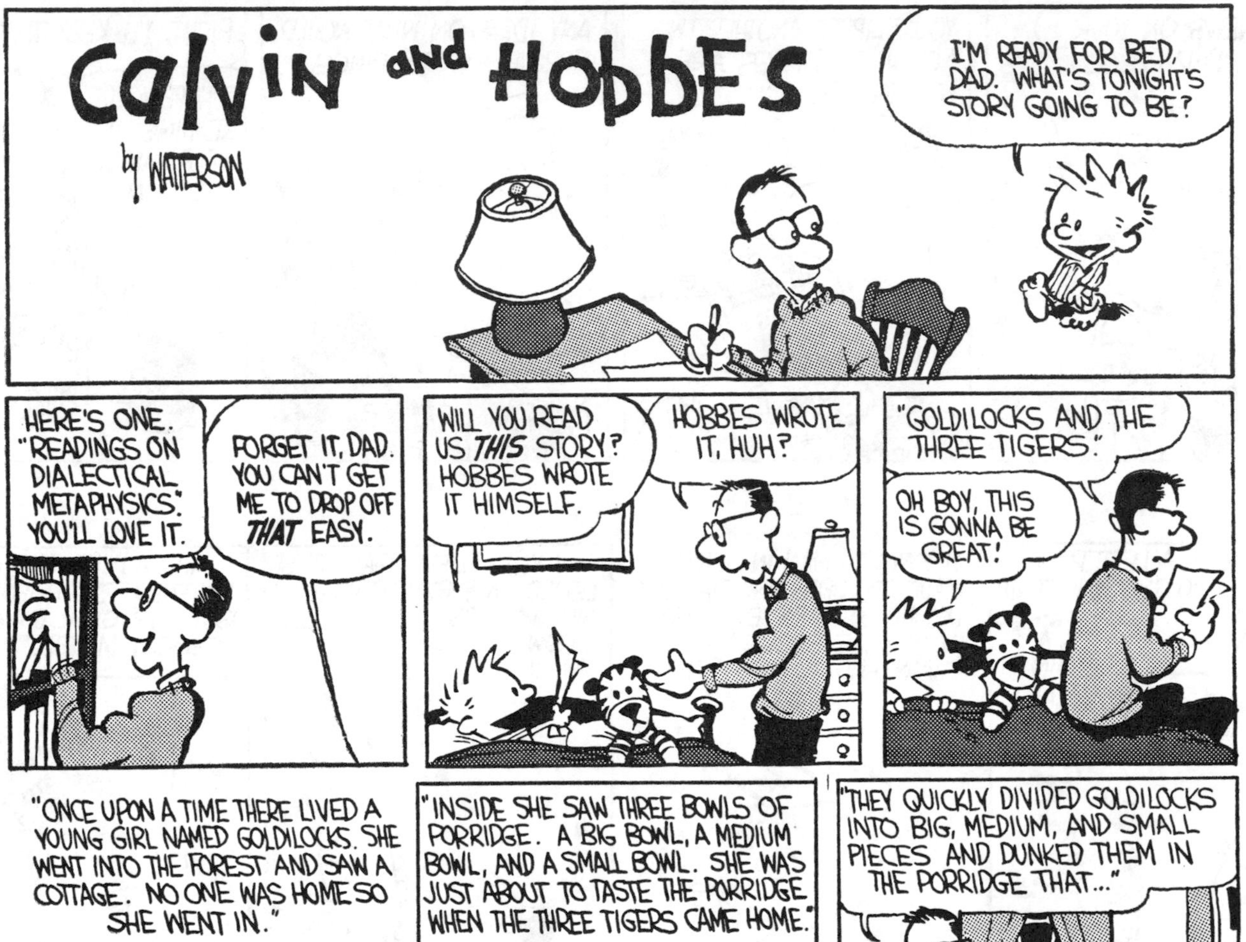
Calvin and HobbEs
by WATTERSON
I'M READY FOR BED, DAD. WHAT'S TONIGHT'S STORY GOING TO BE?
HERE'S ONE. "READINGS ON DIALECTICAL METAPHYSICS." YOU'LL LOVE IT.
FORGET IT, DAD. YOU CAN'T GET ME TO DROP OFF THAT EASY.
WILL YOU READ US THIS STORY? HOBBES WROTE IT HIMSELF.
HOBBES WROTE IT, HUH?
"GOLDILOCKS AND THE THREE TIGERS."
OH BOY, THIS IS GONNA BE GREAT!
"ONCE UPON A TIME THERE LIVED A YOUNG GIRL NAMED GOLDILOCKS. SHE WENT INTO THE FOREST AND SAW A COTTAGE. NO ONE WAS HOME SO SHE WENT IN."
"INSIDE SHE SAW THREE BOWLS OF PORRIDGE. A BIG BOWL, A MEDIUM BOWL, AND A SMALL BOWL. SHE WAS JUST ABOUT TO TASTE THE PORRIDGE WHEN THE THREE TIGERS CAME HOME."
"THEY QUICKLY DIVIDED GOLDILOCKS INTO BIG, MEDIUM, AND SMALL PIECES AND DUNKED THEM IN THE PORRIDGE THAT..."
CALVIN, I'M NOT GOING TO FINISH THIS! THIS IS DISGUSTING!!
I DON'T KNOW WHY I LET YOU TALK ME INTO THIS. GOOD NIGHT!
CLICK
HE DIDN'T EVEN LOOK AT OUR ILLUSTRATIONS.
NOW I'M ALL HUNGRY.

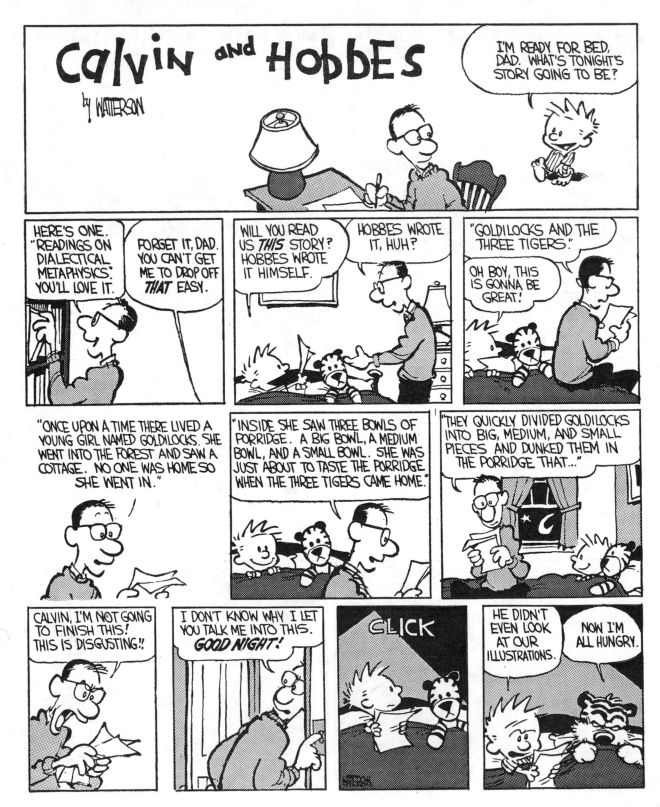

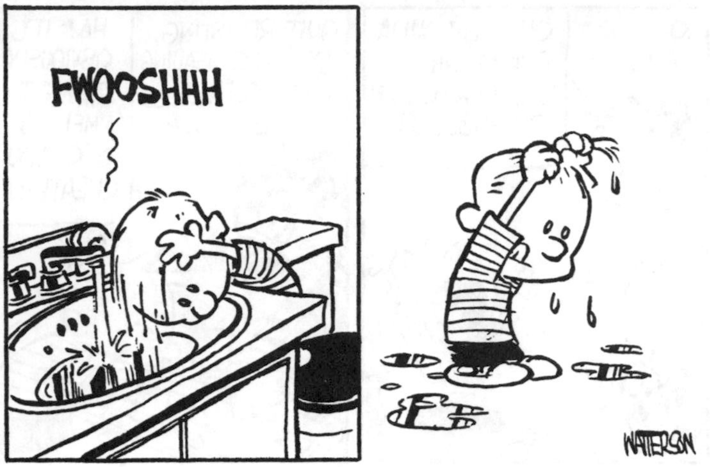
FWOOSHHH
WATTERSON

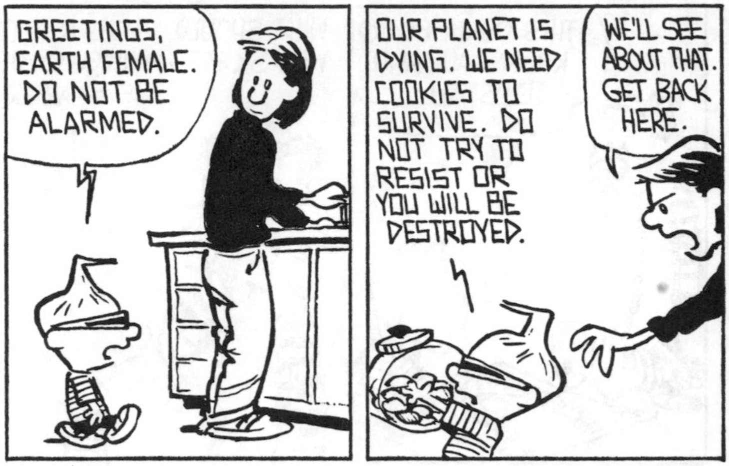
GREETINGS, EARTH FEMALE. DO NOT BE ALARMED.
OUR PLANET IS DYING. WE NEED COOKIES TO SURVIVE. DO NOT TRY TO RESIST OR YOU WILL BE DESTROYED.
WE'LL SEE ABOUT THAT. GET BACK HERE.

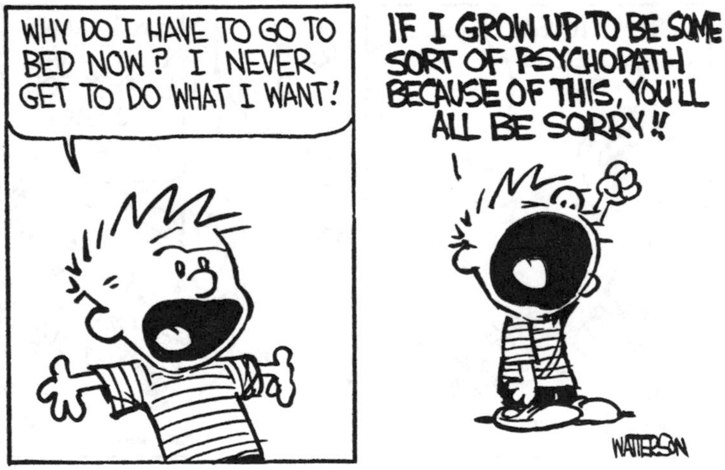
WHY DO I HAVE TO GO TO BED NOW? I NEVER GET TO DO WHAT I WANT!
IF I GROW UP TO BE SOME SORT OF PSYCHOPATH BECAUSE OF THIS, YOU'LL ALL BE SORRY!!
WATTERSON

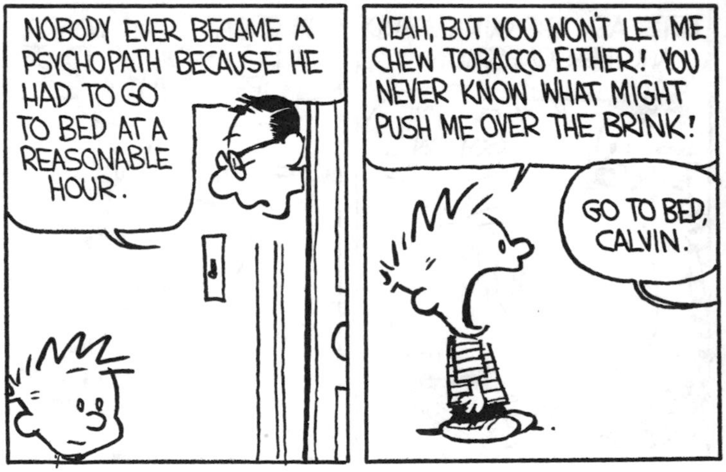
NOBODY EVER BECAME A PSYCHOPATH BECAUSE HE HAD TO GO TO BED AT A REASONABLE HOUR.
YEAH, BUT YOU WON'T LET ME CHEW TOBACCO EITHER! YOU NEVER KNOW WHAT MIGHT PUSH ME OVER THE BRINK!
GO TO BED, CALVIN.

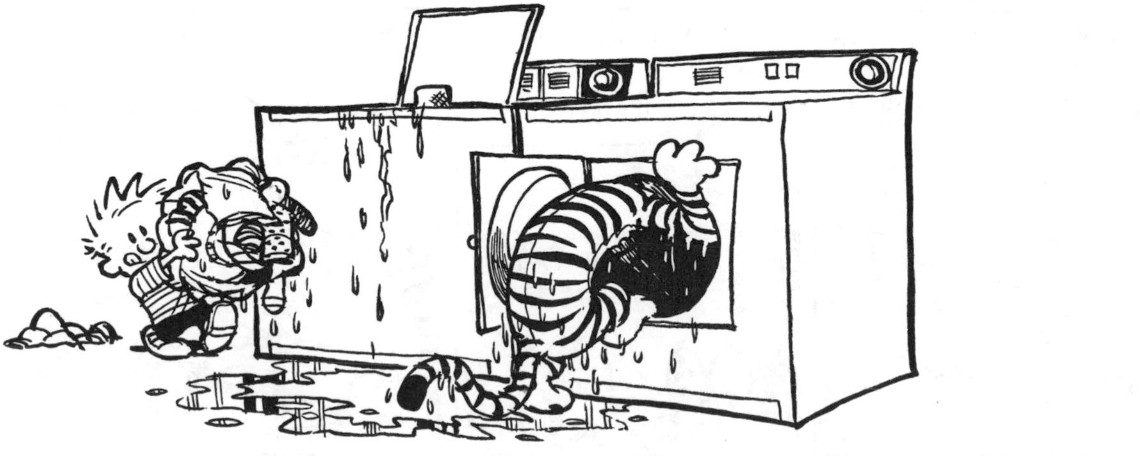

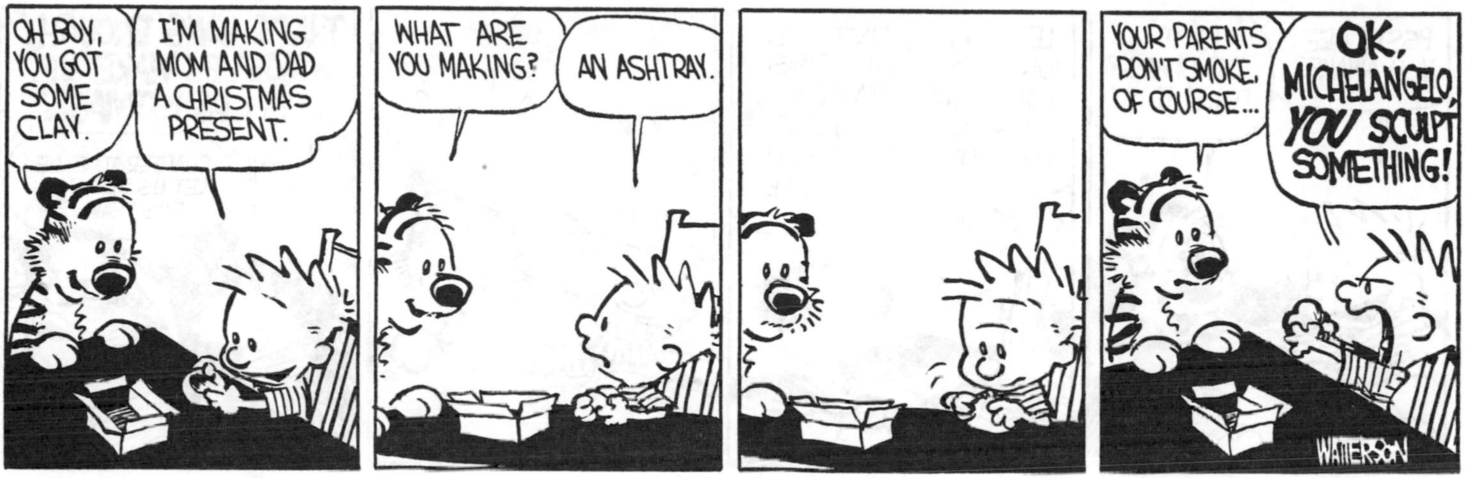
OH BOY, YOU GOT SOME CLAY.
I'M MAKING MOM AND DAD A CHRISTMAS PRESENT.
WHAT ARE YOU MAKING?
AN ASHTRAY.
YOUR PARENTS DON'T SMOKE, OF COURSE...
OK, MICHELANGELO, ***YOU*** SCULPT SOMETHING!
WATTERSON

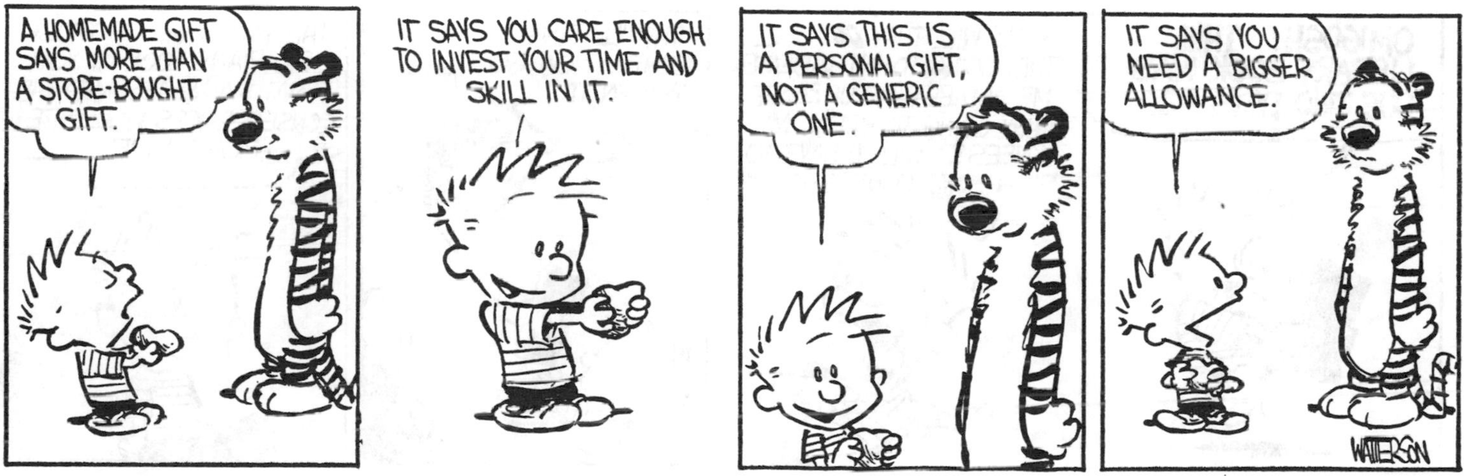
A HOMEMADE GIFT SAYS MORE THAN A STORE-BOUGHT GIFT.
IT SAYS YOU CARE ENOUGH TO INVEST YOUR TIME AND SKILL IN IT.
IT SAYS THIS IS A PERSONAL GIFT, NOT A GENERIC ONE.
IT SAYS YOU NEED A BIGGER ALLOWANCE.
WATTERSON

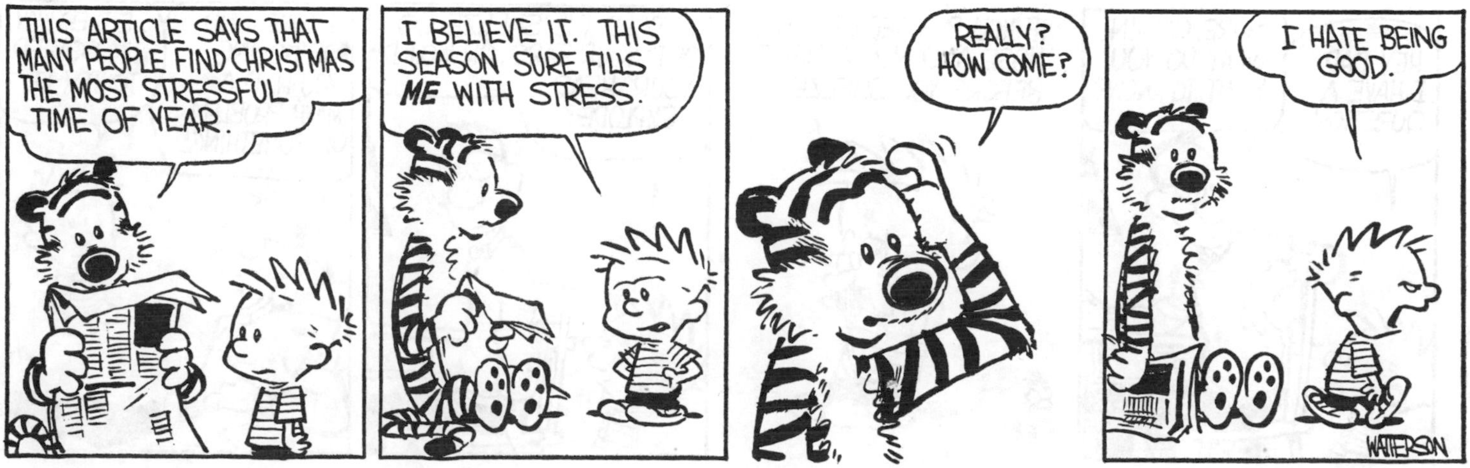
THIS ARTICLE SAYS THAT MANY PEOPLE FIND CHRISTMAS THE MOST STRESSFUL TIME OF YEAR.
I BELIEVE IT. THIS SEASON SURE FILLS ***ME*** WITH STRESS.
REALLY? HOW COME?
I HATE BEING GOOD.
WATTERSON

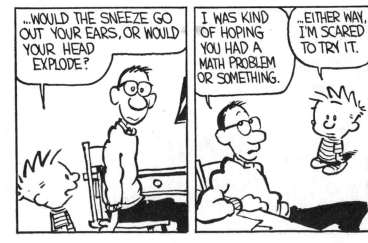

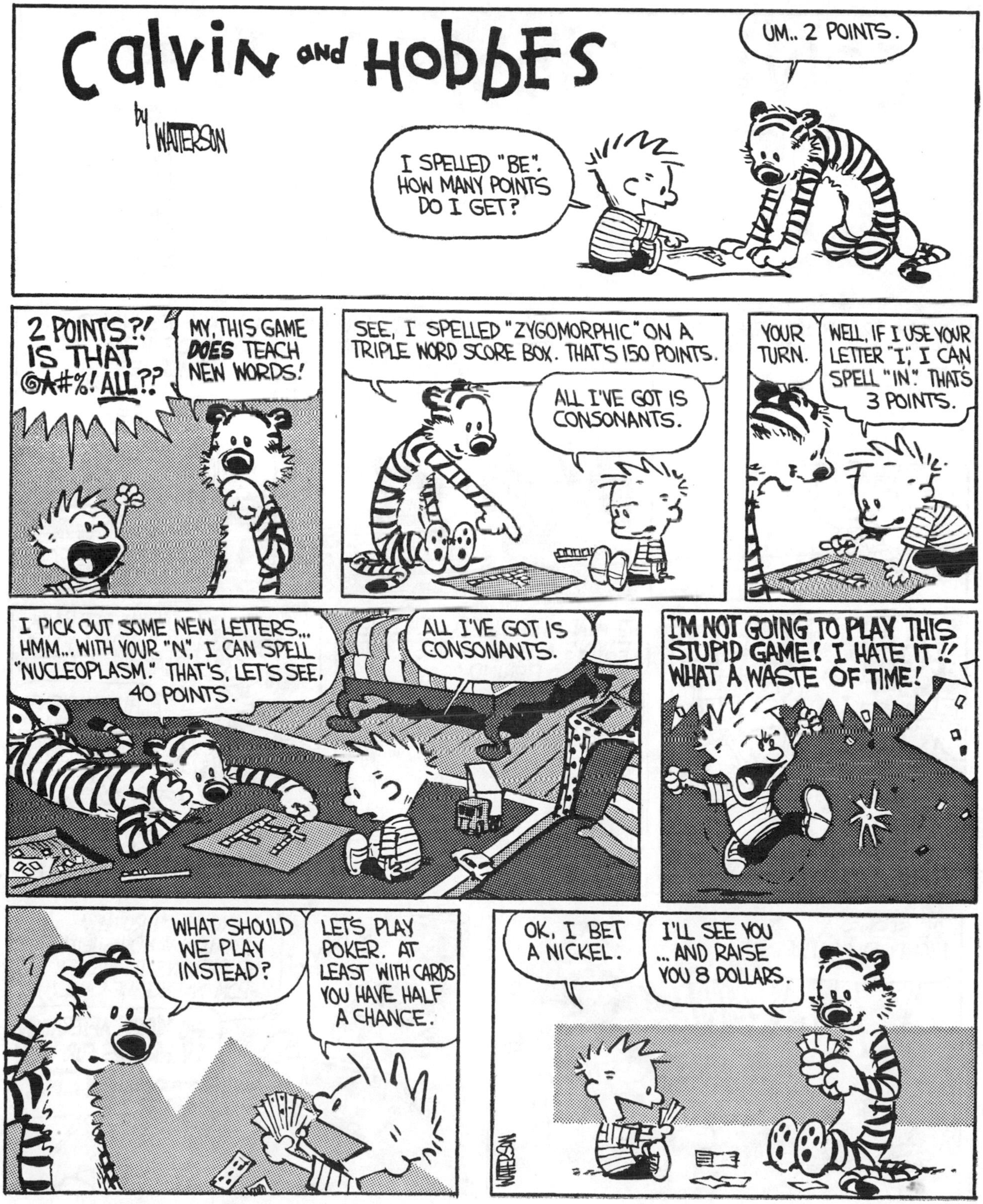
Calvin and HobbES
by WATTERSON
I SPELLED "BE". HOW MANY POINTS DO I GET?
UM.. 2 POINTS.
2 POINTS?! IS THAT @*#%! ALL??
MY, THIS GAME DOES TEACH NEW WORDS!
SEE, I SPELLED "ZYGOMORPHIC" ON A TRIPLE WORD SCORE BOX. THAT'S 150 POINTS.
ALL I'VE GOT IS CONSONANTS.
YOUR TURN.
WELL, IF I USE YOUR LETTER "I", I CAN SPELL "IN." THAT'S 3 POINTS.
I PICK OUT SOME NEW LETTERS... HMM... WITH YOUR "N", I CAN SPELL "NUCLEOPLASM." THAT'S, LET'S SEE, 40 POINTS.
ALL I'VE GOT IS CONSONANTS.
I'M NOT GOING TO PLAY THIS STUPID GAME! I HATE IT!! WHAT A WASTE OF TIME!
WHAT SHOULD WE PLAY INSTEAD?
LET'S PLAY POKER. AT LEAST WITH CARDS YOU HAVE HALF A CHANCE.
OK, I BET A NICKEL.
I'LL SEE YOU ... AND RAISE YOU 8 DOLLARS.
WATTERSON

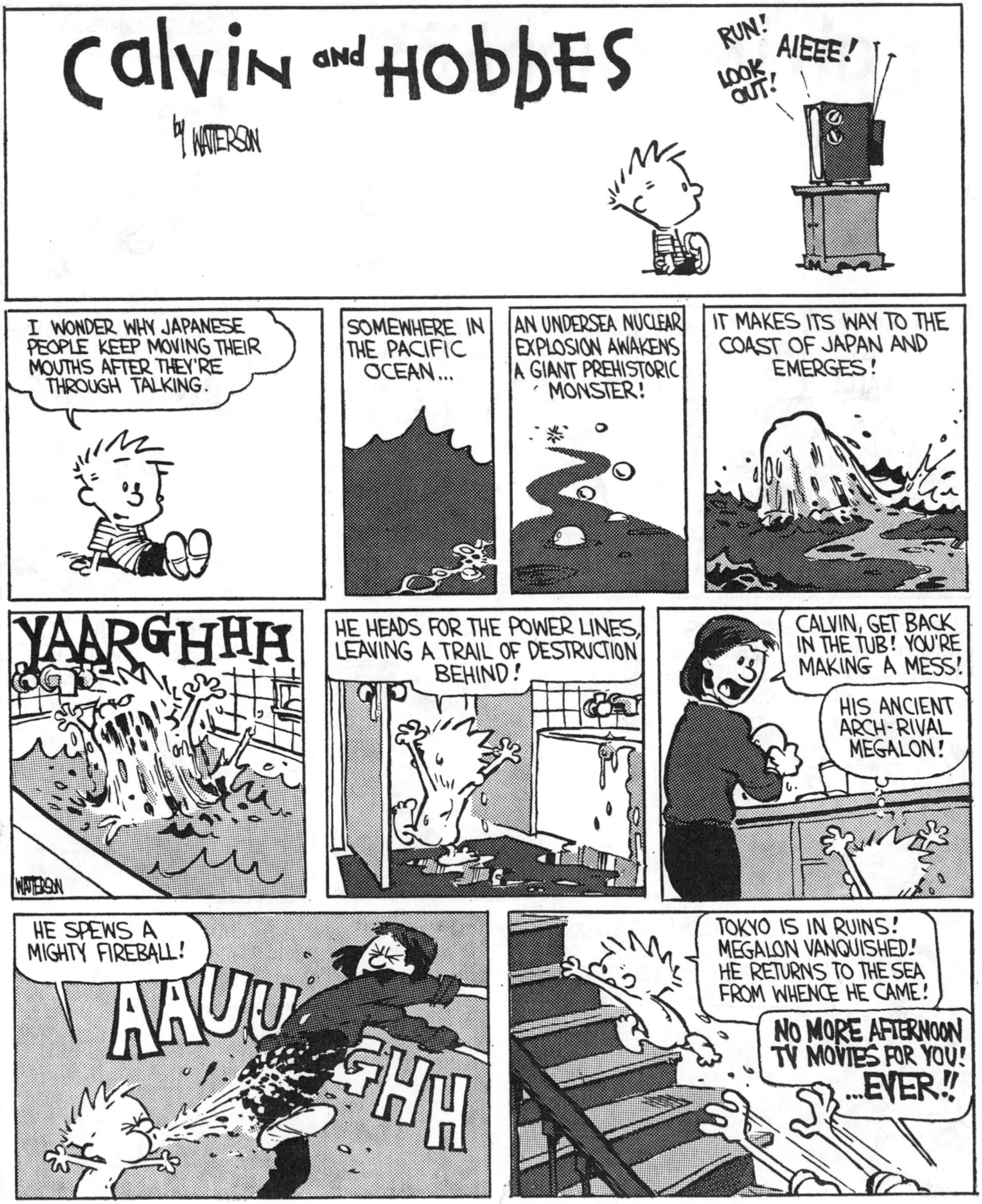
Calvin and HOBBES
by WATTERSON
RUN!
AIEEE!
LOOK OUT!
I WONDER WHY JAPANESE PEOPLE KEEP MOVING THEIR MOUTHS AFTER THEY'RE THROUGH TALKING.
SOMEWHERE IN THE PACIFIC OCEAN...
AN UNDERSEA NUCLEAR EXPLOSION AWAKENS A GIANT PREHISTORIC MONSTER!
IT MAKES ITS WAY TO THE COAST OF JAPAN AND EMERGES!
YAARGHHH
WATTERSON
HE HEADS FOR THE POWER LINES, LEAVING A TRAIL OF DESTRUCTION BEHIND!
CALVIN, GET BACK IN THE TUB! YOU'RE MAKING A MESS!
HIS ANCIENT ARCH-RIVAL MEGALON!
HE SPEWS A MIGHTY FIREBALL!
AAUUGHH
TOKYO IS IN RUINS! MEGALON VANQUISHED! HE RETURNS TO THE SEA FROM WHENCE HE CAME!
NO MORE AFTERNOON TV MOVIES FOR YOU! ...EVER!!

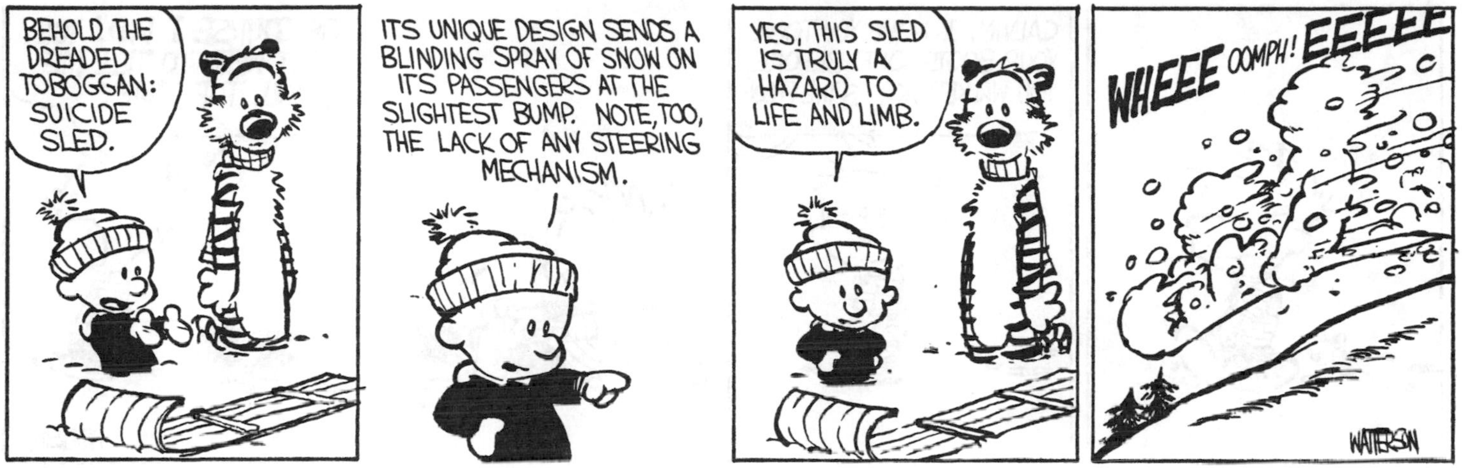
BEHOLD THE DREADED TOBOGGAN: SUICIDE SLED.
ITS UNIQUE DESIGN SENDS A BLINDING SPRAY OF SNOW ON IT'S PASSENGERS AT THE SLIGHTEST BUMP. NOTE, TOO, THE LACK OF ANY STEERING MECHANISM.
YES, THIS SLED IS TRULY A HAZARD TO LIFE AND LIMB.
WHEEE OOMPH! EEEEE
WATTERSON

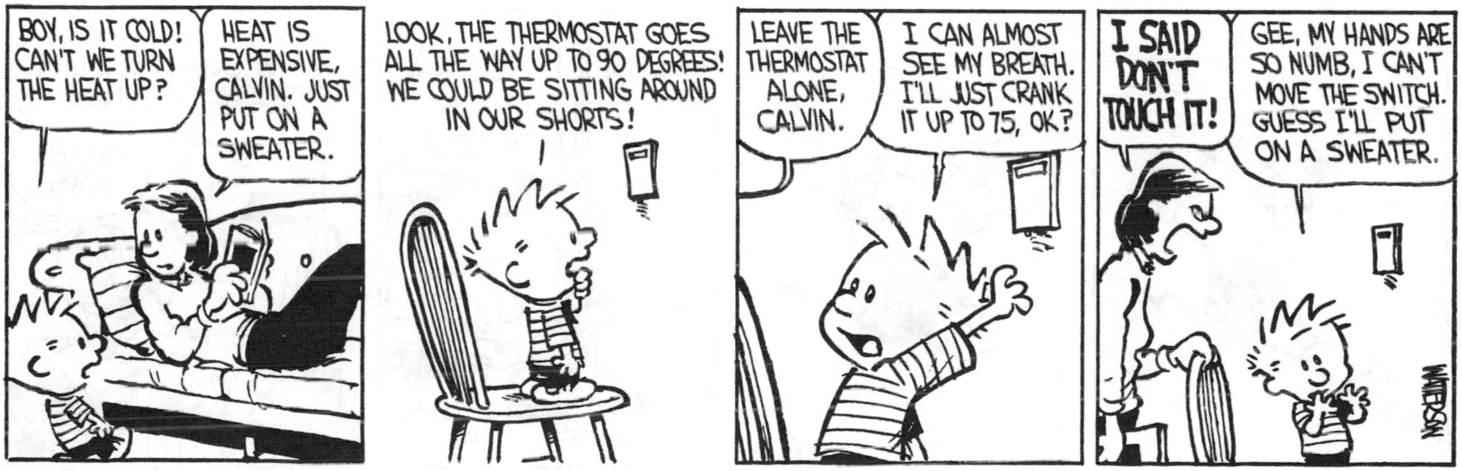
BOY, IS IT COLD! CAN'T WE TURN THE HEAT UP?
HEAT IS EXPENSIVE, CALVIN. JUST PUT ON A SWEATER.
LOOK, THE THERMOSTAT GOES ALL THE WAY UP TO 90 DEGREES! WE COULD BE SITTING AROUND IN OUR SHORTS!
LEAVE THE THERMOSTAT ALONE, CALVIN.
I CAN ALMOST SEE MY BREATH. I'LL JUST CRANK IT UP TO 75, OK?
I SAID DON'T TOUCH IT!
GEE, MY HANDS ARE SO NUMB, I CAN'T MOVE THE SWITCH. GUESS I'LL PUT ON A SWEATER.
WATTERSON

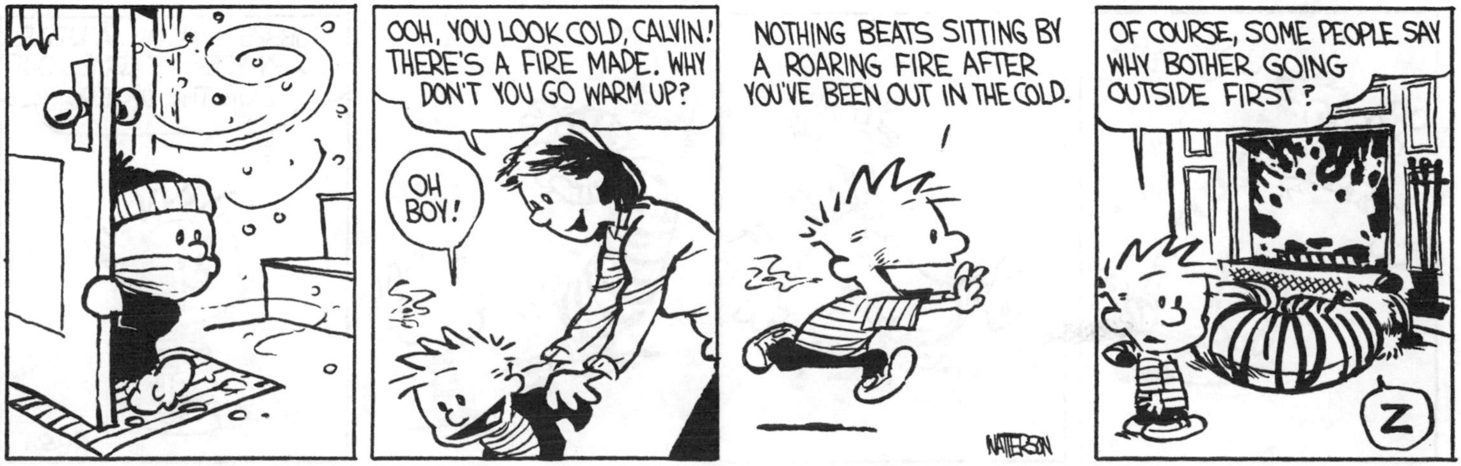
OOH, YOU LOOK COLD, CALVIN! THERE'S A FIRE MADE. WHY DON'T YOU GO WARM UP?
OH BOY!
NOTHING BEATS SITTING BY A ROARING FIRE AFTER YOU'VE BEEN OUT IN THE COLD.
WATTERSON
OF COURSE, SOME PEOPLE SAY WHY BOTHER GOING OUTSIDE FIRST?
Z

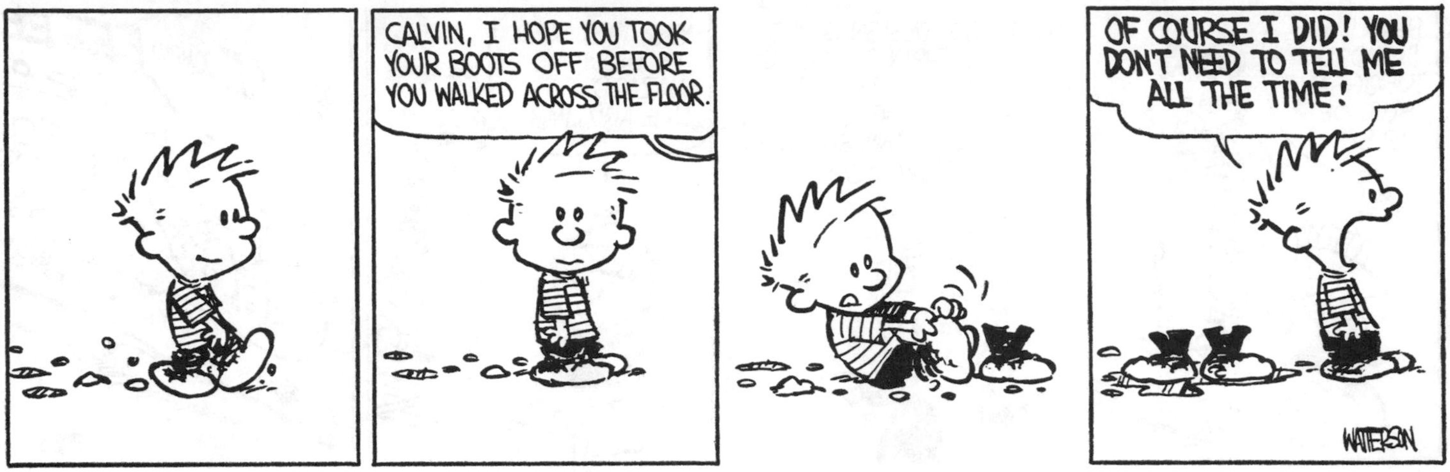
CALVIN, I HOPE YOU TOOK YOUR BOOTS OFF BEFORE YOU WALKED ACROSS THE FLOOR.
OF COURSE I DID! YOU DON'T NEED TO TELL ME ALL THE TIME!
WATTERSON

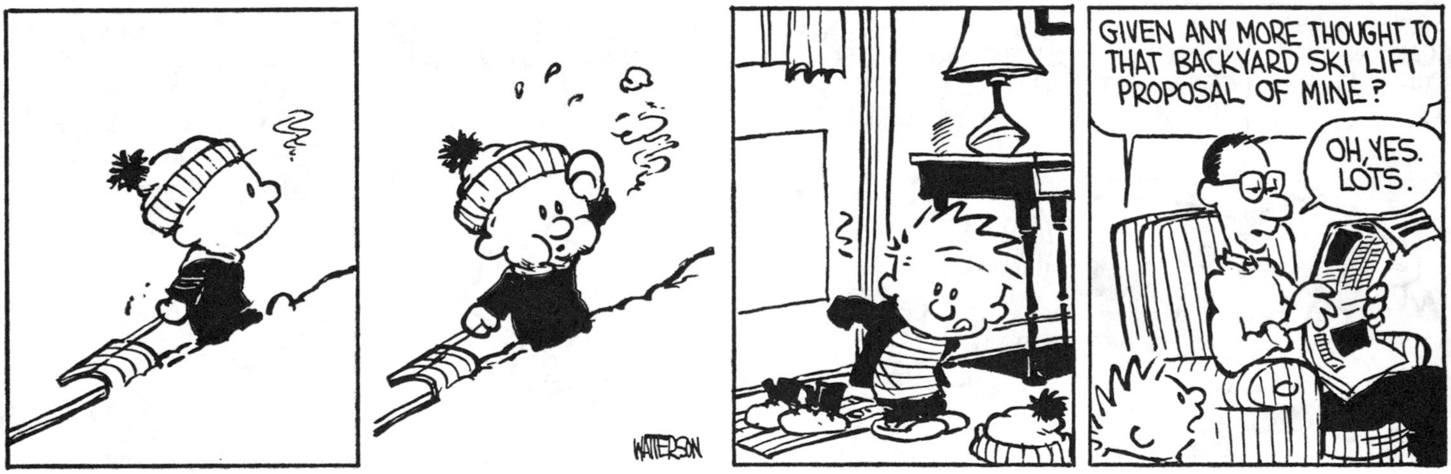
WATTERSON
GIVEN ANY MORE THOUGHT TO THAT BACKYARD SKI LIFT PROPOSAL OF MINE?
OH, YES. LOTS.

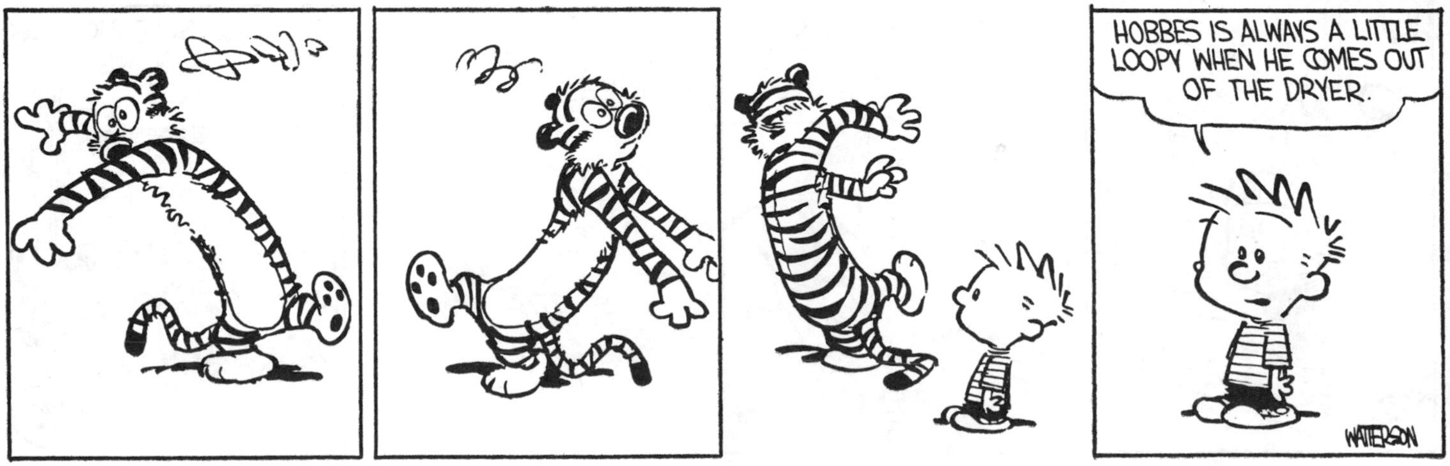
HOBBES IS ALWAYS A LITTLE LOOPY WHEN HE COMES OUT OF THE DRYER.
WATTERSON

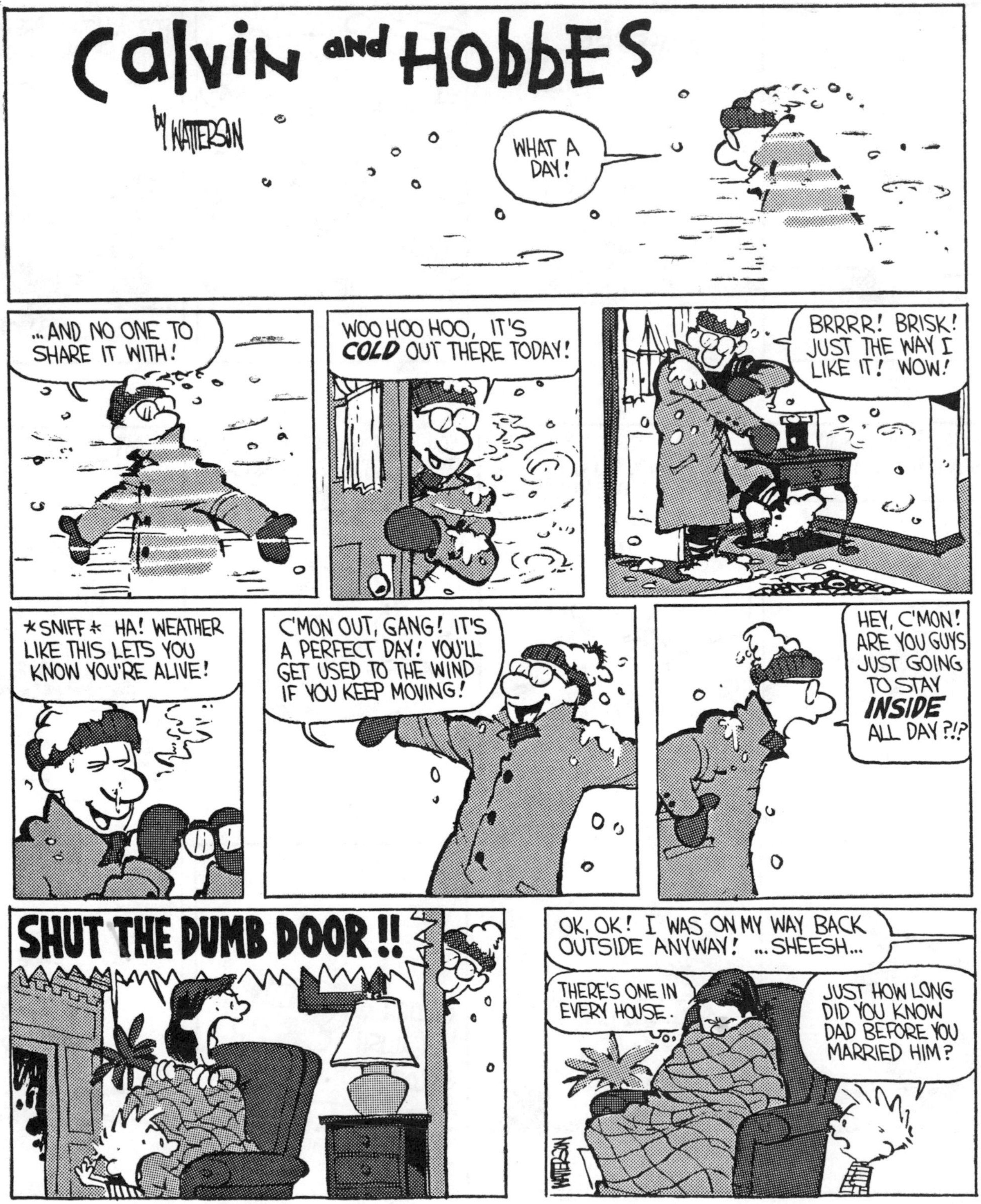
Calvin and HOBBES
by WATTERSON
WHAT A DAY!
...AND NO ONE TO SHARE IT WITH!
WOO HOO HOO, IT'S COLD OUT THERE TODAY!
BRRRR! BRISK! JUST THE WAY I LIKE IT! WOW!
SNIFF HA! WEATHER LIKE THIS LETS YOU KNOW YOU'RE ALIVE!
C'MON OUT, GANG! IT'S A PERFECT DAY! YOU'LL GET USED TO THE WIND IF YOU KEEP MOVING!
HEY, C'MON! ARE YOU GUYS JUST GOING TO STAY INSIDE ALL DAY?!?
SHUT THE DUMB DOOR!!
OK, OK! I WAS ON MY WAY BACK OUTSIDE ANYWAY! ...SHEESH...
THERE'S ONE IN EVERY HOUSE.
JUST HOW LONG DID YOU KNOW DAD BEFORE YOU MARRIED HIM?
WATTERSON

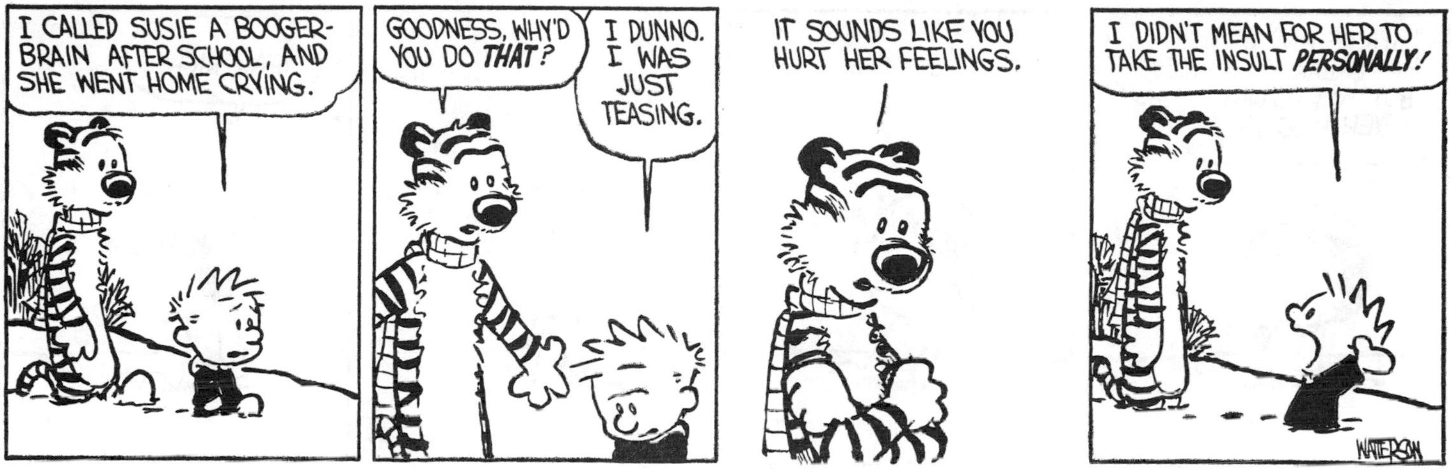
I CALLED SUSIE A BOOGER-BRAIN AFTER SCHOOL, AND SHE WENT HOME CRYING.
GOODNESS, WHY'D YOU DO *THAT*?
I DUNNO. I WAS JUST TEASING.
IT SOUNDS LIKE YOU HURT HER FEELINGS.
I DIDN'T MEAN FOR HER TO TAKE THE INSULT *PERSONALLY*!
WATTERSON

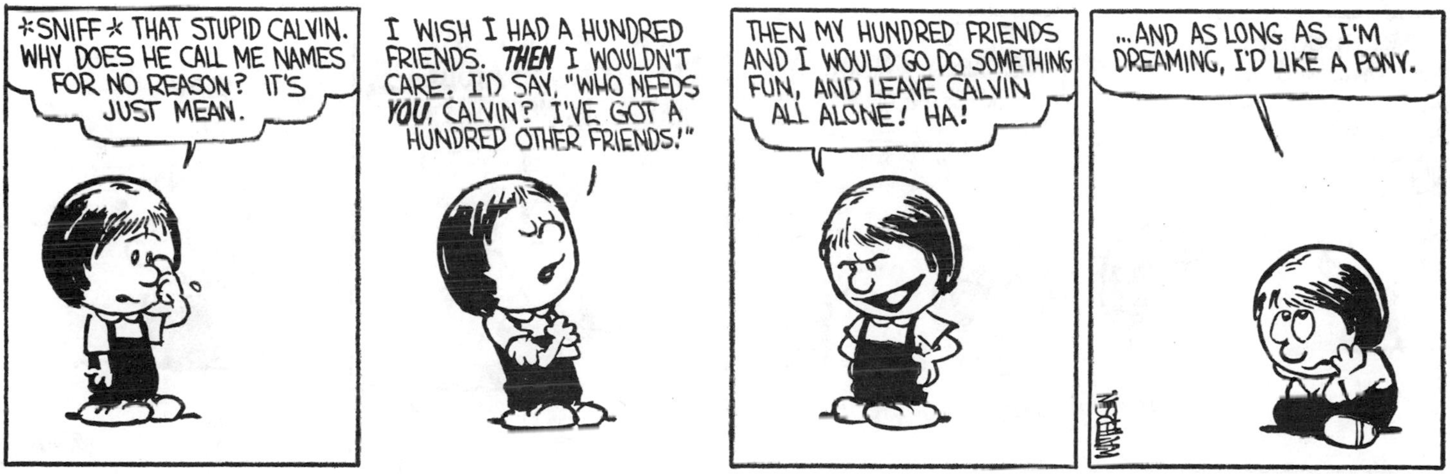
SNIFF THAT STUPID CALVIN. WHY DOES HE CALL ME NAMES FOR NO REASON? IT'S JUST MEAN.
I WISH I HAD A HUNDRED FRIENDS. *THEN* I WOULDN'T CARE. I'D SAY, "WHO NEEDS *YOU*, CALVIN? I'VE GOT A HUNDRED OTHER FRIENDS!"
THEN MY HUNDRED FRIENDS AND I WOULD GO DO SOMETHING FUN, AND LEAVE CALVIN ALL ALONE! HA!
...AND AS LONG AS I'M DREAMING, I'D LIKE A PONY.
WATTERSON

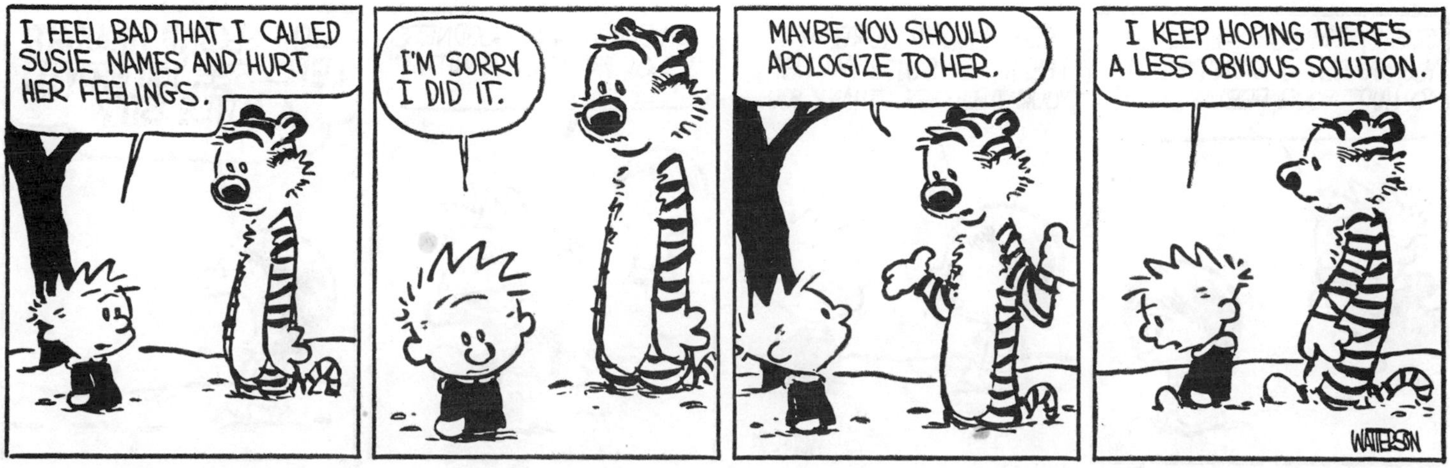
I FEEL BAD THAT I CALLED SUSIE NAMES AND HURT HER FEELINGS.
I'M SORRY I DID IT.
MAYBE YOU SHOULD APOLOGIZE TO HER.
I KEEP HOPING THERE'S A LESS OBVIOUS SOLUTION.
WATTERSON

73

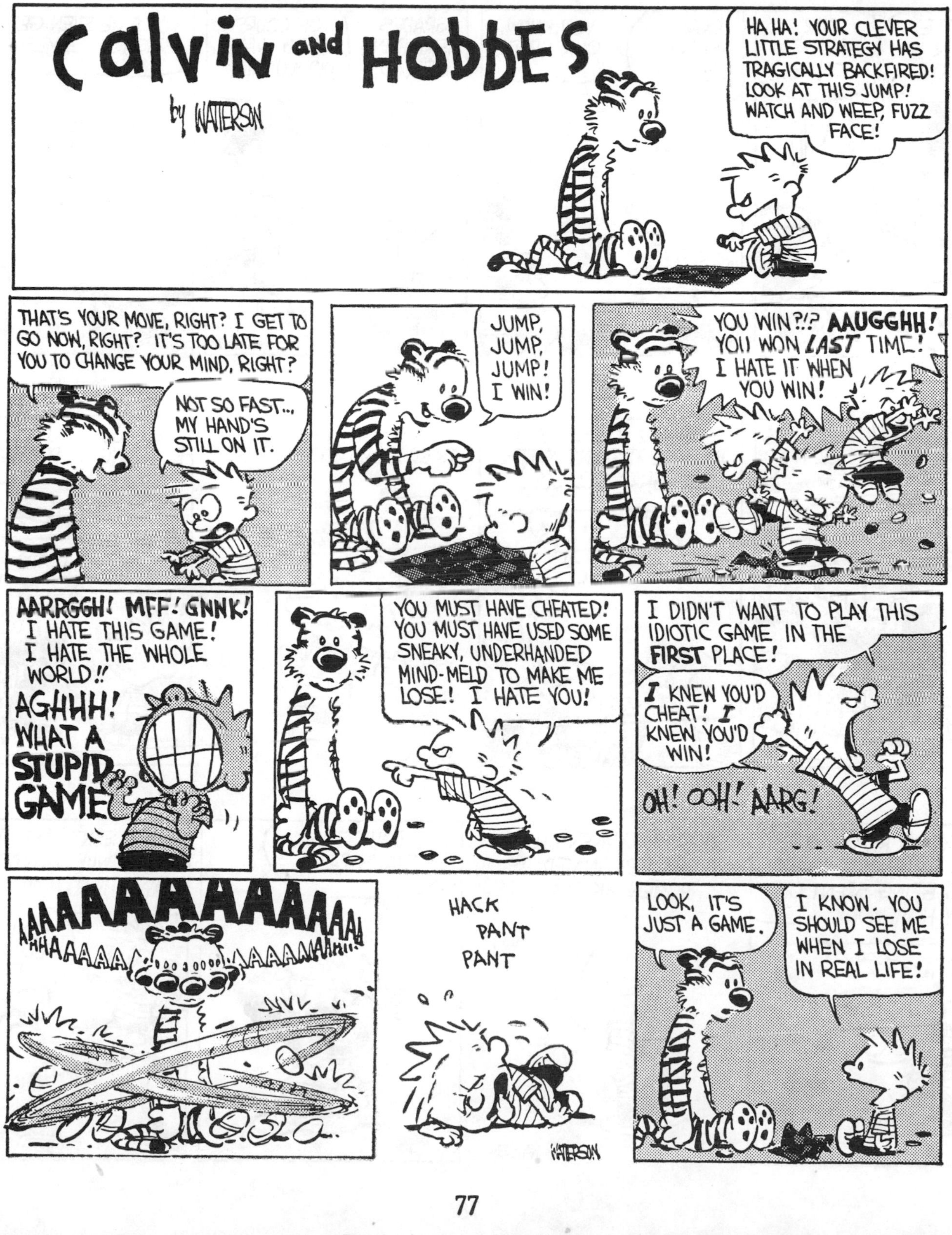
Calvin and HOBBES
by WATTERSON
HA HA! YOUR CLEVER LITTLE STRATEGY HAS TRAGICALLY BACKFIRED! LOOK AT THIS JUMP! WATCH AND WEEP, FUZZ FACE!
THAT'S YOUR MOVE, RIGHT? I GET TO GO NOW, RIGHT? IT'S TOO LATE FOR YOU TO CHANGE YOUR MIND, RIGHT?
NOT SO FAST... MY HAND'S STILL ON IT.
JUMP, JUMP, JUMP! I WIN!
YOU WIN?!? AAUGGHH! YOU WON LAST TIME! I HATE IT WHEN YOU WIN!
AARRGGH! MFF! GNNK! I HATE THIS GAME! I HATE THE WHOLE WORLD!!
AGHHH! WHAT A STUPID GAME
YOU MUST HAVE CHEATED! YOU MUST HAVE USED SOME SNEAKY, UNDERHANDED MIND-MELD TO MAKE ME LOSE! I HATE YOU!
I DIDN'T WANT TO PLAY THIS IDIOTIC GAME IN THE FIRST PLACE!
I KNEW YOU'D CHEAT! I KNEW YOU'D WIN!
OH! OOH! AARG!
AAAAAAAAAAAAAAAA AHHAAAAA AAAAAAHHH!!
HACK PANT PANT
WATTERSON
LOOK, IT'S JUST A GAME.
I KNOW. YOU SHOULD SEE ME WHEN I LOSE IN REAL LIFE!

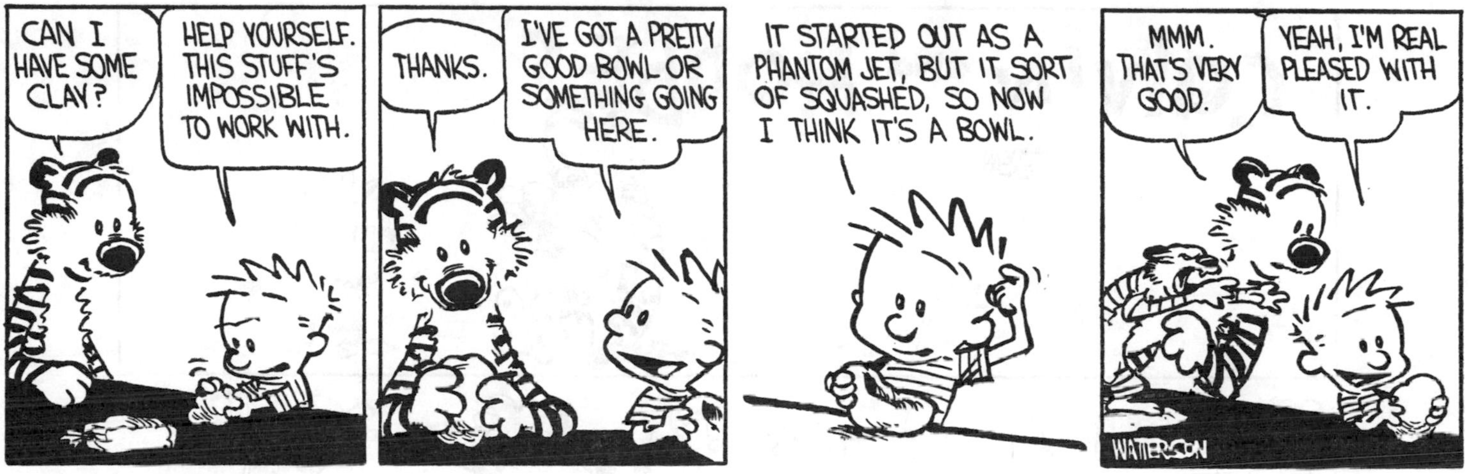
CAN I HAVE SOME CLAY?
HELP YOURSELF. THIS STUFF'S IMPOSSIBLE TO WORK WITH.
THANKS.
I'VE GOT A PRETTY GOOD BOWL OR SOMETHING GOING HERE.
IT STARTED OUT AS A PHANTOM JET, BUT IT SORT OF SQUASHED, SO NOW I THINK IT'S A BOWL.
MMM. THAT'S VERY GOOD.
YEAH, I'M REAL PLEASED WITH IT.
WATTERSON

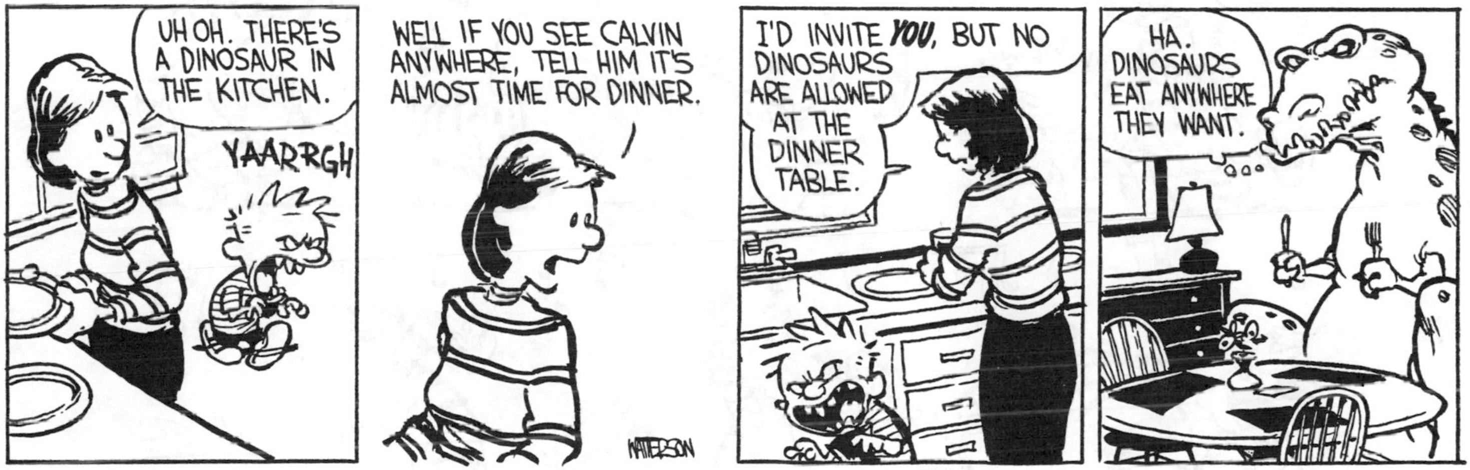
UH OH. THERE'S A DINOSAUR IN THE KITCHEN.
YAARRGH
WELL IF YOU SEE CALVIN ANYWHERE, TELL HIM IT'S ALMOST TIME FOR DINNER.
WATTERSON
I'D INVITE *YOU*, BUT NO DINOSAURS ARE ALLOWED AT THE DINNER TABLE.
HA. DINOSAURS EAT ANYWHERE THEY WANT.

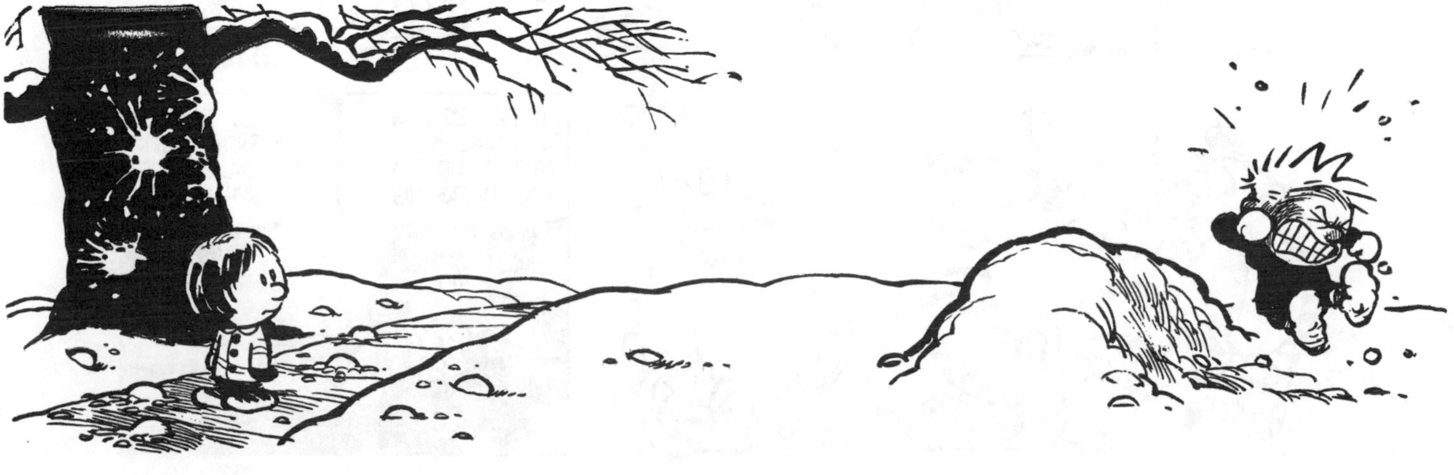

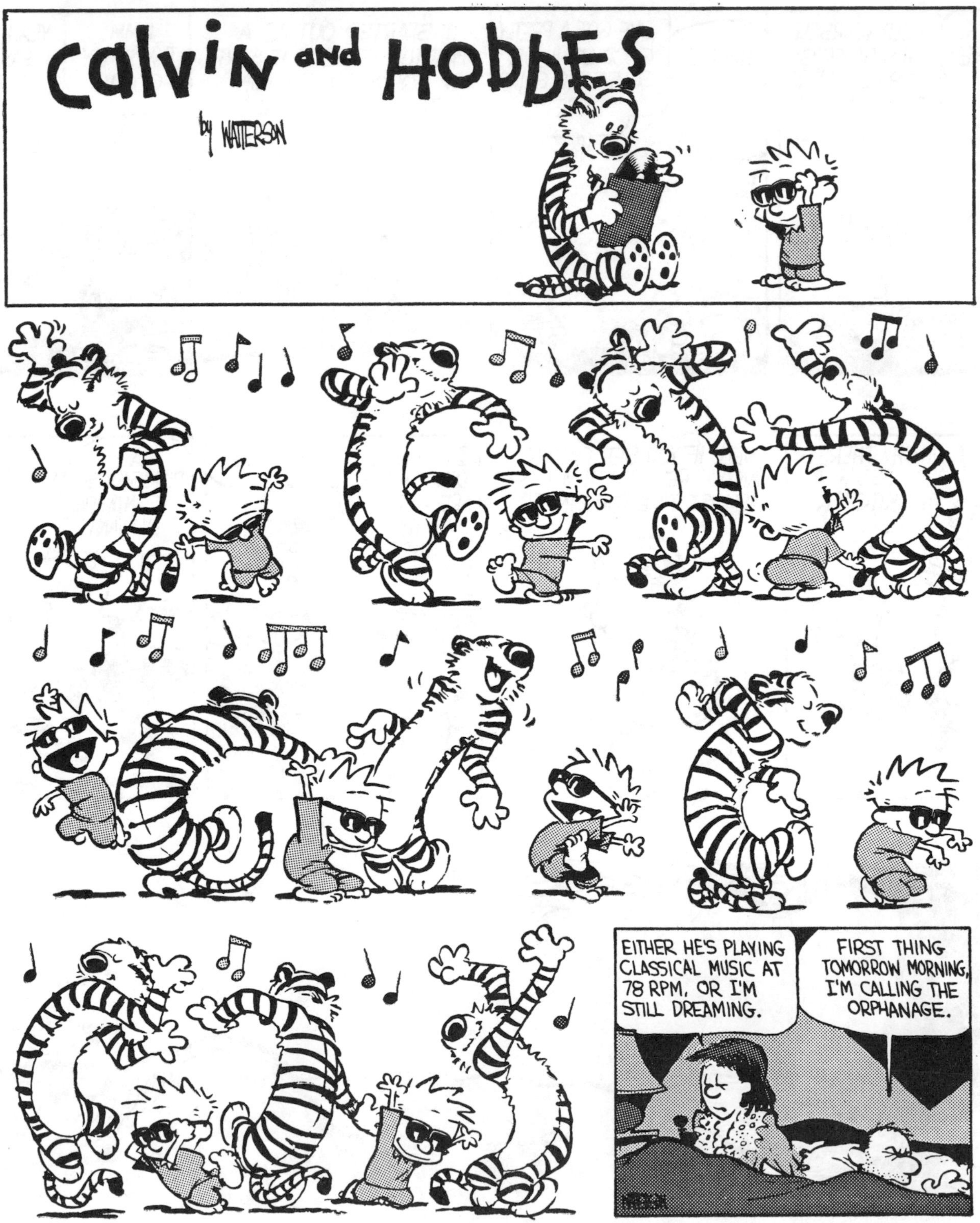
Calvin and HOBBES
by WATTERSON
EITHER HE'S PLAYING CLASSICAL MUSIC AT 78 RPM, OR I'M STILL DREAMING.
FIRST THING TOMORROW MORNING, I'M CALLING THE ORPHANAGE.

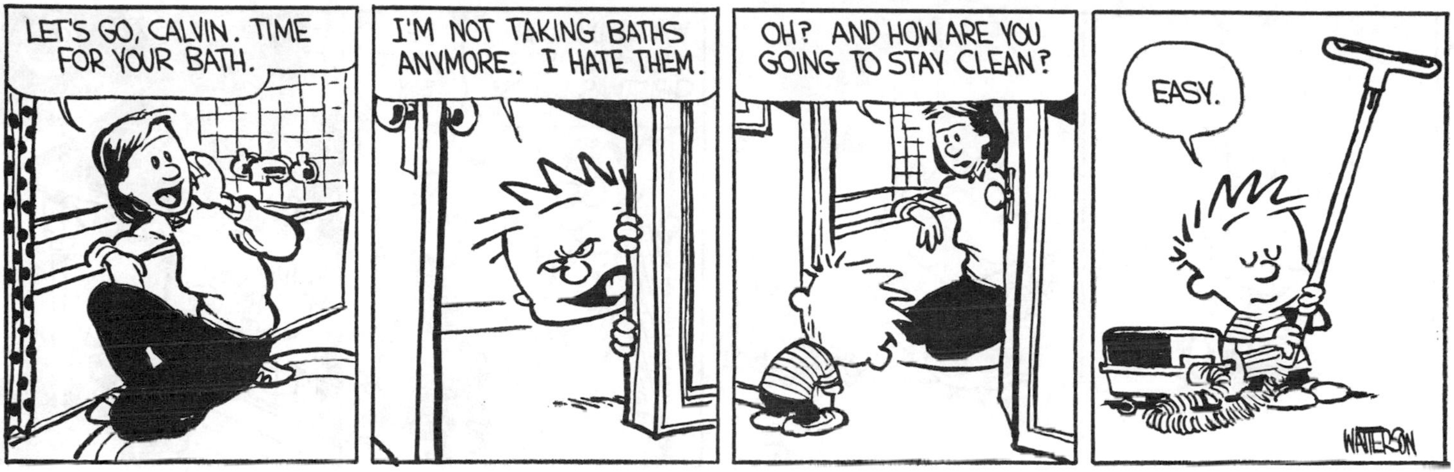
LET'S GO, CALVIN. TIME FOR YOUR BATH.
I'M NOT TAKING BATHS ANYMORE. I HATE THEM.
OH? AND HOW ARE YOU GOING TO STAY CLEAN?
EASY.
WATTERSON

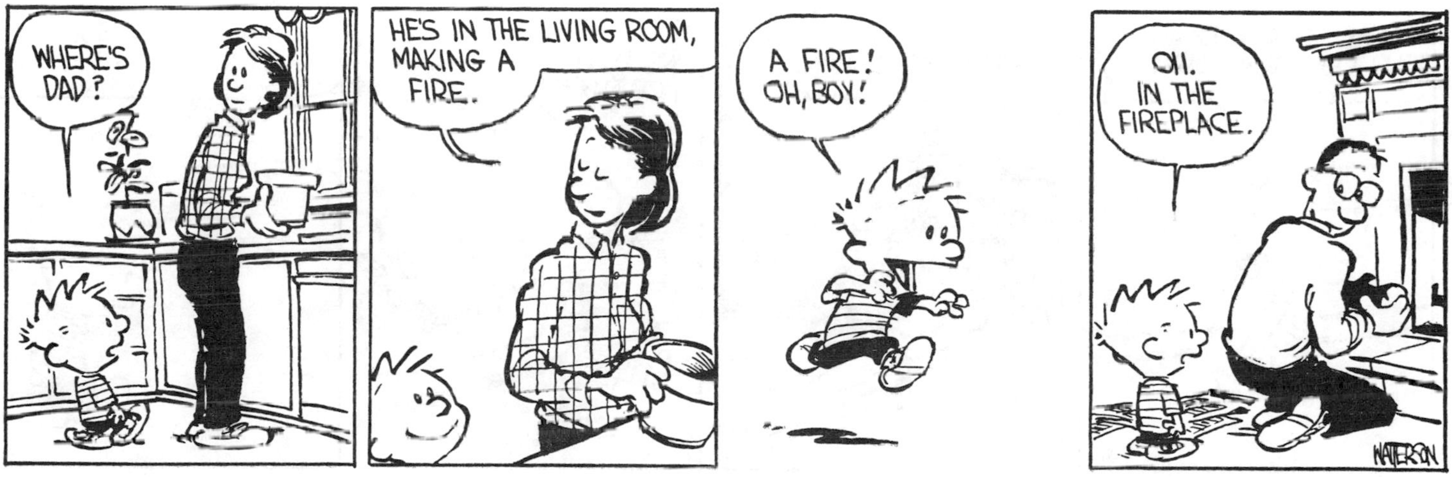
WHERE'S DAD?
HE'S IN THE LIVING ROOM, MAKING A FIRE.
A FIRE! OH, BOY!
OH. IN THE FIREPLACE.
WATTERSON

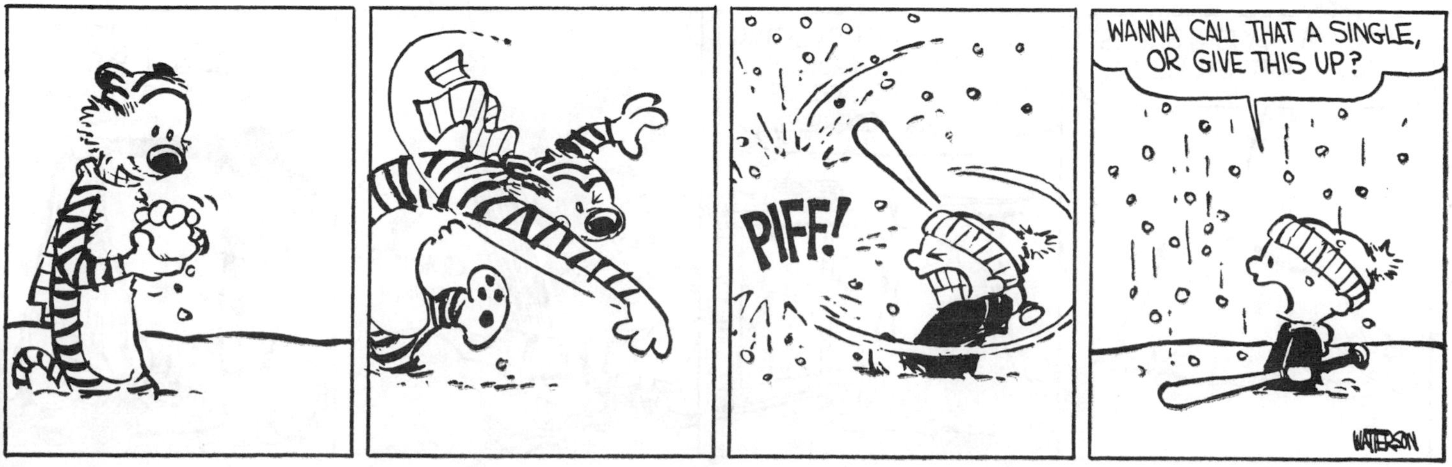
PIFF!
WANNA CALL THAT A SINGLE, OR GIVE THIS UP?
WATTERSON

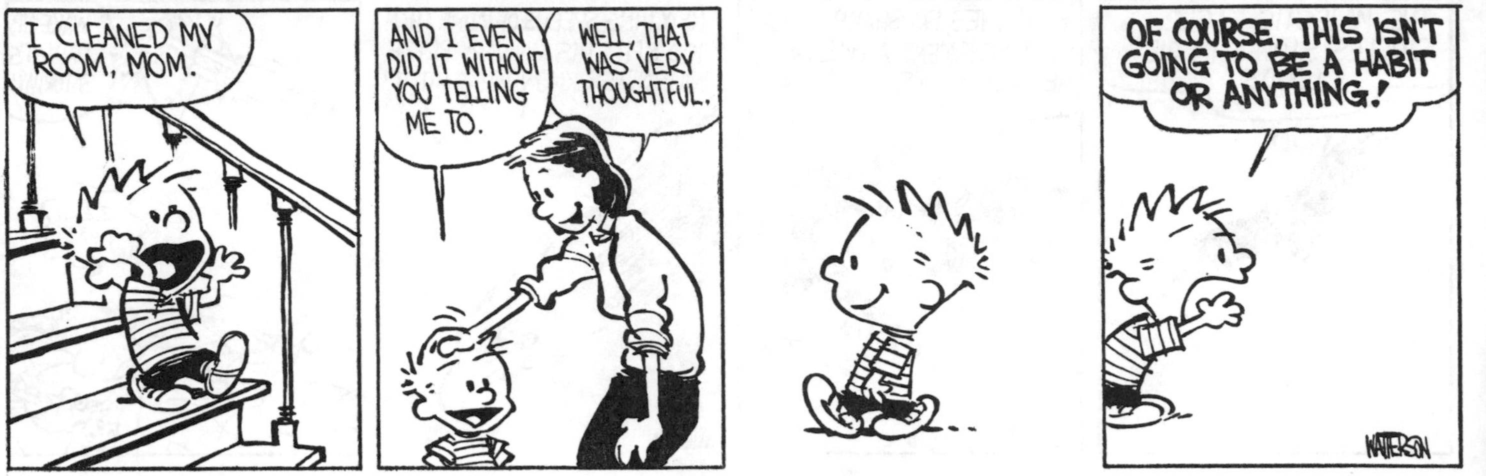
I CLEANED MY ROOM, MOM.
AND I EVEN DID IT WITHOUT YOU TELLING ME TO.
WELL, THAT WAS VERY THOUGHTFUL.
OF COURSE, THIS ISN'T GOING TO BE A HABIT OR ANYTHING!
WATTERSON

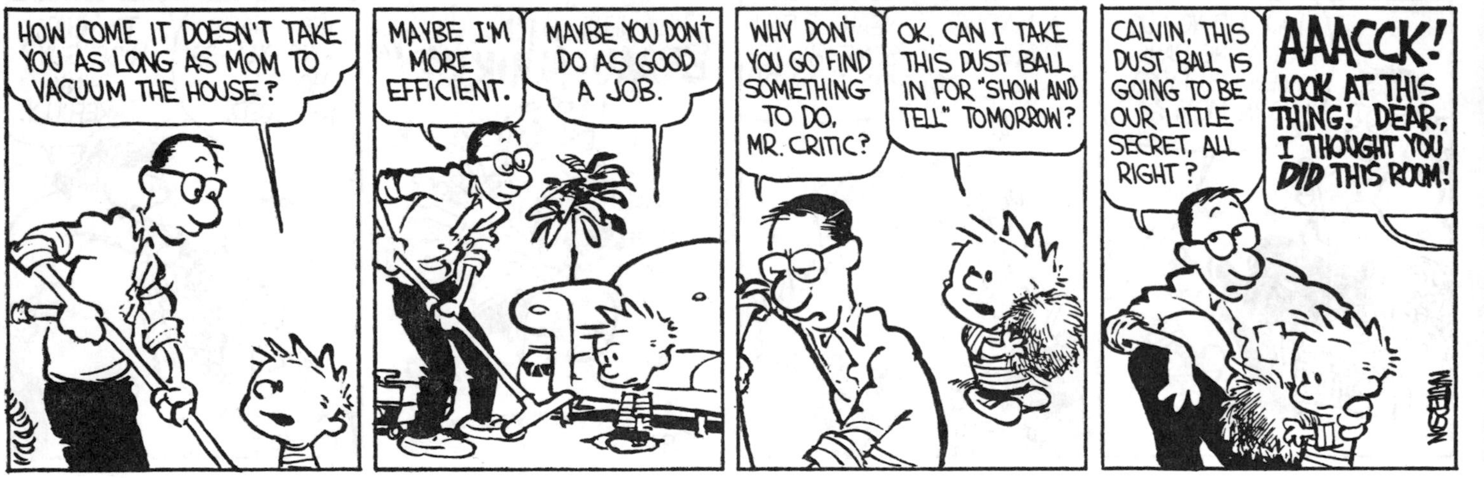
HOW COME IT DOESN'T TAKE YOU AS LONG AS MOM TO VACUUM THE HOUSE?
MAYBE I'M MORE EFFICIENT.
MAYBE YOU DON'T DO AS GOOD A JOB.
WHY DON'T YOU GO FIND SOMETHING TO DO, MR. CRITIC?
OK, CAN I TAKE THIS DUST BALL IN FOR "SHOW AND TELL" TOMORROW?
CALVIN, THIS DUST BALL IS GOING TO BE OUR LITTLE SECRET, ALL RIGHT?
AAACCK! LOOK AT THIS THING! DEAR, I THOUGHT YOU DID THIS ROOM!

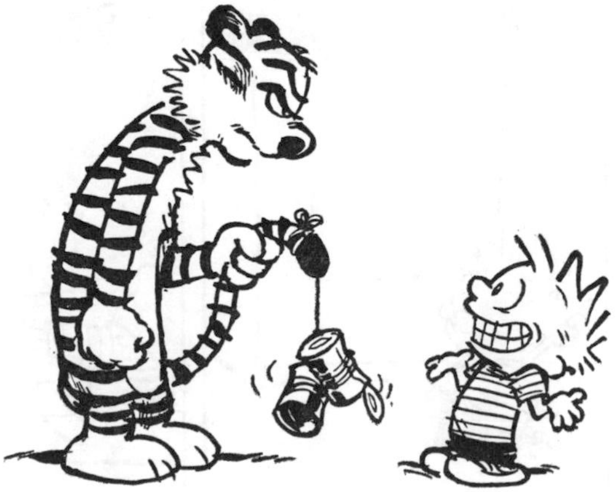

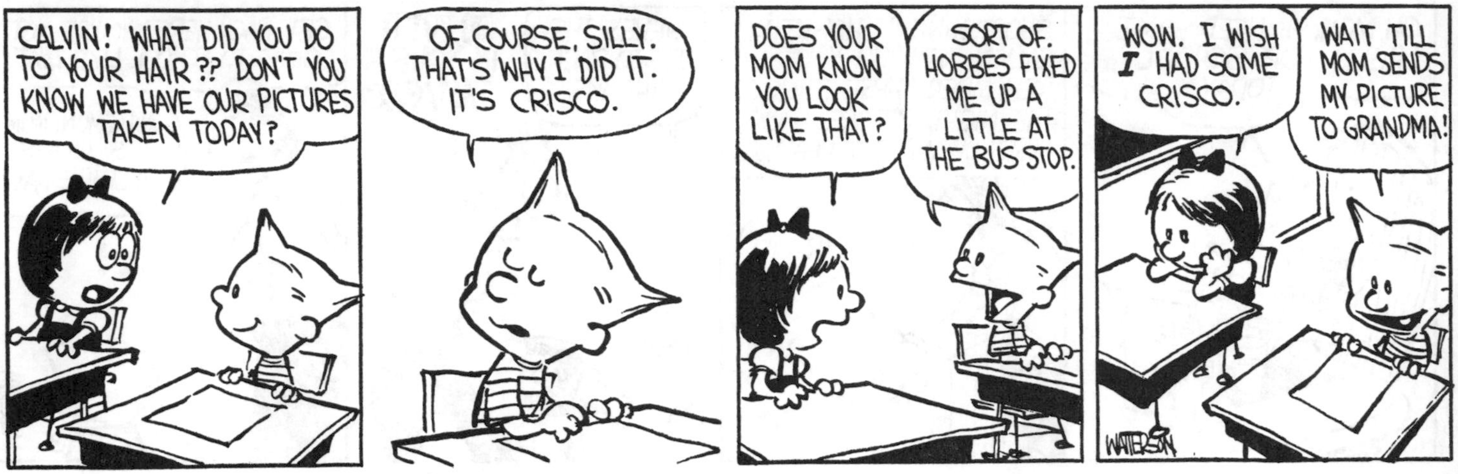
CALVIN! WHAT DID YOU DO TO YOUR HAIR ?? DON'T YOU KNOW WE HAVE OUR PICTURES TAKEN TODAY?
OF COURSE, SILLY. THAT'S WHY I DID IT. IT'S CRISCO.
DOES YOUR MOM KNOW YOU LOOK LIKE THAT?
SORT OF. HOBBES FIXED ME UP A LITTLE AT THE BUS STOP.
WOW. I WISH I HAD SOME CRISCO.
WAIT TILL MOM SENDS MY PICTURE TO GRANDMA!
WATTERSON

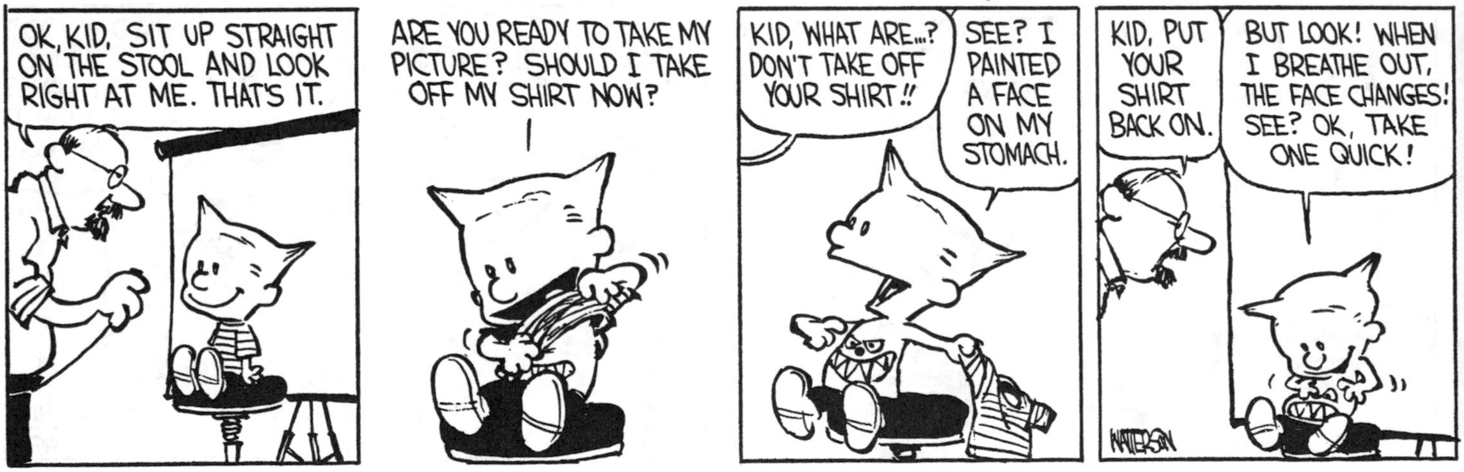
OK, KID, SIT UP STRAIGHT ON THE STOOL AND LOOK RIGHT AT ME. THAT'S IT.
ARE YOU READY TO TAKE MY PICTURE? SHOULD I TAKE OFF MY SHIRT NOW?
KID, WHAT ARE...? DON'T TAKE OFF YOUR SHIRT!!
SEE? I PAINTED A FACE ON MY STOMACH.
KID, PUT YOUR SHIRT BACK ON.
BUT LOOK! WHEN I BREATHE OUT, THE FACE CHANGES! SEE? OK, TAKE ONE QUICK!
WATTERSON

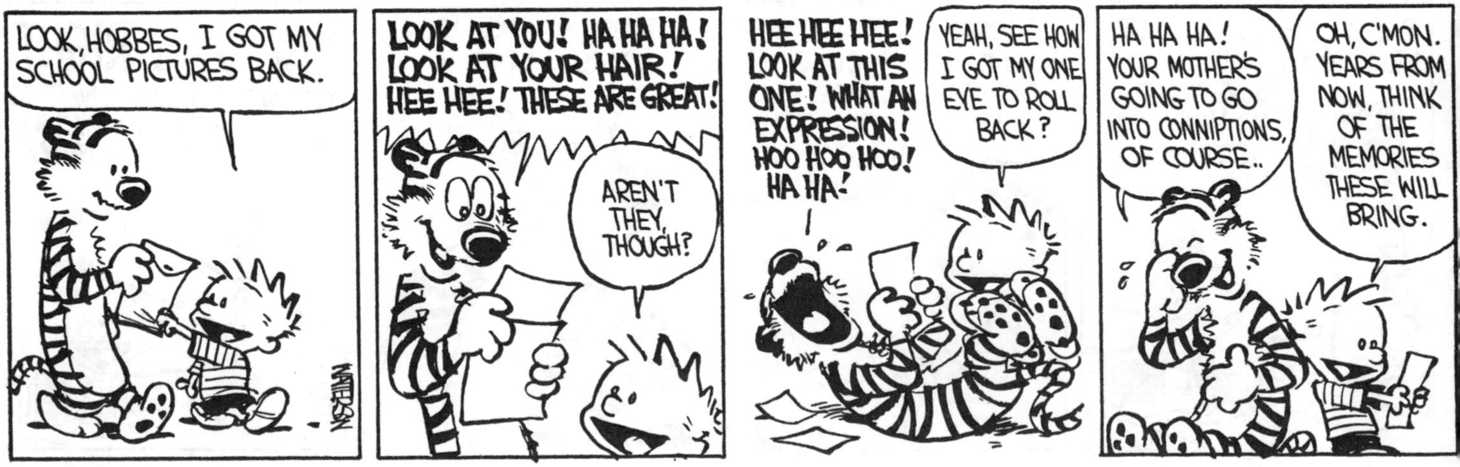
LOOK, HOBBES, I GOT MY SCHOOL PICTURES BACK.
WATTERSON
LOOK AT YOU! HA HA HA! LOOK AT YOUR HAIR! HEE HEE! THESE ARE GREAT!
AREN'T THEY, THOUGH?
HEE HEE HEE! LOOK AT THIS ONE! WHAT AN EXPRESSION! HOO HOO HOO! HA HA!
YEAH, SEE HOW I GOT MY ONE EYE TO ROLL BACK?
HA HA HA! YOUR MOTHER'S GOING TO GO INTO CONNIPTIONS, OF COURSE..
OH, C'MON. YEARS FROM NOW, THINK OF THE MEMORIES THESE WILL BRING.

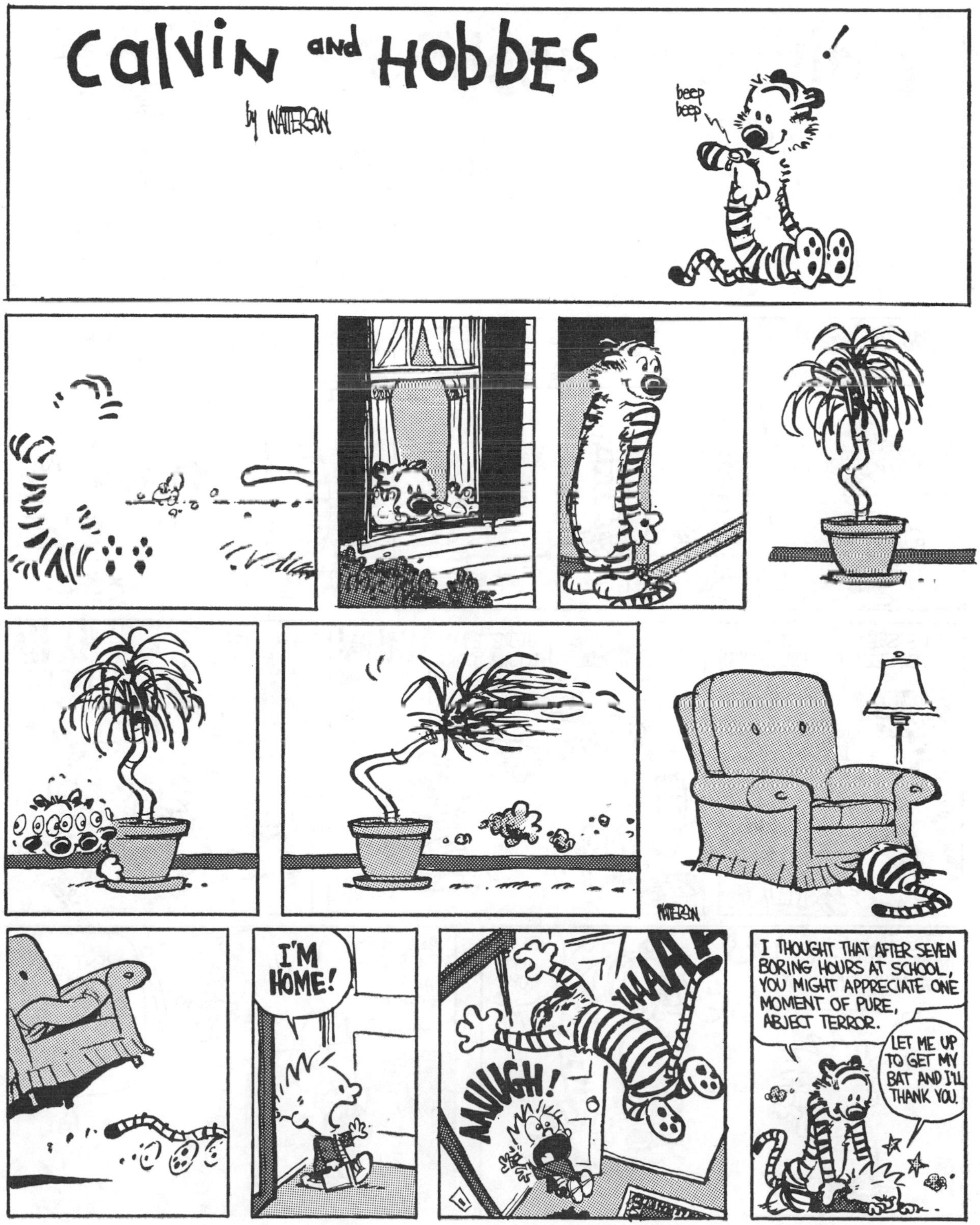
Calvin and HOBBES
by WATTERSON
!
beep beep
WATTERSON
I'M HOME!
AAUUGH!
WAAAA!
I THOUGHT THAT AFTER SEVEN BORING HOURS AT SCHOOL, YOU MIGHT APPRECIATE ONE MOMENT OF PURE, ABJECT TERROR.
LET ME UP TO GET MY BAT AND I'LL THANK YOU.

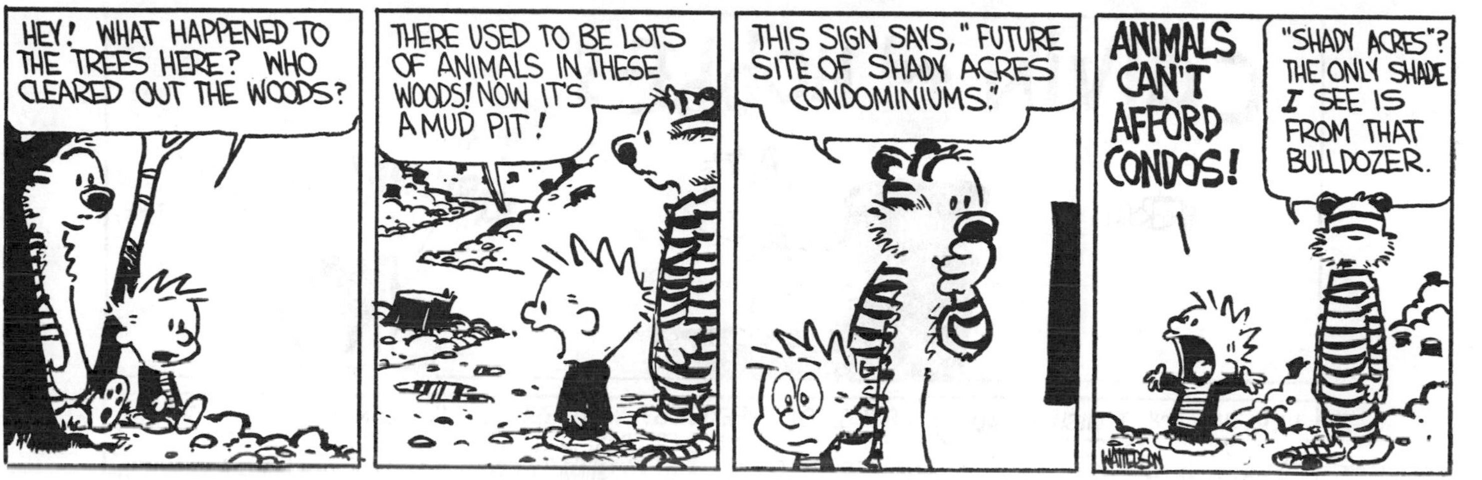
HEY! WHAT HAPPENED TO THE TREES HERE? WHO CLEARED OUT THE WOODS?
THERE USED TO BE LOTS OF ANIMALS IN THESE WOODS! NOW IT'S A MUD PIT!
THIS SIGN SAYS, "FUTURE SITE OF SHADY ACRES CONDOMINIUMS."
ANIMALS CAN'T AFFORD CONDOS!
"SHADY ACRES"? THE ONLY SHADE *I* SEE IS FROM THAT BULLDOZER.

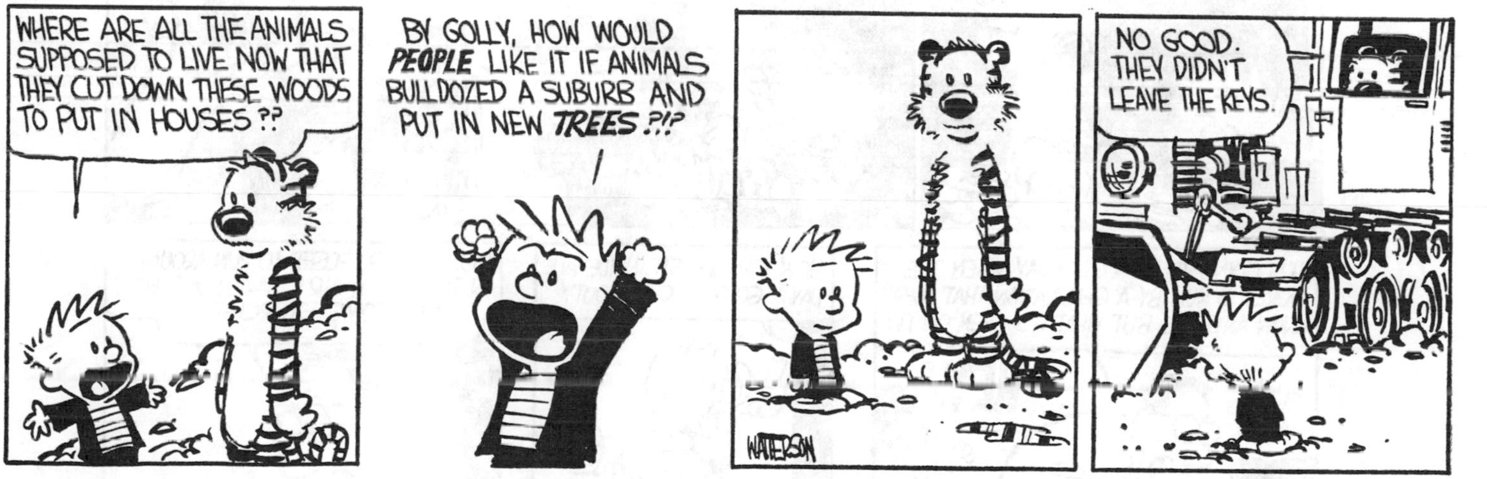
WHERE ARE ALL THE ANIMALS SUPPOSED TO LIVE NOW THAT THEY CUT DOWN THESE WOODS TO PUT IN HOUSES??
BY GOLLY, HOW WOULD **PEOPLE** LIKE IT IF ANIMALS BULLDOZED A SUBURB AND PUT IN NEW **TREES**?!?
NO GOOD. THEY DIDN'T LEAVE THE KEYS.

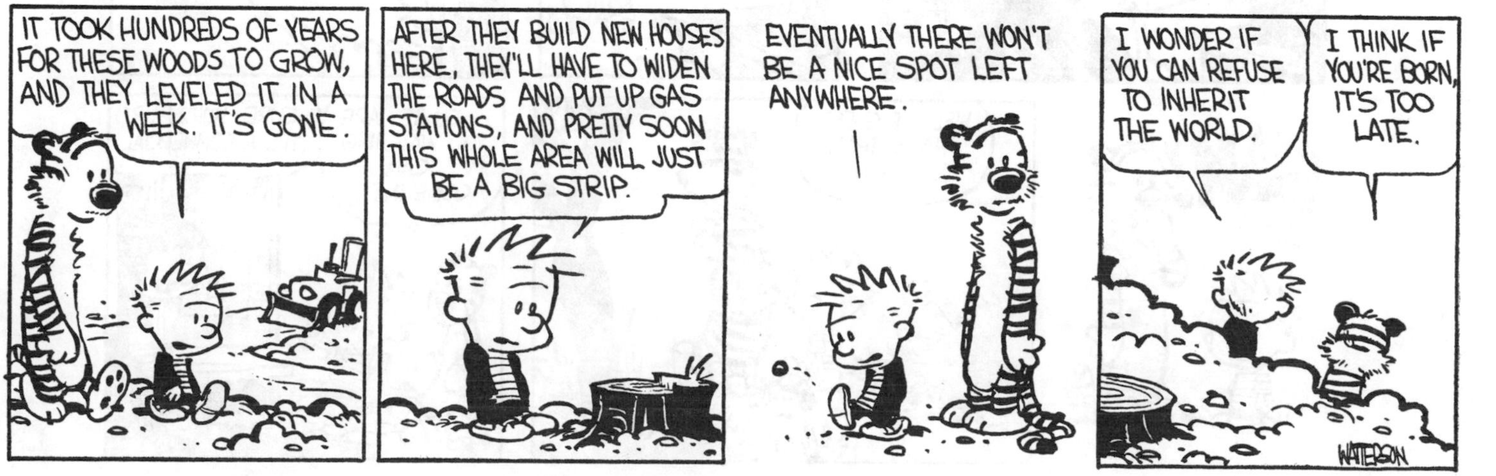
IT TOOK HUNDREDS OF YEARS FOR THESE WOODS TO GROW, AND THEY LEVELED IT IN A WEEK. IT'S GONE.
AFTER THEY BUILD NEW HOUSES HERE, THEY'LL HAVE TO WIDEN THE ROADS AND PUT UP GAS STATIONS, AND PRETTY SOON THIS WHOLE AREA WILL JUST BE A BIG STRIP.
EVENTUALLY THERE WON'T BE A NICE SPOT LEFT ANYWHERE.
I WONDER IF YOU CAN REFUSE TO INHERIT THE WORLD.
I THINK IF YOU'RE BORN, IT'S TOO LATE.

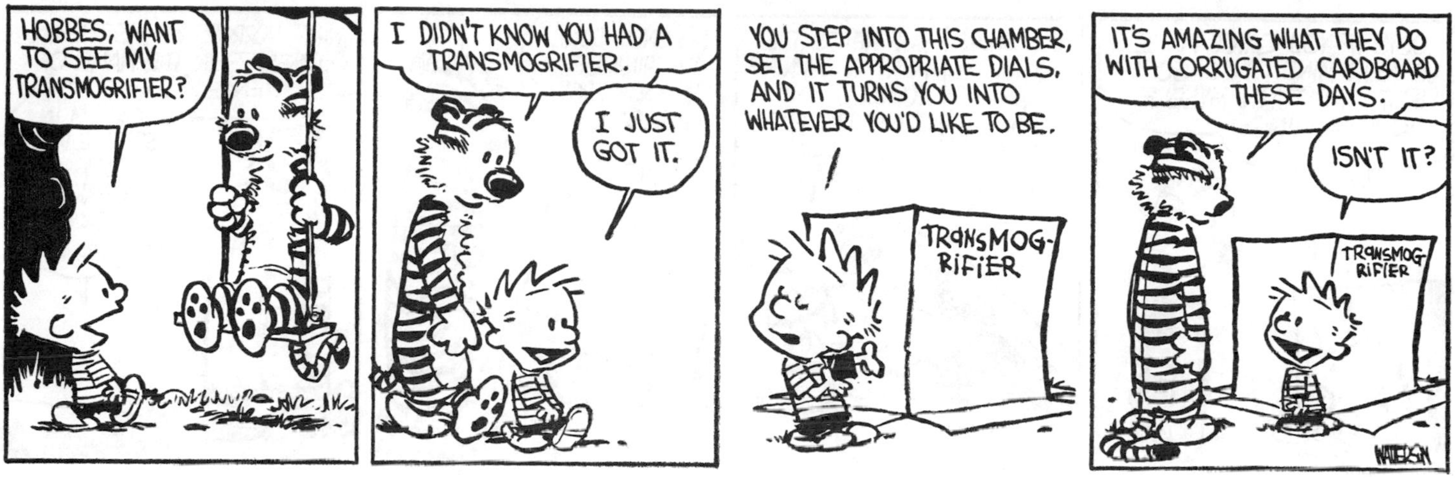
HOBBES, WANT TO SEE MY TRANSMOGRIFIER?
I DIDN'T KNOW YOU HAD A TRANSMOGRIFIER.
I JUST GOT IT.
YOU STEP INTO THIS CHAMBER, SET THE APPROPRIATE DIALS, AND IT TURNS YOU INTO WHATEVER YOU'D LIKE TO BE.
TRANSMOG-RIFIER
IT'S AMAZING WHAT THEY DO WITH CORRUGATED CARDBOARD THESE DAYS.
ISN'T IT?
TRANSMOG-RIFIER
WATTERSON

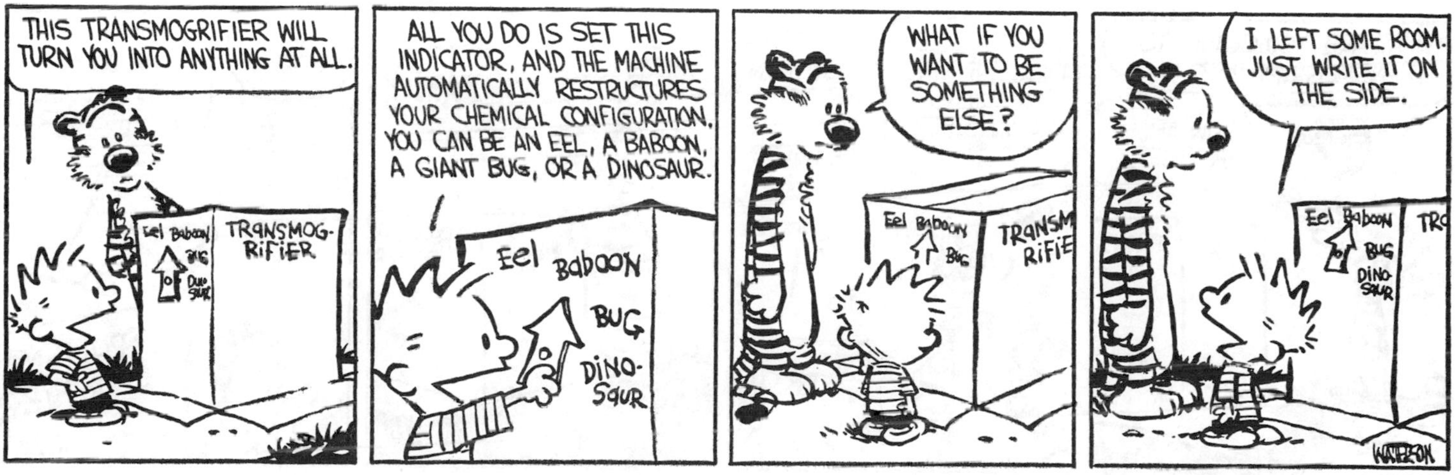
THIS TRANSMOGRIFIER WILL TURN YOU INTO ANYTHING AT ALL.
TRANSMOG-RIFIER
ALL YOU DO IS SET THIS INDICATOR, AND THE MACHINE AUTOMATICALLY RESTRUCTURES YOUR CHEMICAL CONFIGURATION. YOU CAN BE AN EEL, A BABOON, A GIANT BUG, OR A DINOSAUR.
Eel
BABOON
BUG
DINO-SAUR
WHAT IF YOU WANT TO BE SOMETHING ELSE?
I LEFT SOME ROOM. JUST WRITE IT ON THE SIDE.
WATTERSON

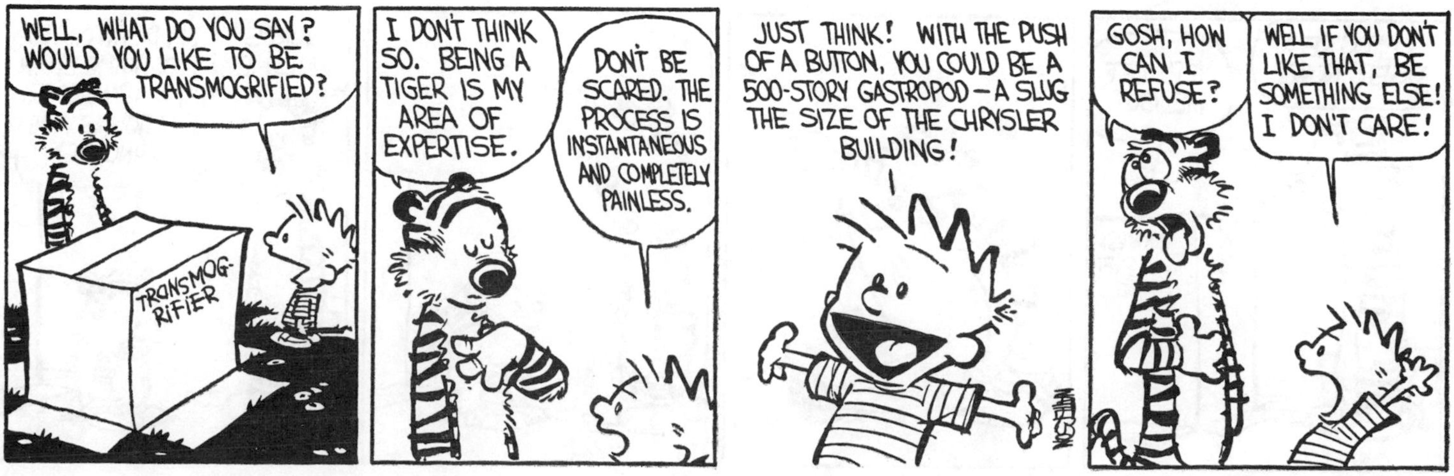
WELL, WHAT DO YOU SAY? WOULD YOU LIKE TO BE TRANSMOGRIFIED?
TRANSMOG-RIFIER
I DON'T THINK SO. BEING A TIGER IS MY AREA OF EXPERTISE.
DON'T BE SCARED. THE PROCESS IS INSTANTANEOUS AND COMPLETELY PAINLESS.
JUST THINK! WITH THE PUSH OF A BUTTON, YOU COULD BE A 500-STORY GASTROPOD — A SLUG THE SIZE OF THE CHRYSLER BUILDING!
WATTERSON
GOSH, HOW CAN I REFUSE?
WELL IF YOU DON'T LIKE THAT, BE SOMETHING ELSE! I DON'T CARE!

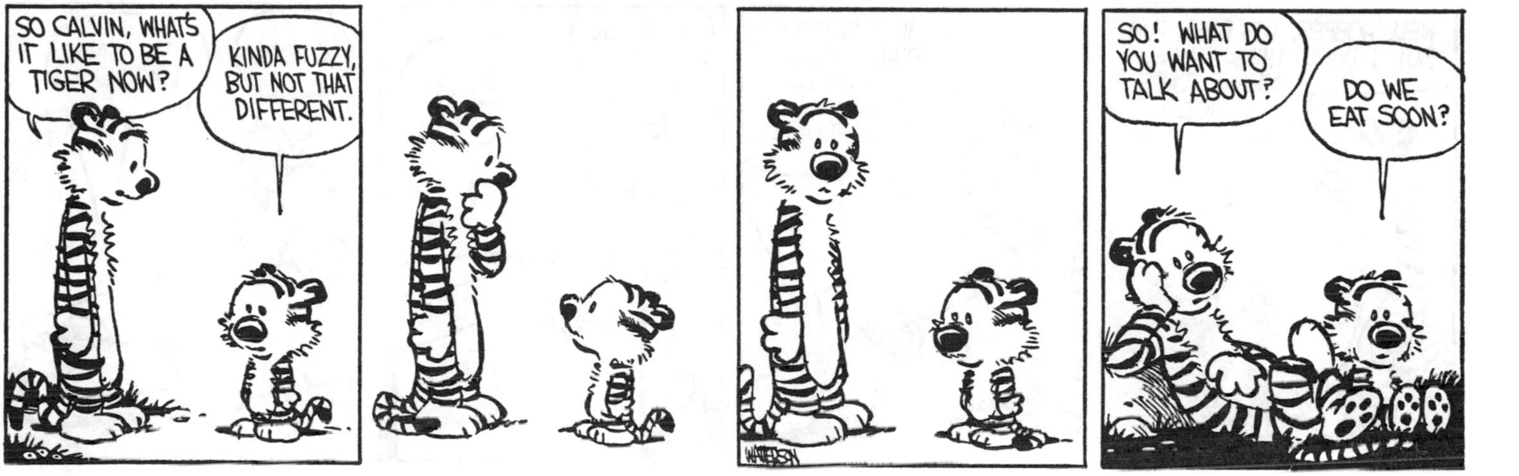
SO CALVIN, WHAT'S IT LIKE TO BE A TIGER NOW?
KINDA FUZZY, BUT NOT THAT DIFFERENT.
SO! WHAT DO YOU WANT TO TALK ABOUT?
DO WE EAT SOON?

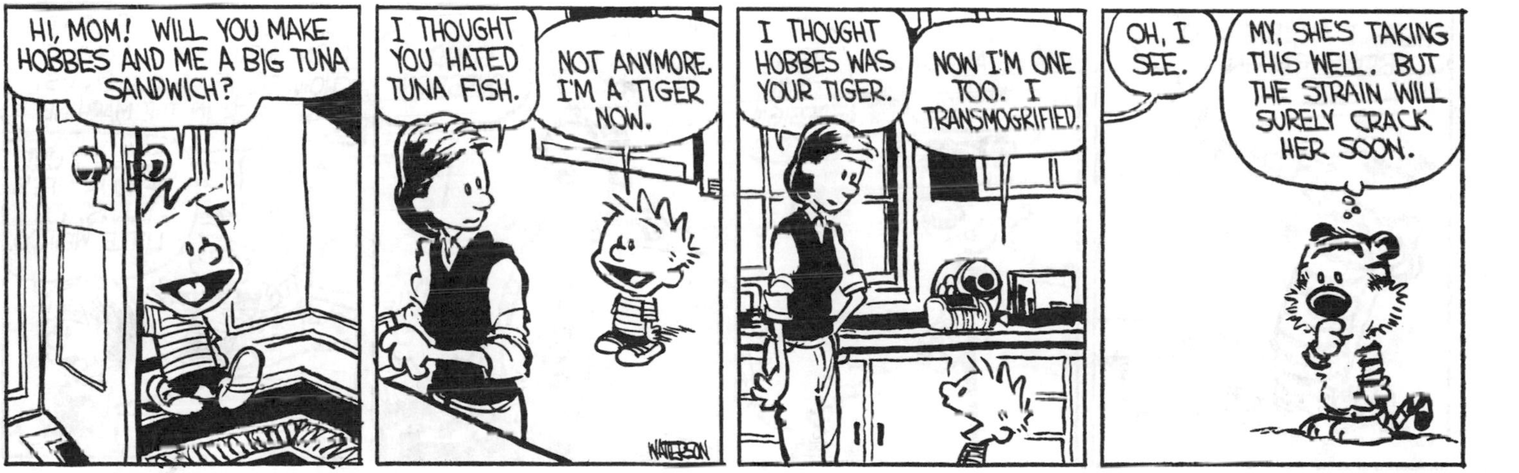
HI, MOM! WILL YOU MAKE HOBBES AND ME A BIG TUNA SANDWICH?
I THOUGHT YOU HATED TUNA FISH.
NOT ANYMORE. I'M A TIGER NOW.
I THOUGHT HOBBES WAS YOUR TIGER.
NOW I'M ONE TOO. I TRANSMOGRIFIED.
OH, I SEE.
MY, SHE'S TAKING THIS WELL. BUT THE STRAIN WILL SURELY CRACK HER SOON.

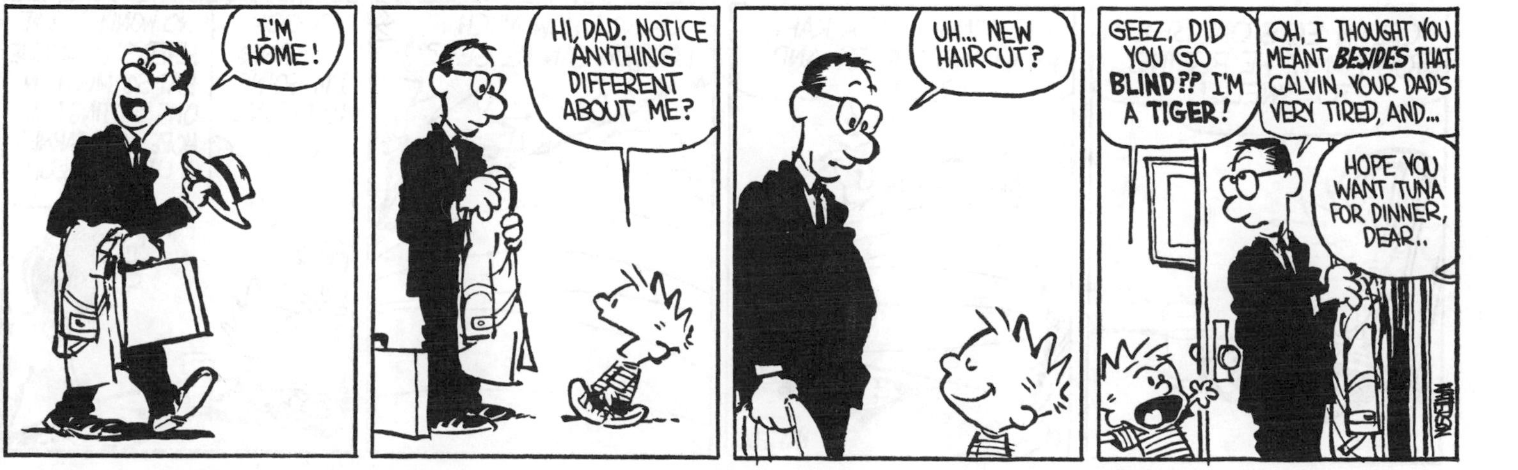
I'M HOME!
HI, DAD. NOTICE ANYTHING DIFFERENT ABOUT ME?
UH... NEW HAIRCUT?
GEEZ, DID YOU GO BLIND?? I'M A TIGER!
OH, I THOUGHT YOU MEANT BESIDES THAT. CALVIN, YOUR DAD'S VERY TIRED, AND...
HOPE YOU WANT TUNA FOR DINNER, DEAR..

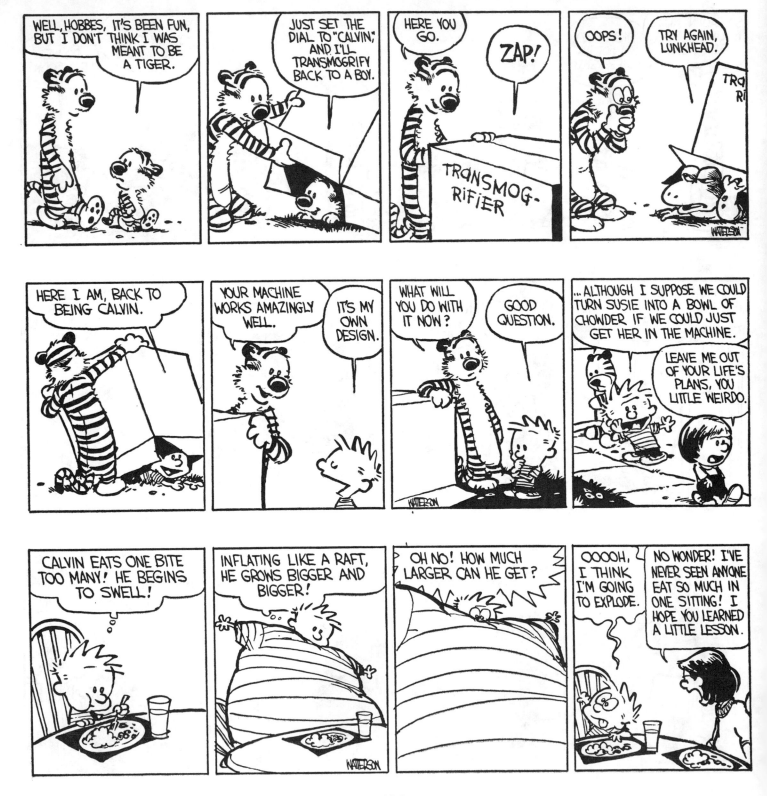

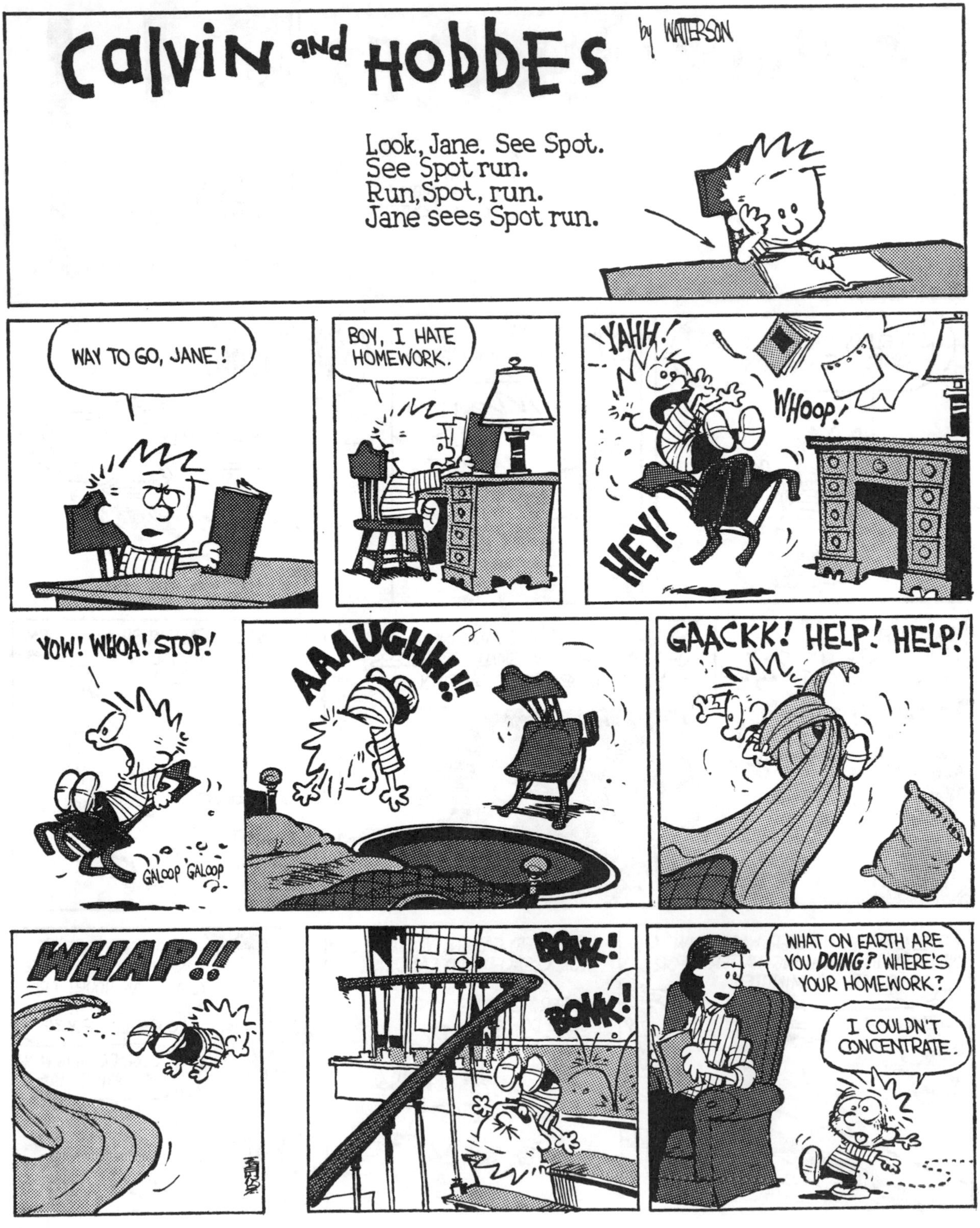
Calvin and HOBBES
by WATTERSON
Look, Jane. See Spot.
See Spot run.
Run, Spot, run.
Jane sees Spot run.
WAY TO GO, JANE!
BOY, I HATE HOMEWORK.
YAHH!
WHOOP!
HEY!
YOW! WHOA! STOP!
GALOOP GALOOP
AAAUGHH!!
GAACKK! HELP! HELP!
WHAP!!
BONK!
BONK!
WHAT ON EARTH ARE YOU DOING? WHERE'S YOUR HOMEWORK?
I COULDN'T CONCENTRATE.

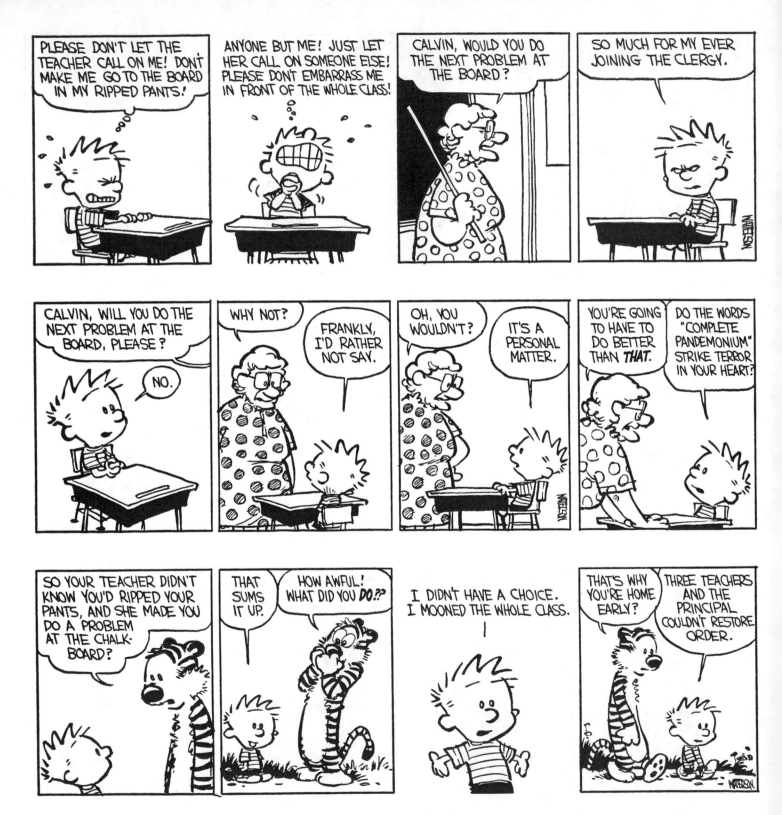

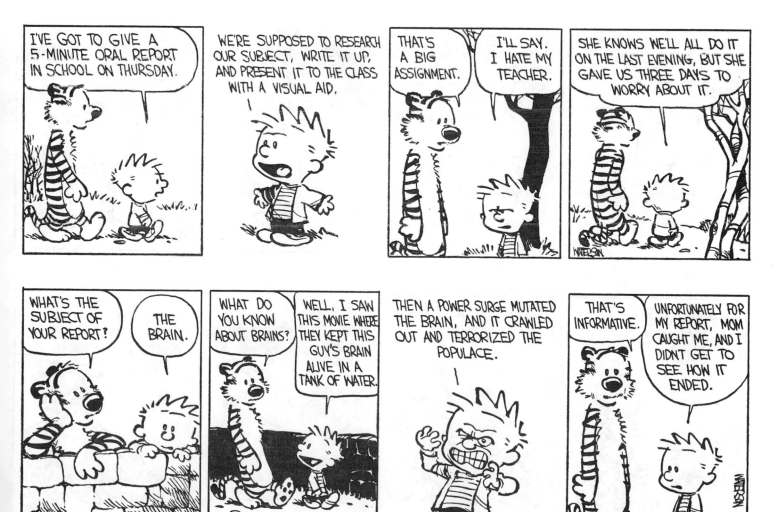

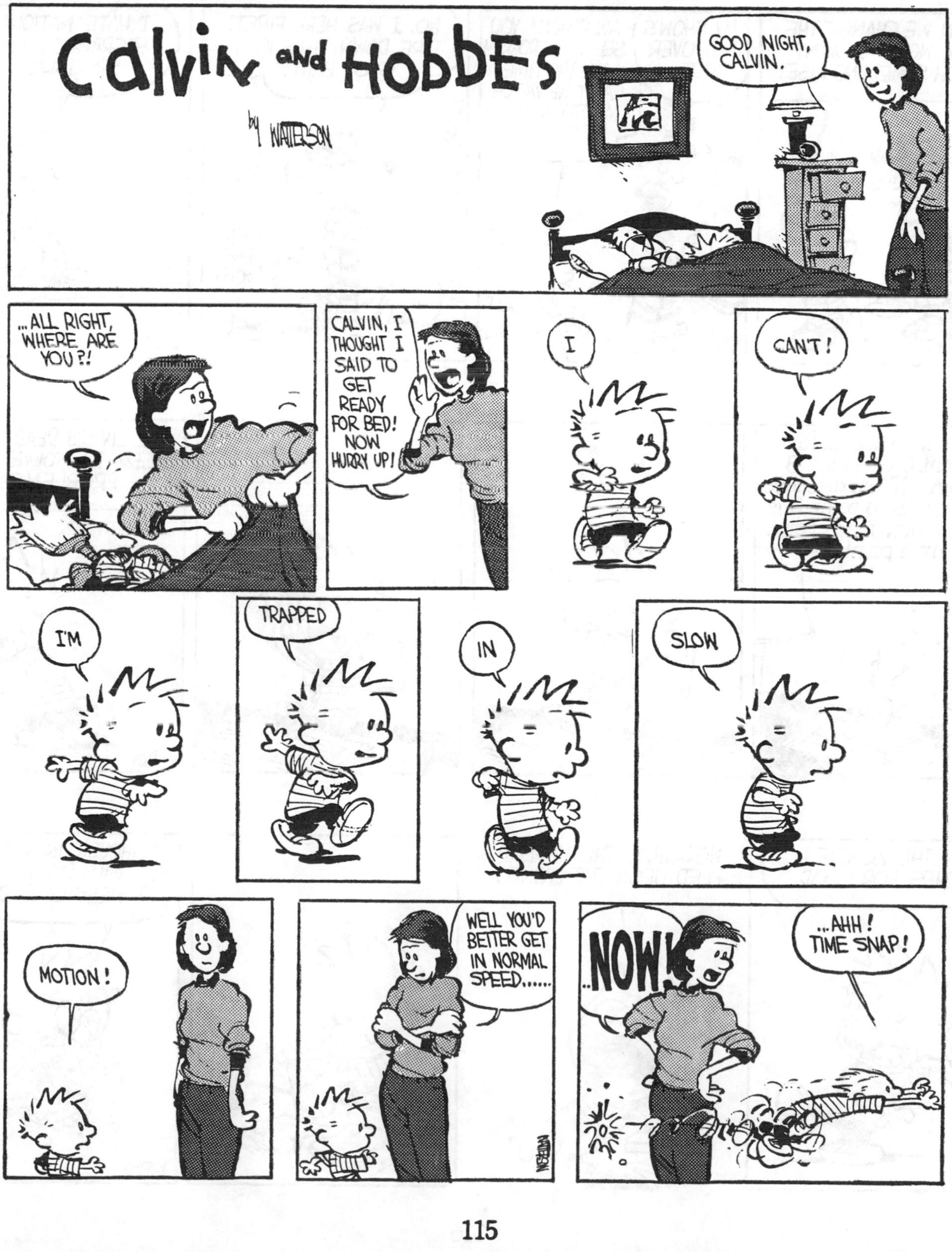
Calvin and Hobbes
by WATTERSON
GOOD NIGHT, CALVIN.
...ALL RIGHT, WHERE ARE YOU?!
CALVIN, I THOUGHT I SAID TO GET READY FOR BED! NOW HURRY UP!
I
CAN'T!
I'M
TRAPPED
IN
SLOW
MOTION!
WELL YOU'D BETTER GET IN NORMAL SPEED......
...NOW!
...AHH! TIME SNAP!

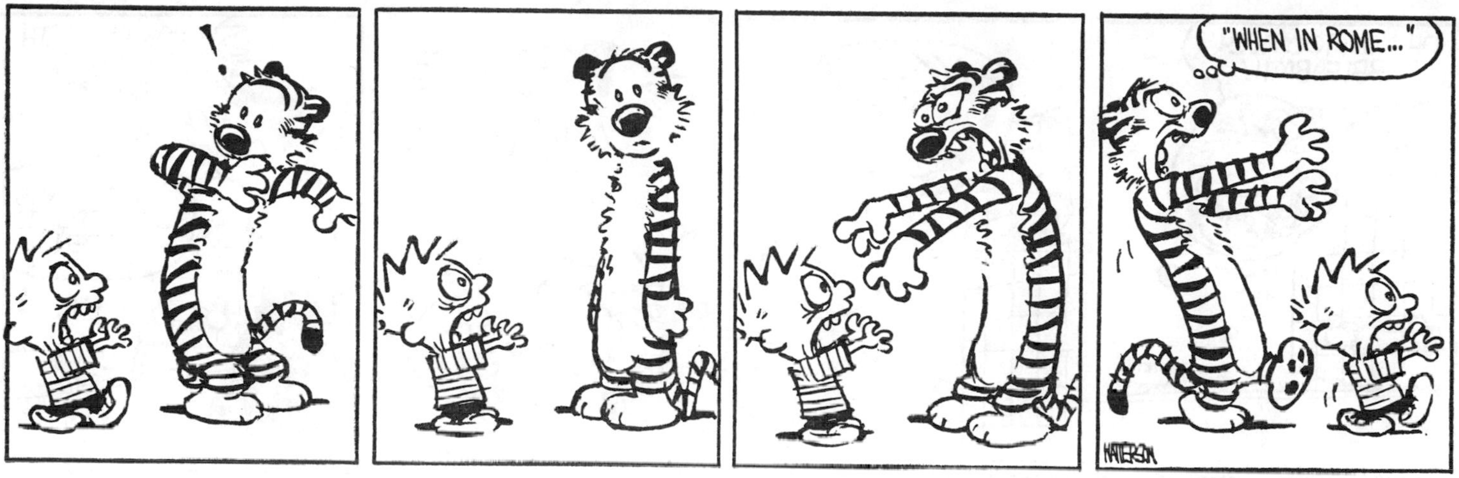
!
"WHEN IN ROME..."
WATTERSON

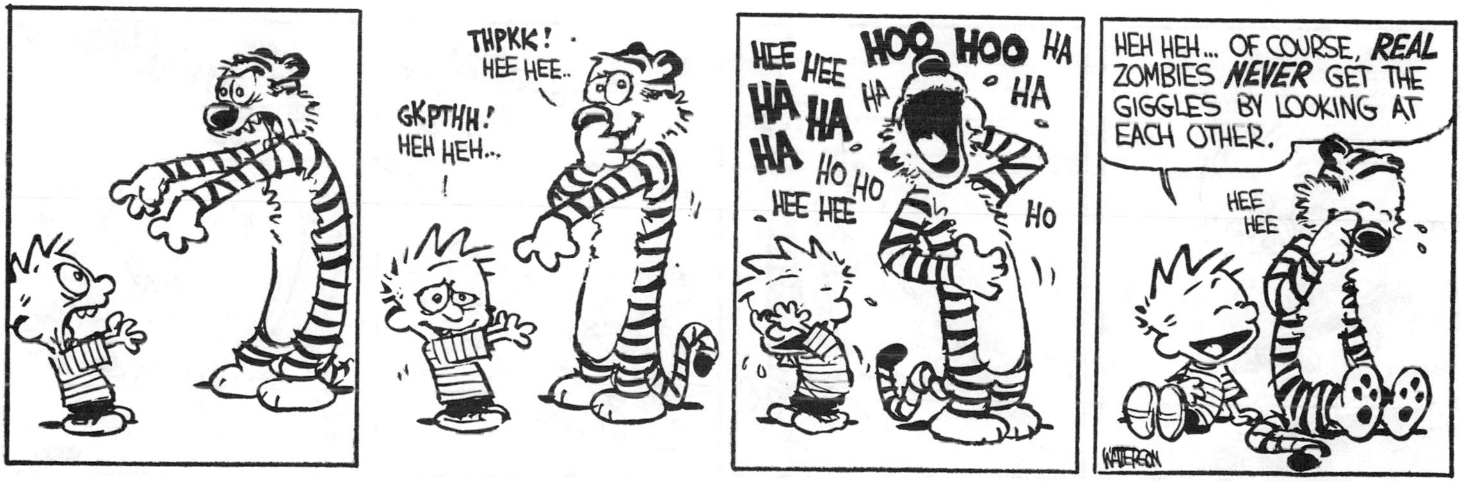
THPKK! HEE HEE..
GKPTHH! HEH HEH..
!
HEE HEE HOO HOO HA
HA HA HA HA HA
HA HO HO HO
HEE HEE HO
HEH HEH... OF COURSE, REAL ZOMBIES NEVER GET THE GIGGLES BY LOOKING AT EACH OTHER.
HEE HEE
WATTERSON

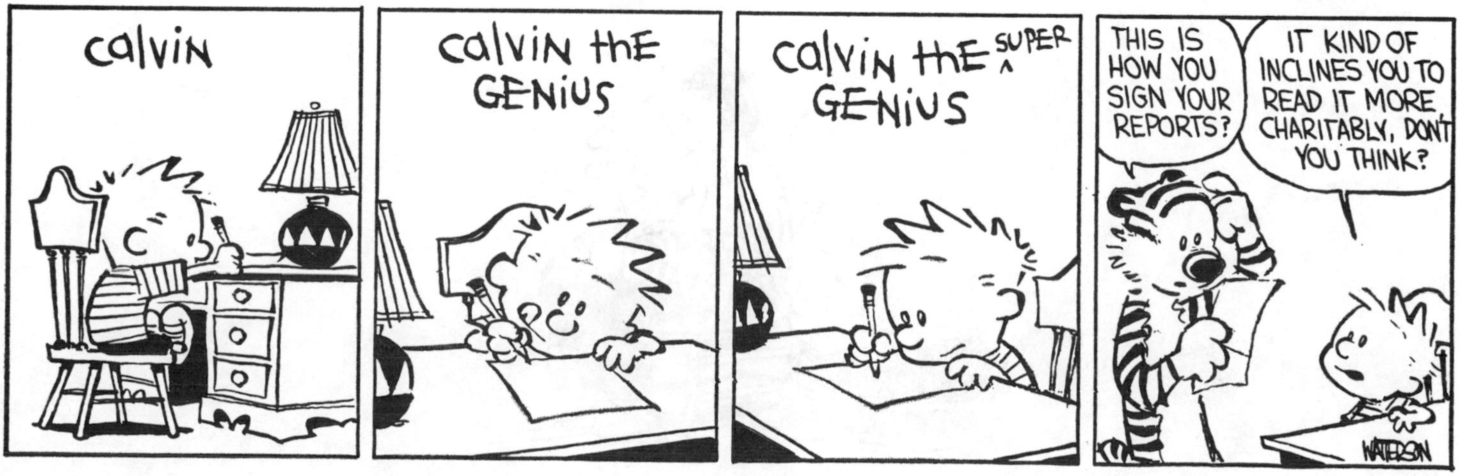
calvin
calvin the GENIUS
calvin the SUPER GENIUS
THIS IS HOW YOU SIGN YOUR REPORTS?
IT KIND OF INCLINES YOU TO READ IT MORE CHARITABLY, DON'T YOU THINK?
WATTERSON

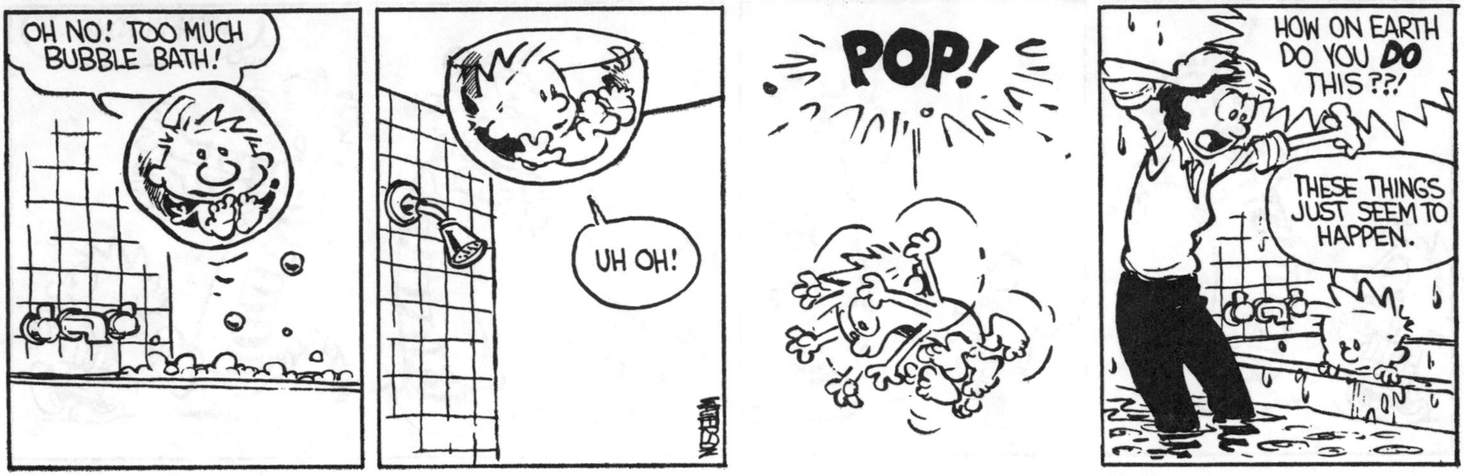
OH NO! TOO MUCH BUBBLE BATH!
UH OH!
POP!
HOW ON EARTH DO YOU DO THIS??!
THESE THINGS JUST SEEM TO HAPPEN.

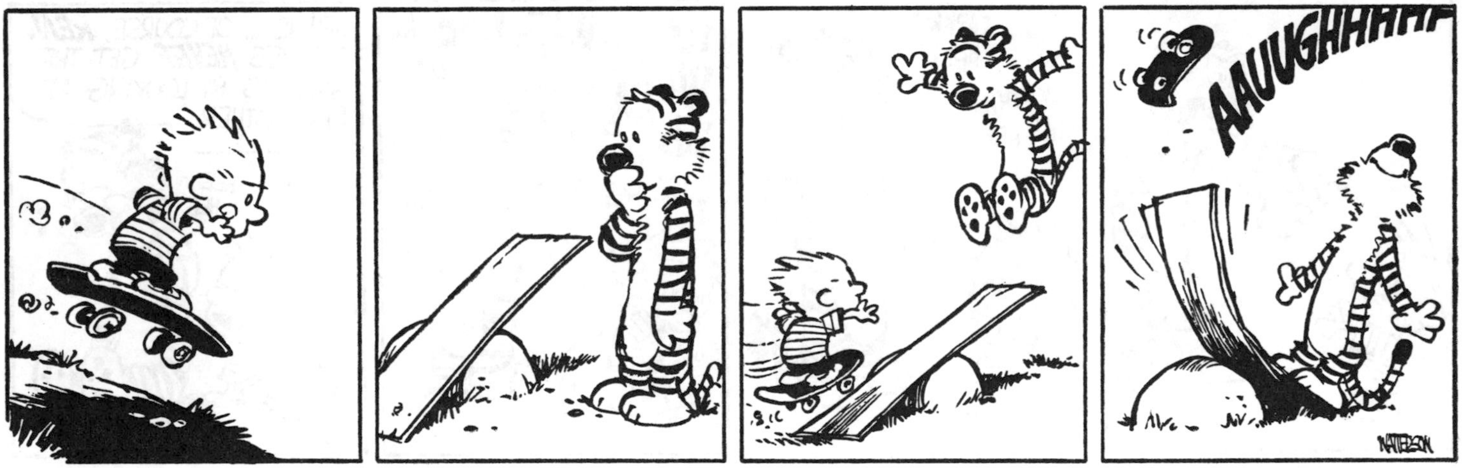
AAUUGHHHH
WATTERSON

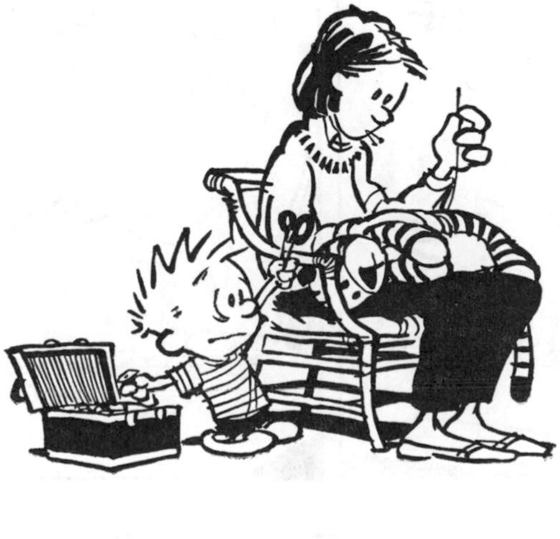

MY CIGARETTE SMOKE MIXED WITH THE SMOKE OF MY .38. IF BUSINESS WAS AS GOOD AS MY AIM, I'D BE ON EASY STREET. INSTEAD, I'VE GOT AN OFFICE ON 49TH STREET AND A NASTY RELATIONSHIP WITH A STRING OF COLLECTION AGENTS.

YEAH, THAT'S ME, TRACER BULLET. I'VE GOT EIGHT SLUGS IN ME. ONE'S LEAD, AND THE REST ARE BOURBON. THE DRINK PACKS A WALLOP, AND I PACK A REVOLVER. I'M A PRIVATE EYE.

SUDDENLY MY DOOR SWUNG OPEN, AND IN WALKED TROUBLE. BRUNETTE, AS USUAL.

TAKE YOUR HAT OFF AT THE DINNER TABLE, CALVIN. IT'S NOT POLITE.

SHE WAS A PUSHY DAME, BUT SHE HAD A CASE..

TAKE YOUR HAT OFF AT THE DINNER TABLE, CALVIN.

HERE COMES THE HURRICANE.

YOU CUT YOUR HAIR!!

NO I DIDN'T. HOBBES DID.

WHY ON EARTH DID YOU CUT YOUR OWN HAIR?! LOOK AT YOU!

I SAID HOBBES CUT IT! YOU THINK I'D DO THIS??

...WELL, I DIDN'T!

SOME BARBER YOU ARE! MOM SAYS THERE'S NOTHING I CAN DO BUT WAIT FOR MY HAIR TO GROW BACK.

IN THE MEANTIME, I'VE GOT TO GO AROUND LOOKING LIKE I'VE GOT MANGE! I HOPE YOU'RE HAPPY.

HAPPY?! YOU STIFFED ME! WHERE'S MY EIGHT BUCKS?!

BOOK REPORT
"Treasure Island"

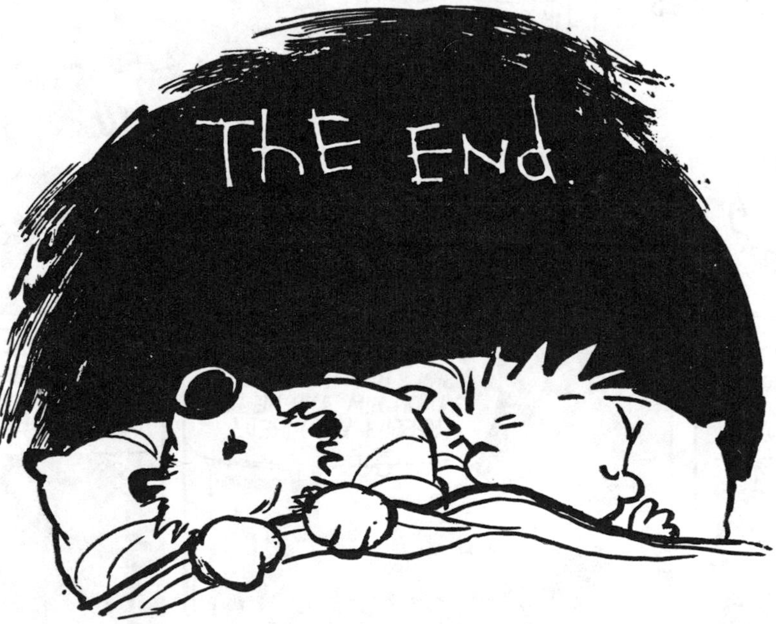
ThE End.